D1189396

# The Scarecrow Author Bibliographies

# Henry David
# THOREAU
## AND THE CRITICS
A Checklist of Criticism,
1900-1978

by
## JEANETTA
## BOSWELL
and
## SARAH
## CROUCH

*The Scarecrow
Author Bibliographies,*

*No. 56*

The Scarecrow Press, Inc.
Metuchen, N.J., & London
1981

**Library of Congress Cataloging in Publication Data**

Boswell, Jeanetta, 1922-
  Henry David Thoreau and the critics.

  (The Scarecrow author bibliographies ; no. 56)
  Includes indexes.
  1. Thoreau, Henry David, 1817-1862--Bibliography.
I. Crouch, Sarah.  II. Title.  III. Series: Scare-
crow author bibliographies ; no. 56.
Z8873.B67  [PS3053]        016.818'309        81-929
ISBN 0-8108-1416-1                            AACR2

To the memories of Betty and Alexi,

whom the gods loved

# CONTENTS

# TRIBUTES

"I liked Thoreau though he was morbid.   I do not
think it was so much a love of woods, streams, and
hills that made him live in the country, as from a
morbid dislike of humanity.   I remember Thoreau say-
ing once, when walking with him in my favorite Brook-
lyn--'What is there in the people?  Pshaw! what do
you (a man who sees as well as anybody) see in all
this cheating political corruption?'  I did not like my
Brooklyn spoken of in this way."
                              --Walt Whitman, 1887


"I will gladly come on Thursday.   Thoreau is to be at
my house, and I shall take the liberty to bring him
with me, unless he has scruples about intruding on
you.   You would find him well worth knowing; he is a
man of thought and originality, with a certain iron-
pokerishness,--an uncompromising stiffness,--in his
mental character, which is interesting, though it grows
rather wearisome on close and frequent acquaintance."
          --Hawthorne, to Henry Wadsworth Longfellow,
          1848


"There is a flower known to botanists, one of the
same genus with our summer plant called 'Life-Ever-
lasting,' a Gnaphalium like that, which grows on the
most inaccessible cliffs of the Tyrolese mountains,
where the chamois dare hardly venture, and which the
hunter, tempted by its beauty, and by his love (for it
is immensely valued by the Swiss maidens), climbs
the cliffs to gather, and is sometimes found dead at
the foot, with the flower in his hand.   It is called by
botanists the Gnaphalium leontopodium, but by the
Swiss Edelweisse, which signifies Noble Purity.   Thoreau seemed to me living in the hope to gather this

plant, which belonged to him of right. The scale on which his studies proceeded was so large as to require longevity, and we were the less prepared for his sudden disappearance. The country knows not yet, or in the least part, how great a son it has lost. It seems an injury that he should leave in the midst his broken task which none else can finish, a kind of indignity to so noble a soul, that he should depart out of Nature before yet he has been really shown to his peers for what he is. But he, at least, is content. His soul was made for the noblest society; he had in his short life exhausted the capabilities of this world; wherever there is knowledge, wherever there is virtue, wherever there is beauty, he will find a home."

> --Ralph Waldo Emerson, "Thoreau," 1862


"I went to the woods because I wished to live deliberately, to front only the essential facts of life, and see if I could not learn what it had to teach, and not, when I came to die, discover that I had not lived."

> --Thoreau, Walden, 1854


"And here I bloom for a short hour unseen,
    Drinking my juices up,
With no root in the land
    To keep my branches green,
        But stand
    In a bare cup."

> --Thoreau, "I Am a Parcel of
> Vain Strivings," 1837

# PREFACE

In the "Foreword" to a handsome reprint edition of Thoreau's Journal (Dover, 1962), Walter Harding remarks on the slim hope that Thoreau had for ever seeing his entire journal--2,000,000 words--in print. Perhaps he cherished the possibility, but almost certainly he would never have expected the critical attention he now enjoys. Thoreau criticism, however, suffers from two serious defects: far too many studies are based upon some premise that puts Thoreau in Emerson's all-too-awesome shadow, and far too many are the worst forms of trivia. Regarding the first complaint, the trend seems to be getting better, and there is hope that eventually Thoreau will stand forth entirely in his own light. As regards the second complaint, we see no real trend, and suspect that the future will bring its share of the "What Thoreau Had for Breakfast" type of article. There is far too much trivia in the criticism of all authors, but this is especially true of Thoreau. It is not necessarily the fault of the critic: magazines encourage this sort of thing, and indirectly colleges and universities encourage it by allowing faculty members to claim such articles as "publications" in their dossiers.

A good deal of work has been done in the interest of Thoreau bibliography, but more should be done. This present book is an attempt to fill the need for an in-depth bibliography of secondary materials covering the better part of the twentieth century. A few nineteenth-century items are included if they have been reprinted in the past few years or are mentioned in the footnotes of a recent work. Likewise, a few foreign-language pieces are given if they have recently appeared in a biography or critical writing. The most recent bibliography on Thoreau is that compiled by Jean Cameron Advena, based on the Thoreau Society Bulletin quarterly bibliographies by Walter Harding. This is an altogether valuable listing except that it has no index, is contained within the limited scope of 1941-69, and perhaps includes too many items of a really ephemeral nature. One of the best bibliographies on Thoreau is that compiled by Francis Henry Allen in 1908, and, thankfully, reprinted in 1967. Although dated, it is a treasure of information from the nineteenth century and is well organized and carefully indexed. Lesser works include that by Christopher A. Hildenbrand, whose scope is 1940-67; one by James F. Lacey, who published a short annotated work on Thoreau in German criticism, 1968; and a checklist of literary criticism of Walden by Annette M. Woodlief, 1975. There are several other bibliographical studies, all listed in our checklist and indexed under "Bibliography."

As usual, our debts of gratitude exceed the limitations of space: to the area libraries and the interlibrary-loan department of the University of Texas at Arlington, who never seem to grow impatient with our efforts; to our friends and families, who also seem to have developed an added measure of tolerance and patience; and to the Electric Company, which kept us cool in this hottest of all Texas summers.

Jeanetta Boswell and Sarah Crouch

Arlington, Texas
August, 1980

# A NOTE
## ON USING THIS BOOK

The first 36 numbered entries are of anonymous authorship and are listed chronologically.

Subarrangements under authors' names are chronological.

### Abbreviations

Two abbreviations are used throughout:

DA          Dissertation Abstracts

PMLA      Publications of the Modern Language Association

# THE CHECKLIST

1 ANONYMOUS (listed chronologically). "Hawthorne and
   Thoreau." TP's Weekly, 6 (September 22, 1905), 369.

2 "Widening Influence of Thoreau." Current Literature, 45
   (August, 1908), 170-171.

3 "New England Nature Studies: Thoreau, Burroughs, Whitman." Edinburgh Review, 208 (October, 1908), 343-
   366.

4 "Thoreau's Early Declaration of Independence for American Literature." Current Opinion, 63 (July, 1917),
   47-48.

5 "Henry David Thoreau, 1817-1917." Seven Arts, 2 (July,
   1917), 383-386.

6 "Thoreau Championed by Emerson's Son." Current Opinion, 63 (September, 1917), 194-195.

7 "The Centenary of Thoreau." Outlook, 117 (September,
   1917), 44.

8 "Thoreau as a Born Supernaturalist." Current Opinion,
   67 (July, 1919), 44.

9 "Thoreau on the Kindly Relations." Scribner's Magazine,
   67 (March, 1920), 379.

10 "Tolstoy's Admiration for Thoreau." New York Times,
   September 29, 1928, p. 6.

11 "In the Week an Incident Relative to Walt Whitman's Be-
   ing Placed in the Hall of Fame." New Republic, 67
   (May 27, 1931), 30.

12 "Theosophist Unaware." Theosophy, 32 (May, June, 1944), 290-295, 330-334.

13 "Thoreau and Music." Thoreau Society Bulletin, 18 (Winter, 1947), 2-3.

14 "The Thoreau Collection of the Pierpont Morgan Library of New York City." Thoreau Society Bulletin, 19 (Spring, 1947), 2.

15 "Thoreau's Plan of a Farm." Thoreau Society Bulletin, 20 (Summer, 1947), 2.

16 "Thoreau's Cabin Site Marked with Granite at Walden Pond." Boston Herald, July 13, 1947, p. 2.

17 "Walden Pond--a Century After Thoreau Lived There." New York Herald Tribune, September 18, 1948, p. 2.

18 "Notes and Comments (on Thoreau)." New Yorker, 25 (May 7, 1949), 23.

19 "An Insight of Thoreau." Think, 17 (July, 1951), 28.

20 "Living in Concord." Times Literary Supplement, 18 (April, 1952), 1-2.

21 "Thoreau in Minnesota." Thoreau Society Bulletin, 57 (Fall, 1956), 1-4.

22 "Aphorisms: Fragments of Old Journals." Emerson Society Quarterly, 7 (1957), 37-39.

23/4 "The 'Save Walden' Campaign." Thoreau Society Bulletin, 61 (Fall, 1957), 1-3.

25 "Help Save Walden Pond." Emerson Society Quarterly, 11 (1958), 1-14. Newspaper coverage.

26 "Save Walden Committee Report." Thoreau Society Bulletin, 67 (Spring, 1959), 2-3.

27 "The Will of H. G. O. Blake." Thoreau Society Bulletin, 68 (Summer, 1959), 2.

28 "Manuscripts in the Clifton Waller Barrett Library of American Literature in the University of Virginia

Library." Thoreau Society Bulletin, 90 (Winter, 1965), 1-2.

29  "Thoreau and the Danish Resistance:  An Anonymous Memoir," in Hicks, John H., ed., Thoreau in Our Season (1966), pp. 20-21.

30  "Early Reviews of Walden, from the Christian Registrar, August 26, 1854." Thoreau Society Bulletin, 118 (Winter, 1972), 7-8.

31  "Note Rejecting Membership in the First Parish of Concord." Thoreau Society Bulletin, 120 (Summer, 1972), 7. Written by Thoreau January 6, 1841.

32  "Notebook by Richard Fuller:  Walk with Thoreau to Wachusett Mt. in 1842." Thoreau Society Bulletin, 121 (Fall, 1972), 1-4.

33  "The Daniel J. Bernstein Collection." Thoreau Society Bulletin, 127 (Spring, 1974), 1.

34  "Another Early Review of Walden." Thoreau Society Bulletin, 129 (Fall, 1974), 8.

35  "Concord in Winter." Thoreau Society Bulletin, 136 (Summer, 1976), 6-8. Reprinted from Springfield Republican, January 20, 1871.

36  "Reminiscences of Thoreau." American Transcendental Quarterly, 36 Supplement (1977), 35-38. Reprinted from The Outlook, December 2, 1899.

37  ABBOTT, Charles C. "Thoreau." Lippincott's Monthly Magazine, 55 (June, 1895), 852-855. Reprinted in Glick, ed., Recognition (1969), pp. 125-130.

38  ADAMS, Alexander B., ed. and illustrated. Thoreau's Guide to Cape Cod. New York: Devin-Adair, 1962.

39  ADAMS, George Matthew. "The Influence of Thoreau," in Adams, Better Than Gold. Introduction by Robert R. Updegraff. New York: Duell, Sloan, 1949, pp. 67-68.

40  ADAMS, J. Donald. "Speaking of Books," column. New

York Times Book Review, January 4, 1942, p. 2.
Thoreau also referred to in the following:
    June 6, 1947, p. 2
    January 11, 1948, p. 2
    March 15, 1953, p. 2
    June 21, 1953, p. 2
    May 6, 1962, p. 2.

41  ADAMS, Raymond William. "Henry David Thoreau's
    Literary Theory and Criticism." Ph. D. diss., North
    Carolina, 1928.

42  _____. "Thoreau and Immortality." Studies in
    Philology, 26 (January, 1929), 58-66.

43  _____. "A Thoreau Checklist, 1908-1930," in A Selec-
    tion of American and English First Editions and Other
    Desirable Books. Chappaqua, N. Y.: Richard M. Sills,
    1930, pp. 35-40.

44  _____. "A Bibliographical Note on Walden." Ameri-
    can Literature, 2 (May, 1930), 166-168.

45  _____. "Thoreau and the Photographers." Photo-Era,
    46 (May, 1931), 239-243.

46  _____. "Thoreau's Literary Apprenticeship." Studies
    in Philology, 29 (October, 1932), 617-629.

47  _____. "Thoreau, Buried Twice." Saturday Review
    of Literature, 10 (September 16, 1933), 111.

48  _____. "The Thoreau Library of Raymond Adams."
    Chapel Hill, N. C.: Mimeographed catalog, 1936.

49  _____. "A Supplement." Chapel Hill, N. C.: Mimeo-
    graphed catalog, 1937.

50  _____. "Thoreau's Burials." American Literature,
    12 (March, 1940), 105-107.

51  _____. "Thoreau at Harvard: Some Unpublished
    Records." New England Quarterly, 13 (March, 1940),
    24-33.

52  _____. "An Irishman on Thoreau: A Stillborn View
    of Walden." New England Quarterly, 13 (December,

1940), 697-699.   By Augustine O'Neill, a New York
lawyer.

53 _____.   "Thoreau at Walden."   University North Carolina Extension Bulletin, 34 (November, 1944), 1-17.

54 _____.   "Thoreau's Diploma."   American Literature,
17 (May, 1945), 174-175.

55 _____.   "Thoreau's Science."   Scientific Monthly, 60
(May, 1945), 379-382.

56 _____.   "Thoreau's Growth at Walden."   Christian
Registrar, 124 (July, 1945), 268-270.

57 _____.   "Thoreau's Sources for 'Resistance to Civil
Government.'"   Studies in Philology, 42 (July, 1945),
640-653.   Reprinted in Coffman, G. R., ed., Studies
in Language and Literature.   Chapel Hill:   University
of North Carolina Press, 1945, pp. 262-275.

58 _____.   "Emerson's House at Walden."   Thoreau
Society Bulletin, 24 (Summer, 1948), 2-6.

59 _____.   "The Bibliographical History of Thoreau's
A Week on the Concord and Merrimack Rivers."   Papers of the Bibliographical Society of America, 43
(1949), 39-47.

60 _____.   "'Civil Disobedience' Gets Printed."   Thoreau
Society Bulletin, 28 (Summer, 1949), 1-2.

61 _____.   "An Early Overlooked Defense of Thoreau."
Thoreau Society Bulletin, 32 (Summer, 1950), 1-2.

62 _____.   "Thoreau, Imitator Plus."   Thoreau Society
Bulletin, 41 (Fall, 1952), 1-2.

63 _____.   "Thoreau and His Neighbors."   Thoreau
Society Bulletin, 44 (Summer, 1953), 1-2.

64 _____.   "Witnessing Walden."   Thoreau Society Bulletin,
48 (Summer, 1954), 1-2.

65 _____.   "Thoreau's Mock-Heroics and the American
Natural History Writers."   Studies in Philology, 52
(January, 1955), 86-97.   An address delivered before

the Grolier Club, New York City, March 16, 1954, in connection with an exhibit marking the centennial of the publication of Walden. Reprinted in Glick, ed., Recognition (1969), pp. 301-315.

66 _____. "Thoreau's Years After Walden." Thoreau Society Bulletin, 52 (Summer, 1955), 1-3.

67 _____. "Hawthorne and a Glimpse of Walden." Essex Institute Historical Collections, 94 (July, 1958), 191-193.

68 _____. "That Claim Again." Thoreau Society Bulletin, 67 (Spring, 1959), 3.

69 _____. "Thoreau's 'Winged Cat.'" Thoreau Society Bulletin, 68 (Summer, 1959), 1-2.

70 _____. "Thoreau's Return to Concord." Thoreau Society Bulletin, 96 (Summer, 1966), 1-3.

71 _____. "Henry Thoreau, Concord, Mass." Thoreau Society Bulletin, 128 (Summer, 1974), 3-5.

72 ADAMS, Richard P. "Romanticism and the American Renaissance." American Literature, 23 (January, 1952), 419-432. Carlyle and Thoreau.

73 _____. "Architecture and the Romantic Tradition." American Quarterly, 9 (Spring, 1957), 46-92. Thoreau and Frank Lloyd Wright.

74 _____. "The American Renaissance: An Epistemological Problem." Emerson Society Quarterly, 35 (1964), 2-7.

75 _____. "Permutations of American Romanticism." Studies in Romanticism, 9 (1970), 249-268.

76 ADIX, Marjorie. "Phoenix at Walden: D. H. Lawrence Calls on Thoreau." Western Humanities Review, 8 (Autumn, 1954), 287-298.

77 ADVENA, Jean Cameron, comp. Introduction by Walter Harding. A Bibliography of the Thoreau Society Bulletin Bibliographies, Edited by Walter Harding, 1941-1969. Troy, N.Y.: Whitson, 1971. 323 pages, listed

alphabetical by author: articles, books, sections of books, many newspaper items, reviews, poems about Thoreau, etc. Is occasionally annotated; has no index, and items are not numbered.

78  AHEARN, Kerry. "Thoreau and John Brown: What to Do About Evil." Thoreau Journal Quarterly, 6 (1974), 24-28.

79  ALBRECHT, Robert Charles. "Thoreau and His Audience: 'A Plea for Capt. John Brown.' " American Literature, 32 (January, 1961), 393-402.

80  _____. "The New England Transcendentalists' Response to the Civil War." Ph. D. diss., Minnesota, 1962. DA, 24 (1964), 4687-4688.

81  _____. "The Theological Response of the Transcendentalists to the Civil War." New England Quarterly, 38 (March, 1965), 21-34. Reprinted in Barbour, American Transcendentalism (1973), pp. 211-221.

82  _____. "Conflict and Resolution: 'Slavery in Massachusetts. ' " Emerson Society Quarterly, 19 (1973), 179-188.

83  ALCOTT, Amos Bronson. Concord Days. Boston: Roberts Brothers, 1872. "Thoreau," excerpt from Concord Days reprinted in Harding, ed., Thoreau: A Century of Criticism (1954), pp. 54-58. Also in Glick, ed., Recognition (1969), pp. 48-51.

84  _____. The Journals of Amos Bronson Alcott, selections edited by Odell Shepard. Boston: Houghton Mifflin, 1938. Thoreau, passim.

85  ALLEN, Francis Henry. A Bibliography of Henry David Thoreau. Boston: Houghton Mifflin, 1908. Reprinted New York: Johnson Reprint Corp., 1967. 200 pages, with subject and author index. Items arranged in sections: Thoreau's books; selections from Thoreau's writings; articles and poems by Thoreau arranged chronologically; biographies (full-length books); books with critical and biographical material; and newspaper and periodical material.

86  _____. "Thoreau's Knowledge of Birds." Nation, 91 (September 22, 1910), 261.

87 _____ . "English as She Is Edited. "  Atlantic,  113
       (March,  1914),  42-45.

88 _____ . "Review of Thoreau's Collected Poems, ed.
       by Carl Bode (1943). "  American Literature,  17 (Nov-
       ember,  1945),  250-267.

89 _____ . "Thoreau's Translation from Pindar. "  Thoreau
       Society Bulletin, 26 (Winter,  1949),  3-4.

90 _____ . "Thoreau's Arms:  A Correction. "  Bulletin
       of Massachusetts Audubon Society,  33 (January,  1950),
       385.

91 _____ . Thoreau's Editors:  History and Reminiscence.
       Monroe,  N. C. :  Nocalore,  1950.  Also published as
       Thoreau Society Booklet,  No. 7 (1950),  21pp.

92 _____ . "The French Translation of Walden. "  Thoreau
       Society Bulletin,  38 (Winter,  1952),  1.

93 _____ , ed.  Notes on New England Birds.  Boston:
       Houghton Mifflin,  1910.  Selections by Henry David
       Thoreau arranged by editor.  Reprinted as Thoreau's
       Bird Lore.  Boston:  Houghton Mifflin,  1925.

94 _____ , ed.  Men of Concord and Some Others as
       Portrayed in the Journal of Henry David Thoreau.
       Illustrated by N. C. Wyeth.  Boston:  Houghton Mifflin,
       1937.

95 ALLEN, Gay Wilson.  "Thoreau's Boots for Mrs. Emer-
       son's Hens. "  Thoreau Journal Quarterly,  5 (1973),
       4-5.

96 ALLEN, M. S. , Earle Osborne, and D. P. Egdell.
       "Walden and How to Teach It. "  College English Asso-
       ciation Newsletter,  9 (December,  1947),  3-4.

97 ALLEN, Walter.  The Urgent West:  The American Dream
       and the Modern Man.  New York:  Dutton,  1969.
       Thoreau, passim.

98 ALLISON, Elliott S.  "Thoreau of Monadnock. "  Thoreau
       Journal Quarterly,  5 (1973),  15-21.

99 ALLISON, Hildreth M.  "Man on a Mountain. "  Appala-
       chia,  27 (June,  1947),  361-363.

100   AMERICAN TRANSCENDENTAL QUARTERLY, 1969.
      Special Index to Christian Examiner, North American
      Review, and New Jerusalem Magazine.

101   AMERICAN TRANSCENDENTAL QUARTERLY, 11 (1971),
      1-91. Thoreau Symposium, ed. John McAleer.

102   ANASTAPLO, George. "On Civil Disobedience:  Thoreau
      and Socrates. " Southwest Review, 54 (1969), 203-
      214.

103   ANDERSON, Barbara.  "Thoreau and Mary Austin. "
      Thoreau Society Bulletin, 126 (Winter, 1974), 7.

104   ANDERSON, Charles R.  "Aspects of Pathological Grief
      and Mourning. "  International Journal of Psycho-
      analysis, 30 (1949), 48-55.  Thoreau, passim; refers
      to the death of Thoreau's brother, John.

105   _____.  "Wit and Metaphor in Thoreau's Walden. "
      USA in Focus:  Recent Re-Interpretations, 2 (1966),
      70-93.  Published by the Nordic Association for
      American Studies, ed. Sigmund Skard.  Oslo:  Uni-
      versitetsford.

106   _____.  "Thoreau Takes a Pot Shot at Carolina
      Sports. "  Georgia Review, 22 (1968), 289-299.

107   _____.  The Magic Circle of Walden.  New York:
      Holt, Rinehart, and Winston, 1968.

108   _____.  "Thoreau's Monastic Vows. "  Etudes Ang-
      laises, 22 (1969), 11-20.

109   _____.  "Thoreau and The Dial:  The Apprentice
      Years, " in Woodress, James, ed. , Essays Mostly
      on Periodical Publication in America:  Essays in
      Honor of Clarence F. Gohdes.  Durham, N. C. :
      Duke University Press, 1973, pp. 92-120.

110   _____, ed. with Introduction.  Walden:  or Life in
      the Woods and "On the Duty of Civil Disobedience. "
      New York:  Collier, 1962.

111   _____, ed.  Thoreau's World:  Miniatures from His
      Journals.  Englewood Cliffs, N. J. :  Prentice-Hall,
      1971.

112 _____, ed. with Introduction. Thoreau's Vision: The Major Essays. Englewood Cliffs, N. J.: Prentice-Hall, 1973.

113 ANDERSON, Esther Howe. "Thoreau and Herbs." The Herbarist, 26 (1960), 25-30.

114 ANDERSON, John P. "Bibliography of Henry David Thoreau," in Salt, Life and Writing (1896).

115 ANDERSON, Quentin. The Imperial Self. New York: Knopf, 1971. Thoreau, pp. 12, 15, and passim.

116 _____. "Thoreau on July 4." New York Times Book Review, July 4, 1971, pp. 1, 16-18.

117 ANGELESCU, Victor. "Henry Thoreau's 'Night and Moonlight.' " Emerson Society Quarterly, 22 (1961), 64-67.

118 ANHORN, Judy Schaaf. "Thoreau in the Beanfield: The Curious Language of Walden." Emerson Society Quarterly, 24 (1978), 179-196.

119 ARMSTRONG, James. "Thoreau as Philosopher of Love," in Harding, ed., Henry David Thoreau: A Profile (1971), pp. 222-243.

120 ARNER, Robert D. "The Deserted Village of Walden Woods: Thoreau's Ruin Piece." American Transcendental Quarterly, 14 (1972), 13-15.

121 _____. "The Story of Hannah Duston: Cotton Mather to Thoreau." American Transcendental Quarterly, 18 (1973), 19-23.

122 ARNSTEIN, Felix. "Henry Thoreau, American." Snowy Egret, 26 (August, 1962), 12-19.

123 ATKINSON, Justin Brooks. "Thoreau, the Radical." Freeman, 1 (July 28, 1920), 468-469.

124 _____. "Concerning Thoreau's Style." Freeman, 6 (September 12, 1922), 8-10.

125 _____. Henry Thoreau: The Cosmic Yankee. New York: Knopf, 1927.

126    _____, ed. with Introduction; Foreword by Townsend
       Scudder. Walden and Other Writings. New York:
       Random House, 1937. Modern Library edition.

127    _____, ed. with Introduction. Thoreau's Walden: A
       Photographic Register by Henry Bugbee Kane. New
       York: Knopf, 1946.

128    AUSTIN, Thomas D. "Thoreau, the First Hippie."
       ANKH, 1 (Spring, 1968), 12-21.

129    BAATZ, Wilmer H. "Henry David Thoreau." Roches-
       ter Library Bulletin, 5 (Winter, 1950), 35-39.

130    BABCOCK, C. Merton. "Henry David Thoreau: In
       Defense of the Wilderness." University College
       Quarterly, 16 (1971), 25-28.

131    BABCOCK, Frederic L. "Adventure in Living." Chris-
       tian Century, 62 (March 28, 1945), 395-396.

132    _____. "Thoreau's House." New York Herald-
       Tribune, September 4, 1947, p. 2.

133    BAILEY, Carolyn Sherwin. "The Boy Who Made Pen-
       cils," in Children of the Handcrafts. New York:
       Viking, 1935, pp. 126-135.

134    BAIRD, Theodore. "Corn Grows in the Night." Mas-
       sachusetts Review, 4 (1962), 93-103. Reprinted in
       Hicks, John H. , ed. , Thoreau in Our Season (1966),
       pp. 68-78.

135    BAKER, Gail. "The Organic Unity of Henry David
       Thoreau's A Week on the Concord and Merrimack
       Rivers." Ph. D. diss. , New Mexico, 1970. DA,
       31 (1971), 5349A-5350A.

136    _____. "Friendship in Thoreau's Week." Thoreau
       Journal Quarterly, 7 (1975), 3-15.

137    BALOTĂ, Nicolae. "Walden." România Literară, 26
       (June, 1974), 20.

138    BARATE, Justo. "Thoreau in the Spanish Language:
       A Bibliography." Thoreau Society Booklet, 24 (1970),
       24 (1970), 28pp.

139   BARBOUR, Brian M., ed. with Introduction. American
      Transcendentalism: An Anthology of Criticism. Notre
      Dame, Ind.: University of Notre Dame Press, 1973.
      "The Theological Response of the Transcendentalists
      to the Civil War," by Robert Charles Albrecht, pp.
      211-221.

140   BARITZ, Loren. "The Idea of the West." American
      Historical Review, 66 (April, 1961), 618-640.

141   _____. City on a Hill: A History of Ideas and
      Myths in America. New York: Wiley, 1965. Tho-
      reau, passim.

142   BARNES, Carlotta. "Thoreau in the Eyes of Today's
      Concord." Thoreau Society Bulletin, 125 (Fall, 1973),
      5-6.

143   BARTLETT, Irving H. "Political and Social Thought in
      the American Democracy," in Bartlett, The American
      Mind in the Mid-Nineteenth Century. New York:
      Crowell, 1967, pp. 32-72. Crowell's American His-
      tory series.

144   BARTON, W. G. "Thoreau, Flagg, and Burroughs."
      Emerson Society Quarterly, 15 (1959), 51-64. Re-
      printed from Essex Institute Historical Collections,
      1885.

145   BASILE, Joseph Lawrence. "Technology and the Artist
      in A Week." American Transcendental Quarterly, 11
      (1911), 87-91.

146   _____. "Man and Machine in Thoreau." Ph.D.
      diss., Louisiana State, 1971. DA, 33 (1972), 2314A.

147   _____. "Narcissus in the World of Machines."
      Southern Review, 32 (1976), 10-13.

148   BASSETT, Charles W. "Katahdin, Wachusett, and
      Kilimanjaro: The Symbolic Mountains of Thoreau
      and Hemingway." Thoreau Journal Quarterly, 3
      (1971), 1-10.

149   BAYLOP, Adrienne. "Music Is the Sound of Universal
      Laws Promulgated." College English Association
      Journal, 39 (1976), 11-15.

150  BAYM, Nina Z.  "The Paradoxical Hero in Henry David
     Thoreau's Writings. "  Ph. D.  diss. , Harvard, 1963.

151  _____.  "Thoreau's View of Science. "  Journal of
     History of Ideas, 26 (April-June, 1965), 221-234.

152  _____.  "From Metaphysics to Metaphor:  The Image
     of Water in Emerson and Thoreau. "  Studies in Ro-
     manticism, 5 (1966), 231-243.

153  BAZALGETTI, Léon.  Henry David Thoreau:  Bachelor
     of Nature.  Translated from French by Van Wyck
     Brooks.  New York: Dutton, 1924.  Reprinted Port
     Washington, N. Y.:  Kennikat, 1969.  Published origi-
     nally as Henry Thoreau:  Sauvage.  Paris, 1914.

154  BEARDSLEE, Martin.  "A Walk to Walden. "  Thoreau
     Journal Quarterly, 1 (1969), 17-21.

155  BEARDSLEY, George.  "Thoreau as a Humorist. "
     Dial, 28 (April 1, 1900), 241-243.

156  BEAULIEU, Linda H.  "Robert Francis on Henry
     Thoreau. "  Thoreau Society Bulletin, 139 (Spring,
     1977), 3-4.

157  BEAVER, Harold.  "The Transcendental Savage. "  Times
     Literary Supplement (London), 9 (October, 1978), 1115.
     Review-essay.

158  BEAVER, John.  "Thoreau's Stylistic Use of the Nega-
     tive. "  American Transcendental Quarterly, 32 (1976),
     21.

159  BECKER, Isadore H.  "Thoreau's Princely Leisure. "
     Husson Review, 3 (1970), 161-167.

160  BEERS, Henry Augustin.  Four Americans:  Roosevelt,
     Hawthorne, Emerson, Whitman.  New Haven:  Yale
     University Press, 1919.  Reprinted Freeport, N. Y.:
     Books for Libraries, 1968.  Emerson in "Pilgrim in
     Concord, " pp. 59-83.  Thoreau, passim.  Printed
     earlier in Yale Review, 3 (1914), 673-688.

161  BENNETT, Fordyce Richard.   "Thoreau and Alcott's
     Papers of Government. "  Thoreau Society Bulletin,
     138 (Winter, 1977), 4.

162 BENNETT, James O'Donnell. "Thoreau's Walden," in
    Bennett, Much Loved Books. New York: Liveright,
    1927, pp. 318-326. Reprinted in shorter version, New
    York: Fawcett, 1959. Thoreau omitted in reprint
    version.

163 BENOIT, Raymond. "Walden as God's Drop." Ameri-
    can Literature, 43 (1971), 122-124. Reprinted in
    Benoit, Single Nature's Double Name. Atlantic High-
    lands, N. J.: Humanities, 1973, pp. 76-83.

164 BENSON, Adolph B. "Scandinavian Influence in the
    Writings of Thoreau." Scandinavian Studies (Univer-
    sity of Wisconsin), 16 (May, August, 1941), 201-211,
    241-256.

165 BERGER, Patrick Frederick. "Margaret Fuller: Criti-
    cal Realist as Seen in Her Works." Ph. D. diss.,
    St. Louis, 1972. DA, 34 (1974), 5157A.

166 BERKOWITZ, Morton S. "Thoreau and Richard Baxter."
    Thoreau Society Bulletin, 131 (Spring, 1975), 4.

167          . "Thoreau, Rice, and Vose on the Commer-
    cial Spirit." Thoreau Society Bulletin, 141 (Fall,
    1977), 1-5. 1837 Harvard Commencement speeches.

168 BESTON, Henry. Henry David Thoreau. New York:
    Rinehart, 1951.

169 BETTELHEIM, Bruno. "The Problem of Generations,"
    in Erikson, Erik, ed., The Challenge of Youth.
    Garden City, N. Y.: Doubleday, 1963, pp. 76-109.
    Thoreau, passim.

170 BHATIA, Kamala. The Mysticism of Thoreau and Its
    Affinity with Indian Thought. New Delhi: New India,
    1966.

171          . "Thoreau and India," in Harding, et al.,
    Henry David Thoreau: Studies (1972), pp. 117-132.

172 BICKMAN, Martin. "Flawed Words and the Stubborn
    Sounds: Another Look at Structure and Meaning in
    Walden." Southern Humanities Review, 8 (1974),
    153-162.

173   BIDDLE, Arthur W. "Letter from A. Bronson Alcott."
      American Transcendental Quarterly, 13 (1972), 36-
      37. Comments on Thoreau.

174   BIER, Jesse. "Weberism, Franklin, and the Transcen-
      dental Style." New England Quarterly, 43 (1970),
      179-192.

175   BIGELOW, Gordon E. "Summer Under Snow: Thoreau's
      'A Winter Walk.' " Emerson Society Quarterly, 56
      (1969), 13-16.

176   _____. "Thoreau's Melting Sandbank: Birth of a
      Symbol." International Journal of Symbology, 2
      (1971), 7-13.

177   BIRNEY, Gaylord Adrian. "The Poetics of American
      Space: Aspects of the Topographical in Nineteenth
      Century American Literature." Ph. D. diss., Cali-
      fornia (San Diego), 1967. DA, 28 (1968), 5043A-
      5044A.

178   BIRSS, John Howard. "Thoreau and Thomas Carew."
      Notes and Queries, 164 (January 28, 1933), 63.

179   BISHOP, Jonathan. Emerson on the Soul. Cambridge:
      Harvard University Press, 1964. Thoreau, passim.

180   _____. "The Experience of the Sacred in Thoreau's
      Week." English Literary History, 33 (1966), 66-91.

181   BLACK, August B. "Thoreau and the Lawyer." Tho-
      reau Journal Quarterly, 7 (1975), 26-27.

182   BLAIR, John G., and Augustus Trowbridge. "Thoreau
      on Katahdin." American Quarterly, 12 (Winter,
      1960), 508-517.

183   BLAKE, Harrison G. O., ed. Early Spring in Massa-
      chusetts: From Thoreau's Journals. Boston: Hough-
      ton Mifflin, 1881.

184   _____, ed. Summer: From Thoreau's Journals.
      Boston: Houghton Mifflin, 1884.

185   _____, ed. Winter: From Thoreau's Journals.
      Boston: Houghton Mifflin, 1888.

186        _____, ed. Autumn:  From Thoreau's Journals.
           Boston:  Houghton Mifflin, 1892.

187        _____, ed. Thoreau's Complete Works, 5 vols.
           Boston:  Houghton Mifflin, 1929.  Concord edition.

188   BLANCH, Robert J.  "The Synchronized Clocks of Berg-
           son and Thoreau. "  Revue des Langues Vivantes, 33
           (September-October, 1967), 489-492.  In French.

189   BLANDING, Thomas.  "Walton and Walden. "  Thoreau
           Society Bulletin, 107 (Spring, 1969), 3.

190        _____. "Letter from Sophia Thoreau About Her Late
           Brother, May, 1866. "  Concord Saunterer, 7 (Sum-
           mer, 1972), 1-6.

191        _____. "Daniel Ricketson's Reminiscences of Tho-
           reau. "  Concord Saunterer, 8 (Spring, 1973), 7-11.

192        _____. "Of New Bedford 'Feelosofers' and Concord
           Real Estate. "  Concord Saunterer, 8 (Summer, 1973),
           2-8.  Includes unpublished Thoreau letter.

193        _____. "Passages from John Thoreau Jr. 's Journal. "
           Thoreau Society Bulletin, 136 (Summer, 1976).

194        _____. "Thoreau Letter to George Thatcher. "  Con-
           cord Saunterer, 12 (Summer, 1977), 21-22.

195        _____. "Daniel Ricketson's Sketch Book, " in Myer-
           son, ed., Studies in the American Renaissance:  1977
           (1978), pp. 327-338.  Illustrated.

196   BLASING, Mutlu K.  "The Economics of Walden. "
           Texas Studies in Literature and Language, 17 (1976),
           759-775.  Reprinted in Blasing, The Art of Life:
           Studies in American Autobiographical Literature.
           Austin and London:  University of Texas Press, 1977,
           pp. 1-23.

197   BLAU, Joseph L.  "Henry David Thoreau:  Anarchist, "
           in Blau, Men and Movements in American Philosophy.
           New York:  Prentice-Hall, 1952, pp. 131-141.

198   BLINDERMAN, Abraham.  American Writers on Educa-
           tion Before 1865.  Boston:  Twayne, 1975.  Emerson,
           Alcott, Thoreau, pp. 133-151 and passim.

199   BLIVIN, Bruce. "Mr. Thoreau of Walden Pond."
      Reader's Digest, 79 (December, 1961), 225-234.

200   BODE, Carl J. "Henry David Thoreau as a Poet, With
      a Critical Edition of the Poems." Ph. D. diss.,
      Northwestern, 1941.

201        . "Thoreau's Last Letter (Dated April 2,
      1862)." New England Quarterly, 19 (June, 1946),
      244.

202        . "Thoreau Finds a House." Saturday Review
      of Literature, 29 (July 20, 1946), 15. A letter.

203        . "A New College Manuscript of Thoreau's."
      American Literature, 21 (November, 1949), 311-320.

204        . "Thoreau and His Last Publishers." New
      England Quarterly, 26 (September, 1953), 383-387.

205        . "Thoreau the Actor." American Quarterly,
      5 (Fall, 1953), 247-252. Reprinted in Bode, The
      Half-World of American Culture (1965), pp. 54-62.

206        . The American Lyceum: Town Meeting of
      the Mind. New York: Oxford University Press,
      1956. Reprinted Carbondale: Southern Illinois Uni-
      versity Press, 1968. Thoreau, pp. 225-228 and pas-
      sim.

207        . "Thoreau with Advice." American Literature,
      28 (March, 1956), 77-78. Letter of 1860 to S. R.
      Bartlett.

208        . "Thoreau's Manuscript Poems in Private
      Hands." Emerson Society Quarterly, 14 (1959), 17-
      18.

209        . "Thoreau's Unpublished Poems." Thoreau
      Society Bulletin, 66 (Winter, 1959), 1. Analysis of
      a sales catalog.

210        . "The Half-Hidden Thoreau." Massachusetts
      Review, 4 (1962), 68-80. Reprinted in Bode, The
      Half-World of American Culture (1965), pp. 3-15.
      Also reprinted in Hicks, John H., ed., Thoreau in
      Our Season (1966), pp. 104-116.

211          . The Half-World of American Culture:  A
Miscellany.  Preface by C. P. Snow.  Carbondale:
Southern Illinois University Press, 1965.  "Thoreau's
Young Ideas," pp. 95-105.  Also reprints earlier
essays on Thoreau.

212          . American Life in the 1840's.  New York:
New York University Press; Garden City, N. Y.:
Anchor, 1967.  "Making a Home," pp. 55-56.

213          . "Thoreau and the Borrowed Reeds," in
Browne, Ray B., and Donald Pizer, eds., Themes
and Directions in American Literature:  Essays in
Honor of Leon Howard.  Lafayette, Ind.:  Purdue
Research Foundation, 1969, pp. 58-68.

214          . "A Problem in Arithmetic."  Thoreau Society
Bulletin, 130 (Winter, 1975), 3.  See Howarth, ed.,
The Literary Manuscripts of Thoreau (1974).

215          , ed.  Collected Poems of Henry Thoreau.
Chicago:  University of Chicago Press, 1943.  Reprinted Baltimore:  Johns Hopkins University Press,
1964.  Reprints 1943 text without revision; adds 13
new poems.

216          , ed. with Introduction.  The Portable Thoreau.
New York:  Viking, 1947.  Revised edition, 1964.

217          , ed.  The Young Rebel in American Literature:
Seven Lectures.  London:  Heinemann, 1959; New
York:  Praeger, 1959.  "Thoreau:  The Double Nega-
tive," pp. 3-22.

218          , ed. with Foreword.  Selected Journals of
Henry David Thoreau.  New York:  New American
Library, 1967.  Reprinted as The Best of Thoreau's
Journals.  Carbondale:  Southern Illinois University
Press; London:  Feffer and Simons, 1971.

219          , and Walter Harding, eds.  The Correspondence
of Henry David Thoreau.  New York:  New York University Press, 1958.

220  BOEWE, Charles.  "Thoreau's 1854 Lecture in Philadelphia."  English Language Notes, 2 (December,
1964), 115-122.

221   BOIES, Jack Jay. "Circular Imagery in Thoreau's
      Week." College English, 26 (February, 1965), 350-
      355.

222   BOLLER, Paul F., Jr. American Transcendentalism,
      1830-1860: An Intellectual Inquiry. New York: Put-
      nam, 1974. Thoreau, pp. 29-31 and passim.

223   BOND, Brian C. "Thoreau's A Week on the Concord
      and Merrimack Rivers: A Generic Study." Ph. D.
      diss., Bowling Green, 1972. DA, 33 (1973), 3574A.

224   BONNER, Willard Hallam. "Mariners and Terreners:
      Some Aspects of Nautical Imagery in Thoreau."
      American Literature, 34 (January, 1963), 507-519.

225   _____. "Captain Thoreau: Gubernator to a Piece of
      Wood." New England Quarterly, 39 (March, 1966),
      26-46. Sailing images in Thoreau.

226   _____. "Thoreau's Other Telegraph Figure." Amer-
      ican Notes and Queries, 7 (1969), 99-100.

227   _____. "Thalassa! Thalassa! Thoreau at Newport?"
      Thoreau Society Bulletin, 120 (Summer, 1972), 7-8.

228   _____. "The Harvest of Thought in Thoreau's 'Au-
      tumnal Tints.' " Emerson Society Quarterly, 22
      (1976), 78-84.

229   _____, and Mary Alice Budge. "Thoreau and Robin-
      son Crusoe: An Overview." Thoreau Journal Quar-
      terly, 5 (Summer, 1973), 16-18.

230   BOOTH, Edward Townsend. God Made the Country.
      New York: Knopf, 1946. "Concord Alluvial: Emer-
      son, Thoreau, and Alcott," pp. 186-201.

231   BORCK, Jim Springer, and Herbert B. Rothschild, Jr.
      "Meditative Discoveries in Thoreau's 'The Pond in
      Winter.' " Texas Studies in Literature and Language,
      20 (1978), 93-106.

232   BORN, Helena. Whitman's Ideal Democracy and Other
      Writings, ed. with Biographical Sketch of Helena
      Born by Helen Tufts. Boston: Everett, 1902.
      "Thoreau's Joy in Nature," pp. 20-30.

233 BORST, Raymond. "Thoreau Advertisements from The
      Atlantic Monthly: 1862-1868." Thoreau Society Bul-
      letin, 129 (Fall, 1974), 4-6.

234 _____. "Footnotes on Thoreau Taken from The
      Critic." Thoreau Society Bulletin, 133 (Fall, 1975),
      3-6. Refers to a periodical published 1844-1863.

235 BOTTORFF, William K., and David G. Hoch. "Thoreau
      and Ether." Thoreau Society Bulletin, 136 (Summer,
      1976), 6.

236 BOUDREAU, Gordon V. "Henry Thoreau's Sound Sense."
      Oral English (Le Moyne College, N.Y.), 1 (1972),
      7-12.

237 _____. "Henry David Thoreau, William Gilpin, and
      the Metaphysical Ground of the Picturesque." Ameri-
      can Literature, 45 (1973), 357-369.

238 _____. " 'Remember the Creator': Thoreau and St.
      Augustine." Emerson Society Quarterly, 19 (1973),
      149-160.

239 _____. "Thoreau and Richard C. French: Conjec-
      tures on the Pickerel Passage in Walden." Emerson
      Society Quarterly, 20 (1974), 117-124.

240 _____. "Seeds." Concord Saunterer, 10 (Winter,
      1975), 9-11.

241 BOWDEN, Larry R. "Transcendence in Walden."
      Religion in Life, 46 (1977), 166-171.

242 BOWLING, Lawrence. "Thoreau's Social Criticism as
      Poetry." Yale Review, 55 (Winter, 1966), 255-264.

243 BOYD, David. "Thoreau, the Rebel Idealist." Ameri-
      cana, 30 (January, April, 1936), 89-118, 286-323.

244 BOYNTON, Percy H. A History of American Literature.
      Boston: Ginn, 1919. Thoreau, pp. 221-235.

245 BRADFORD, Robert W. "Thoreau and Therien."
      American Literature, 34 (January, 1963), 499-506.

246 BRANCH, E. Douglas. The Sentimental Years: 1836-

1860. New York: Appleton-Century, 1934. Thoreau, passim.

247   BRASHERS, Charles. "Franklin, Thoreau, and the
      Decline of Pleasure." Recovering Literature, 6
      (1977), 31-42.

248   BRATTON, F. G. "New England Unitarianism," in
      Legacy of the Liberal Spirit. New York: Scribner,
      1943, pp. 183-200.

249   BRAUN, Frederic W. "Allegash--1974." Thoreau So-
      ciety Bulletin, 131 (Spring, 1975), 4-5. Refers to a
      locale in Maine.

250   BRAWNER, James P. "Thoreau as Wit and Humorist."
      South Atlantic Quarterly, 44 (April, 1945), 170-194.

251   _____. "Thoreau." Times Literary Supplement
      (London), 4 (February, 1972), 128-129.

252   BRENNER, Gerry. "Thoreau's 'Brute Neighbors': Four
      Levels of Nature." Emerson Society Quarterly, 39
      (1965), 37-40.

253   BRESSLER, Leo A. "Walden, Neglected American
      Classic." English Journal, 51 (January, 1962),
      14-20.

254   BRICKETT, Elsie F. "Studies in the Poets and Poetry
      of New England Transcendentalism." Ph. D. diss.,
      Yale, 1934. Thoreau, passim.

255   BRIDGES, William E., ed. Spokesmen for the Self:
      Emerson Thoreau, and Whitman. Scranton, Pa.:
      Chandler, 1971. Thoreau, pp. 82-150. Quotations,
      excerpts, passages from the works of the authors.

256   BRIDGMAN, Richard. "Holmes, Thoreau, and Ponds."
      Thoreau Society Bulletin, 83 (Spring, 1963), 1-2.

257   BRODERICK, John C. "Henry David Thoreau's Principle
      of Simplicity as Shown in His Attitudes Toward Cities,
      Government, and Industrialism." Ph. D. diss., North
      Carolina, 1953.

258   _____. "Imagery in Walden." University of Texas
      Studies in English, 33 (1954), 80-89.

259 _____. "Thoreau and My Prisons." Boston Public
        Library Quarterly, 7 (January, 1955), 48-50.

260 _____. "The Thoreau Family and Concord Fires."
        Thoreau Society Bulletin, 51 (Spring, 1955), 2.

261 _____. "Thoreau's Proposals for Legislation."
        American Quarterly, 7 (Fall, 1955), 285-290.

262 _____. "Young Thoreau Asserts Himself." Thoreau
        Society Bulletin, 53 (Fall, 1955), 2.

263 _____. "American Reviews of Thoreau's Posthumous
        Books, 1863-1866: Checklist and Analysis." Univer-
        sity of Texas Studies in English, 34 (1955), 125-139.

264 _____. "Thoreau, Alcott, and the Poll Tax." Studies
        in Philology, 53 (October, 1956), 612-626.

265 _____. "The Movement of Thoreau's Prose." Amer-
        ican Literature, 33 (May, 1961), 133-142. Reprinted
        in Glick, ed., Recognition (1969), pp. 324-334.

266 _____. "Emerson, Thoreau, and Transcendentalism,"
        a review of current scholarship in American Literary
        Scholarship, 1967, pp. 3-16; 1968, pp. 3-18; 1969, pp.
        3-18; 1970, pp. 3-17; 1971, pp. 3-23.

267 _____. "Flynndependence." Thoreau Society Bul-
        letin, 113 (Fall, 1970), 5. On Errol Flynn's diary
        and possible influence of Thoreau on the actor's de-
        sire for independence.

268 BROGAN, Katherine Doherty. "Thoreau's First Ex-
        perience with Myth in A Week." Thoreau Journal
        Quarterly, 7 (1975), 3-9.

269 BROOKS, Van Wyck. The Flowering of New England,
        1815-1865. New York: Dutton, 1937. Revised edi-
        tion, 1940. Fourth edition, New York: Ronald,
        1948. "Thoreau," pp. 286-302. Had been earlier
        printed in Morgan, S. S., and W. H. Thomas, eds.,
        Opinions and Attitudes in the Twentieth Century.
        New York: Nelson, 1934, pp. 91-105. Revised edi-
        tion, pp. 244-258.

270 _____. "Thoreau at Walden," in Brooks, The Flow-
    ering (1937), pp. 359-373.  Also in Balch, M., ed.,
    Modern Short Biographies and Autobiographies.  New
    York: Harcourt, Brace, 1935, pp. 255-273.  Also
    in Essay Annual, 1937, pp. 87-101.

271 _____. "Concord in the Fifties," in Brooks, The
    Flowering (1937), pp. 422-442.

272 _____. "Thoreau, Master of Simplicity." Reader's
    Digest, 30 (May, 1937), 25.

273 BROWN, Gilbert. "Thoreau's Mountain: Monadnock."
    Literarische Wochenschrift, 31 (1968), 45-47.

274 BROWN, Mary Hosmer. Memories of Concord. Bos-
    ton: Houghton Mifflin, 1926.

275 BROWN, Theodore M. "Thoreau's Prophetic Architec-
    tural Program." New England Quarterly, 38 (1935),
    3-20.

276 BROWN, Thomas H. "The Significant Opening of Wal-
    den." American Transcendental Quarterly, 17 (1973),
    16.

277 BRUCCOLI, Matthew J., ed. The Chief Glory of Every
    People: Essays on Classic American Writers. Car-
    bondale: Southern Illinois University Press, 1973.
    "Henry Thoreau and the Reverend Poluphloisboios
    Thalassa," by Joel Porte, pp. 191-210.

278 BRUEL, Andrée. "Ralph Waldo Emerson et Thoreau."
    Paris: Les Presses Modernes, 1929. Ph.D. diss.,
    Paris, 1929. In French.

279 BUBER, Martin. "Man's Duty as Man," translated
    from German by John Harland Hicks, in Hicks, ed.,
    Thoreau in Our Season (1966), p. 19.

280 BUCKELL, H. "A Thoreau Pilgrimage." North Ameri-
    can Review, 238 (October, 1934), 376-377.

281 BUCKLEY, Frank. "Thoreau and the Irish." New
    England Quarterly, 13 (September, 1940), 389-400.

282 BUELL, Lawrence. "Transcendental Catalog Rhetoric:

Vision Versus Form." American Literature, 40
(1968), 325-339.

283 _____. "Review of The Recognition of Henry David
Thoreau, ed. Wendell Glick (1969)." New England
Quarterly, 44 (1971), 323-325.

284 _____. Literary Transcendentalism: Style and
Vision in the American Renaissance. Ithaca, N.Y.:
Cornell University Press, 1973. "Thoreau and the
Literary Excursion," pp. 188-207; "Thoreau's A
Week," pp. 208-238; and "Emerson and Thoreau:
Soul Versus Self," pp. 284-311.

285 _____. "Emerson, Thoreau, and Transcendentalism,"
a review of current scholarship in American Literary
Scholarship, 1974, pp. 3-14; 1975, pp. 3-15.

286 BURANELLI, Vincent. "The Case Against Thoreau."
Ethics, 67 (July, 1957), 257-268.

287 BURBANK, R., and J. B. Moore, eds. Literature of
the American Renaissance. Columbus: Ohio State
University Press, 1969. Thoreau, passim.

288 BURBICK, Joan Susan. "The Art of Days: Perspectives on The Journal of Henry Thoreau." Ph. D.
diss., Brandeis, 1974. DA, 35 (1974), 3672A.

289 BURD, V. A. "A Louisiana Estimate of an 'American
Rebel': Sarah Anne Dorsey on Henry David Thoreau."
Louisiana History, 5 (Summer, 1964), 296-309.

290 BURNHAM, Philip E., and Carvel Collins. "Contribu-
tions to a Bibliography of Thoreau, 1938-1945."
Bulletin of Bibliography, 19 (September-December,
1946), 16-19; (January-April, 1947), 37-39.

291 BURNS, John Robert. "Thoreau's Use of the Bible."
Ph. D. diss., Notre Dame, 1966. DA, 27 (1967), 3864A.

292 BURR, Gray. "The One and Only," a poem. Massachusetts Review, 4 (1962), 92. Reprinted in Hicks,
ed., Thoreau in Our Season (1966), p. 79.

293 BURR, Michael A. "Thoreau's Love and Doubt: An
Anagram." American Transcendental Quarterly 24
Supplement 1 (1974), 22-25.

294  BURRESS, Lee A., III. "Thoreau on Ether and Psy-
     chedelic Drugs." American Notes and Queries, 12
     (1974), 99-100.

295  BURROUGHS, John. "Henry David Thoreau." Century
     Magazine, July, 1882, pp. 368-379. Reprinted in
     The Writings of John Burroughs. Boston: Houghton
     Mifflin, 1904. Vol. VIII, Indoor Studies, pp. 3-48.
     Also reprinted Hartford, Conn.: Emerson Society,
     1962.

296  _____. "Thoreau's Wildness," in Literary Values.
     Boston: Houghton Mifflin, 1902, pp. 217-223. Re-
     printed in Harding, ed., A Century (1954), pp. 87-90.

297  _____. "A Critical Glance into Thoreau." Atlantic,
     123 (July, 1919), 777-786.

298  _____. The Last Harvest. Boston: Houghton Mifflin,
     1922. "Another Word on Thoreau," pp. 103-171.

299  _____. "Henry David Thoreau with Selections," in
     Columbia University Course, Vol. 17; Warner Li-
     brary, Vol. 24. 1930.

300  BURROUGHS, Julian. "Burroughs and Thoreau."
     Thoreau Society Bulletin, 21 (Fall, 1947), 2.

301  BUSCH, Frederick. "Thoreau and Melville as Cell-
     mates." Modern Fiction Studies, 23 (1977), 239-
     242. A study of "Bartleby" and "Civil Disobedience."

302  BUSH, Rev. Trevor N. W. "Thoreau in South Africa:
     A Letter to John H. Hicks." Massachusetts Re-
     view, 4 (Autumn, 1962), 90-91. Reprinted in Hicks,
     John H., ed., Thoreau in Our Season (1966), pp.
     27-28.

303  BUTKISS, John F. "Hecker and Thoreau: Their Cor-
     respondence." Thoreau Journal Quarterly, 8
     (1976), 17-23.

304  BUTLER, Albert F. "Thoreau's Three Thousand
     Bluets." Thoreau Society Bulletin, 117 (Fall, 1971),
     4.

305  BUTTER, Gerald J. "Comment on Brasher's Re-ap-

praisal of Franklin and Thoreau. " <u>Recovering Lit-</u>
<u>erature</u>, 6 (1977), 43-45.

306 BYRON, Gilbert. "The Proggers. " <u>Thoreau Society</u>
<u>Bulletin</u>, 89 (Fall, 1964), 1-2. Thoreau and local
outdoor philosophers.

307 _____. "Henry Thoreau: Boatman. " <u>Thoreau</u>
<u>Journal Quarterly</u>, 1 (1969), 9-14.

308 C., W. A. "A Week on the Frontier. " <u>Thoreau Society</u>
<u>Bulletin</u>, 57 (Fall, 1956), 1-4.

309 CADY, Lyman V. "Thoreau's Quotations from the Confucian Books in <u>Walden.</u> " <u>American Literature</u>, 33
(March 1961), 20-32.

310 CAHOON, Herbert, Thomas V. Lange, and Charles
Ryskamp, eds. <u>American Literary Autographs:</u>
<u>From Washington Irving to Henry James.</u> New York:
Dover, 1977. Thoreau, pp. 45-47.

311 CAIRNS, William B. <u>A History of American Literature.</u>
New York and London: Oxford University Press,
1912. Thoreau, pp. 238-242.

312 CALLAHAN, Robert D. "<u>Walden:</u> Portrait of the
Critics' Saint as a Young Daydreamer. " <u>Paunch,</u>
24 (1965), 27-39. Argues that Thoreau represents
futility, not hope.

313 CALLOW, James T., and Robert J. Reilly. <u>Guide to</u>
<u>American Literature from Its Beginnings Through</u>
<u>Walt Whitman.</u> New York: Barnes and Noble, 1976.
Contains long bibliographies.

314 CAMERON, Kenneth Walter. <u>Emerson the Essayist:</u>
<u>An Outline of His Philosophical Development Through</u>
<u>1836,</u> 2 vols. Raleigh, N. C. : Thistle, 1945. Third
and enlarged edition, Hartford, Conn. : Transcendental, 1971. Thoreau, passim.

315 _____. "Emerson, Thoreau, and the Society of
Natural History. " <u>American Literature</u>, 24 (March,
1952), 21-30.

316 _____. "Thoreau Discovers Emerson:  A College
Reading Record. "  Bulletin of the New York Public
Library,  57 (June, 1953), 319-334.

317 _____. "Thoreau, Sir Vita, and Harvardiana. "   Thoreau Society Bulletin, 49 (Fall, 1954), 1.

318 _____. "Emerson, Thoreau, and the Poet Henry
Sutton. "  Emerson Society Quarterly (ESQ), 1
(1955), 10-16.

319 _____. "The Whereabouts of Thoreau's Natural
History Collection. "  Emerson Society Quarterly, 2
(1956), 15.

320 _____. "Thoreau and the Folklore of Walden Pond. "
Emerson Society Quarterly, 3 (1956), 10-12.

321 _____. "Thoreau's Three Months Out of Harvard
and His First Publication. "  Emerson Society Quarterly, 5 (1956), 2-12.

322 _____. "Four Uncollected Thoreau Poems with Notes
on the Canon. "  ESQ, 5 (1956), 13-16.

323 _____. "Two Thoreau Journal Fragments of 1851. "
ESQ, 5 (1956), 16-19.

324 _____. "Emerson, Thoreau, Parson Frost, and
'The Problem. ' "  ESQ, 6 (1957), 16.

325 _____. "Emerson, Thoreau, Elegant Extracts and
Proverb Lore. "  ESQ, 6 (1957), 26-39.

326 _____. "Helen Thoreau Writes to Dr. Shattuck in
1838. "  ESQ, 6 (1957), 48.

327 _____. "Four Uncollected Thoreau Poems--A Correction. "  ESQ,  6 (1957), 48.

328 _____. "Thoreau's Gift to the Massachusetts Historical Society in 1846. "  ESQ, 6 (1957), 48.

329 _____. "The Solitary Thoreau of the Alumni Notes. "
ESQ, 7 (1957), 48.

330 _____. "Jones Very and Thoreau--the 'Greek' Myth. "
ESQ, 7 (1957), 39-40.

331  _____. "Thoreau, Parker, and Emerson's 'Mouse-
trap' in The Monitor (1862)." ESQ, 7 (1957), 42-46.

332  _____. "Thoreau Bills His Pupils at the Concord
Academy." ESQ, 7 (1957), 47-50.

333  _____. "Thoreau's Newspaper Clippings in the Morgan College Notebook." ESQ, 7 (1957), 51-52.

334  _____. "Thoreaus in the Evangelical Missionary Society of Concord." ESQ, 7 (1957), 52-53.

335  _____. "A Brief Glance at the Thoreau Society."
ESQ, 7 (1957), 54.

336  _____. "Emerson, Thoreau, and the Town and
Country Club." ESQ, 8 (1957), 2-17.

337  _____. "Freshman Thoreau Opposes Harvard's Marking System." ESQ, 8 (1957), 17-18.

338  _____. "A Manuscript Fragment of Thoreau's Quebec
Journey of 1850." ESQ, 8 (1957), 19.

339  _____. "Thoreau's Early Compositions in the Ancient
Languages." ESQ, 8 (1957), 20-29.

340  _____. "Ralph Cudworth and Thoreau's Translations
of an Orphic Hymn." ESQ, 8 (1957), 31-36.

341  _____. "An Unidentified French Passage in Thoreau's Notebook (H. M. 13201)." ESQ, 8 (1957),
36.

342  _____. "Young Henry Thoreau in the Annals of the
Concord Academy (1829-1833)." ESQ, 9 (1957), 1-
42.

343  _____. "Thoreau Witnesses Emerson Purchase Land
at Walden." ESQ, 10 (1958), 15-16.

344  _____. "Thoreau and Barzillai Frost." ESQ, 10
(1958), 42-46.

345  _____. "Harvard Records of Thoreau's Closest College Friends." ESQ, 10 (1958), 47-48.

346        _____ . "The Thoreau Family in Probate Records. "
           ESQ, 11 (1958), 17-24.

347        _____ . "Memorabilia of Thoreau's Concord Academy
           Friends. " ESQ, 11 (1958), 24-26.

348        _____ . "A Checklist of Concord Academy Students in
           Thoreau's Day. " ESQ, 11 (1958), 46-48.

349        _____ . "Articles of Possible Interest to Emerson
           and Thoreau in Concord Newspapers. " ESQ, 12
           (1958), 48-49.

350        _____ . "The Little Pond--What It Means to Us. "
           ESQ, 13 (1958), 48-49.

351        _____ . "Thoreau's 'Love's Invalides are not those
           of Common Wars'--A Correction. " ESQ, 13 (1958),
           26.

352        _____ . "Thoreau and Walden Pond in Early News-
           papers. " ESQ, 13 (1958), 46.

353        _____ . "An Epitaph on the Cover of a Thoreau Jour-
           nal. " ESQ, 13 (1958), 93-95.

354        _____ . "The Recent Sale of Thoreau Manuscripts. "
           ESQ, 13 (1958), 98-114.

355        _____ . Emerson and Thoreau as Readers.   Hartford,
           Conn. : Transcendental, 1958.  Reissued in enlarged
           edition, 1972.

356        _____ . "Thoreau's New Poems (Unlisted Manu-
           scripts). " ESQ, 14 (1959), 21-32.

357        _____ . "Lectures in Boston During Thoreau's Senior
           Year. " ESQ, 14 (1959), 43-48.

358        _____ . "Thoreau's Diploma Again. " ESQ, 14 (1959),
           48-49.

359        _____ . "Thoreau and Emerson in Channing's Letters
           to the Watsons. " ESQ, 14 (1959), 77-85.

360        _____ . "Thoreau in the Court of Common Pleas
           (1854). " ESQ, 14 (1959), 86-89.

361          . "Chronology of Thoreau's Harvard Years."
ESQ, 15 (1959), 2-108. Also published as book,
Thoreau's Harvard Years. Hartford, Conn.: Tran-
scendental, 1959. See also a similar work in 1966.

362          . "A New Thoreau Poem--'To Edith.' " ESQ,
18 (1960), 40-41.

363          . "Historical Notes on the Concord Academy."
ESQ, 19 (1960), 46-51.

364          . "Emerson, Thoreau, and Concord in Early
Newspapers." ESQ, 21 (1960), 1-57. Also published as book, Hartford, Conn.: Transcendental,
1958.

365          . "Henry Thoreau's Stepgrandmother." ESQ,
22 (1961), 54-56.

366          . "Emerson's Walden Woodlots and the Fitch-
burg Railroad." ESQ, 22 (1961), 67-68.

367          . "Thoreau's Notes from Dubuat's Principes."
ESQ, 22 (1961), 68-76.

368          . "Thoreau's Walden Pond." ESQ, 22 (1961),
77-80. Reprints 1960 news item about saving Walden
Pond.

369          . "Emerson's Fight for His Walden Woodlots."
ESQ, 22 (1961), 90-95.

370          . "A Bundle of Emerson Letters." ESQ, 22
(1961), 95-96. Thoreau, passim.

371          . "Books Thoreau Desired to Purchase in
1859." ESQ, 23 (1961), 16.

372          . "Thoreau's Harvard Textbooks." ESQ, 23
(1961), 19-119. Visual survey of contents. Also
published as book, Hartford, Conn.: Transcendental,
1961.

373          . "Annotations on Thoreau's Correspondence."
ESQ, 24 (1961), 6-105. Refers to work ed. by Bode
and Harding (1958). Published as book in 1964.

374 _____ . "Thoreau's Disciple at Walden:  Edmond S. Hotham. "  ESQ, 26 (1962), 34-45.

375 _____ .  "Emerson, Thoreau, and the Atlantic Cable. " ESQ,  26 (1962), 45-87.

376 _____ .  "Thoreau Manuscripts--Ungathered and Migrant. "  ESQ, 35 (1964), 84-86.

377 _____ .  "Anti-Slavery Song Books in Thoreau's Library. "  ESQ, 36 (1964), 52-121.  Photo-reproduction.

378 _____ .  "Introduction to the Publication of Thoreau's Literary Notebook in the Library of Congress. "  ESQ, 37 (1964), 55-59.

379 _____ .  Companion to Thoreau's Correspondence. Hartford, Conn. :  Transcendental, 1964.

380 _____ .  "Thoreau's Two Books of Pindar. "  ESQ, 38 (1965), 96-112.  Mostly facsimile reproduction of books owned by Thoreau, with marginalia.

381 _____ .  "Henry Thoreau and the Entomology of Kirby and Spence. "  ESQ, 38 (1965), 138-142.  A work that Thoreau knew and used.

382 _____ .  "Thoreau on Harvard College--A Debt to Marshall Tufts?"  ESQ, 43 (1966), 2-3.  Followed by reproduction of source.

383 _____ .  "Thoreau, Edward Tyrrel Channing and College Themes. "  ESQ, 43 (1966), 15-34.

384 _____ .  "Thoreau and Stearns Wheeler:  Four Letters and a Reading Record. "  ESQ, 48 (1967), 73-81.

385 _____ .  "Sophomore Thoreau and Religious Improvement. "  ESQ, 48 (1967), 82-85.

386 _____ .  "Reflections of Thoreau at Harvard. "  ESQ, 48 (1967), 87-89.

387 _____ .  "Scattered Thoreau Manuscripts, I. "  ESQ, 48 (1967), 145-149.  See American Transcendental Quarterly, 14 (1972), 189-194 for Part II.  Location of rare items.

388 _____. "A Tabular View of Thoreau's Harvard Curriculum." ESQ, 51 (1968), 10-25.

389 _____. "Thoreau and Orestes Brownson." ESQ, 51 (1968), 53-65.

390 _____. "Thoreau's Harvard Friends and Temperance." ESQ, 51 (1968), 137-141.

391 _____. "Thoreau and Frank Bellew in Concord." ESQ, 51 (1968), 141-143.

392 _____. "Harvard Rules and Certificates of Thoreau's Day." ESQ, 52 (1968), 86-87.

393 _____. "Thoreau's Notes on the Shipwreck at Fire Island." ESQ, 52 (1968), 97-99.

394 _____. "What Thoreau Taught in 1837." ESQ, 52 (1968), 100.

395 _____. "Damning National Publicity for Thoreau in 1849." American Transcendental Quarterly (ATQ), 2 (1969), 18-27.

396 _____. "Thoreau's Walden and Alcott's Vegetarianism." ATQ, 2 (1969), 27-28.

397 _____. "Thoreau on the Limitations of Great Circle Sailing." ATQ, 14 (1972), 70-71.

398 _____. "Tribute to Thoreau in the National Anti-Slavery Standard (1866)." ATQ, 14 (1972), 73-75.

399 _____. "Thoreau and Hiram Leonard." ATQ, 14 (1972), 135-147.

400 _____. "Emerson and Thoreau Lecture at Lynn." ATQ, 14 (1972), 158-164.

401 _____. "Some Scattered Thoreau Manuscripts, II." ATQ, 14 (1972), 189-194.

402 _____. "Thoreau and the Biography of John Brown." ATQ, 17 (1973), 17.

403 _____. "Thoreau in the Pulpit: Report of a Lost Address." ATQ, 20 Supplement (1973), 1.

404 _____. "Two Thoreau Poems: Variant Readings."
ATQ, 20 Supplement (1973), 128-129. "Annus Mira-
bilis" and "Inspiration."

405 _____. "Thoreau's Declaration at the Concord
Academy." ATQ, 20 Supplement (1973), 140-144.

406 _____. Transcendental Apprenticeship: Notes on
Young Henry Thoreau's Reading: A Contexture with
a Researcher's Index. Hartford, Conn.: Transcendental, 1976.

407 _____. "Nathaniel Seefurth: Friend of Thoreau."
ATQ, 32 (1976), 5-10.

408 _____. "Thoreau's Schoolmate, Alfred Munroe,
Remembers Concord." ATQ, 36 (1977), 10-38.

409 _____. "The Lyceum in Massachusetts: Emerson,
Thoreau, and Others at Newburyport (1848-1855)."
ATQ, 36 (1977), 39-42.

410 _____. "Loyalty to Emerson, Thoreau, and Transcendentalism at Harvard in 1854-1855." ATQ, 36
(1977), 51-60.

411 _____. "Thoreau's Lecture on 'Misspent Lives' and
the Evolution of 'Life Without Principle.'" ATQ,
36 (1977), 75-79.

412 _____. "Association or Presentation Copies of
Thoreau's Books." ATQ, 36 (1977), 80-82.

413 _____. "More Ungathered or Migrant Thoreau Manuscripts." ATQ, 36 (1977), 82-84.

414 _____. Transcendentalism and American Renaissance
Bibliographies. Hartford, Conn.: Transcendental,
1977. Lists 66 publications with summaries of primary works published by Transcendental Books.

415 _____, ed. Emerson, Thoreau, and Concord in
Early Newspapers: Biographical and Historical Lore
for the Scholar and General Reader. Hartford,
Conn.: Transcendental, 1958.

416 _____, ed. The Transcendentalists and Minerva:

Cultural Background of the American Renaissance with
Fresh Discoveries in the Intellectual Climate of Emer-
son, Alcott, and Thoreau, 3 vols.  Hartford, Conn. :
Transcendental, 1958.

417          , ed.  Transcendental Climate:  New Resources
for the Study of Emerson, Thoreau, and Their Contemporaries, 3 vols.  Hartford, Conn. :  Transcendental, 1963.

418          , ed.  Thoreau's Literary Notebook in the Library of Congress.  Facsimile text, with Index.
Hartford, Conn. :  Transcendental, 1964.

419          , ed. with Notes.  Over Thoreau's Desk:  New
Correspondence, 1838-1861.  Hartford, Conn. :  Transcendental, 1965.  Family business, etc. , not Thoreau as author.

420          , ed. with Commentary and Index.  Thoreau and
His Harvard Classmates:  Henry Williams' "Memorials
of the Class of 1837. "  Hartford, Conn. :  Transcendental, 1965.  Reprinted in ATQ, 3 (1969), 5-132.

421          , ed.  Transcendental Epilogue:  Primary
Materials for Research in Emerson, Thoreau, Literary New England, the Influence of German Theology,
and Higher Biblical Criticism.  Hartford, Conn. :
Transcendental, 1965.

422          , ed. with Annotation and Index.  Thoreau's
Fact Book in the Harry Elkins Widener Collection in
the Harvard College Library, 2 vols.  Hartford,
Conn. :  Transcendental, 1966.

423          , ed.  Thoreau's Harvard Years:  Materials
Introductory to New Explorations:  Record of Fact
and Background.  Hartford, Conn. :  Transcendental,
1966.

424          , ed.  The Massachusetts Lyceum During the
American Renaissance:  Materials for the Study of
the Oral Tradition in American Letters:  Emerson,
Thoreau, Hawthorne, and Other New England Lec-
turers.  Hartford, Conn. :  Transcendental, 1969.
Reprinted as Emerson and Thoreau Speak:  Lecturing
in Concord and Lincoln During the American Renaissance.  Hartford, Conn. :  Transcendental, 1972.

425 _____, ed. Transcendental Log. Hartford, Conn.:
Transcendental, 1973. Reprinted in ATQ, 28 (1975),
1-345.

426 _____, ed. Response to Transcendental Concord:
The Last Decades of the Era of Emerson, Thoreau,
and the Concord School as Recorded in Newspapers.
Hartford, Conn.: Transcendental, 1974.

427 _____, ed. with Notes and Index. Sixty Years of
Concord, 1855-1915: Life, People, Institutions, and
Transcendental Philosophy in Massachusetts--with
Memories of Emerson, Thoreau, Alcott, Channing,
and Others, by F. B. Sanborn. Hartford, Conn.:
Transcendental, 1976.

428 CAMPBELL, Charles L. "An American Tragedy: or,
Death in the Woods." Modern Fiction Studies, 15
(Summer, 1969), 251-259. Dreiser's interest in
Thoreau.

429 CANBY, Henry Seidel. "The Modern Thoreau." Dial,
59 (July 15, 1915), 54-55.

430 _____. "Thoreau, the Great Eccentric." Saturday
Review of Literature, 4 (November 26, 1927), 337-
339.

431 _____. "Henry David Thoreau," in Classic Americans. New York: Harcourt, Brace, 1931. Reprinted New York: Russell and Russell, 1959, pp.
184-225.

432 _____. "Thoreau," in American Estimates. New
York: Harcourt, Brace, 1929, pp. 97-109.

433 _____. "Thoreau and the Machine Age." Yale Review, 20 (March, 1931), 517-531. Similar to material in Classic Americans. Reprinted in Sizer, Theodore, et al., eds., Aspects of the Social History of
America. Chapel Hill: University of North Carolina
Press, 1931, pp. 95-116.

434 _____. "Back to Walden." Catholic World, 134
(January, 1932), 478-480.

435 _____. "The Man Who Did What He Wanted: A Pro-

posed Definition of Thoreau." Saturday Review of
Literature, 15 (December 16, 1936), 3-4, 15.

436 _____. "Thoreau in History." Saturday Review of
Literature, 20 (July 15, 1939), 3-4, 14-15.

437 _____. "Thoreau in Search of a Public." American
Scholar, 8 (August, 1939), 431-444.

438 _____. "Two Women." North American Review,
248 (August, 1939), 18-32. Thoreau and Lucy Jackson Brown and Lidian Jackson Emerson.

439 _____. "American Challenge: A Study of Walden."
Saturday Review of Literature, 20 (September 2, 1939),
10-12, 16.

440 _____. Thoreau. Boston: Houghton Mifflin, 1939.
Reprinted Boston: Beacon, 1958. Also reprinted
Gloucester, Mass.: Peter Smith, 1965.

441 _____. "Back to Nature," in The Yale Review
Anthology. New Haven: Yale University Press, 1941,
pp. 116-127.

442 _____. "A Self-Appointed Interpreter to Americans."
Christian Science Monitor, 38 (December 3, 1945), 8.

443 _____. "Thoreau: A New Estimate." Saturday Review of Literature, 22 (December 3, 1949), 15-16.

444 _____. "Walden: One Hundred Years Later."
Saturday Review of Literature, 37 (August 7, 1954),
7-8, 40-41.

445 _____. "Thoreau," excerpt from 1939 Biography, in
Prochnow, Herbert V., ed., Great Stories from Great
Lives. New York: Harper, 1944, pp. 102-107.

446 _____. "Henry David Thoreau: 1817-1862," in Van
Doren, Mark, ed., There Were Giants in the Land.
New York: Farrar and Rinehart, 1942, pp. 161-168.

447 _____. "From Books to Men," in American Memoirs.
Boston: Houghton Mifflin, 1947, pp. 401-408.

448 _____, ed. Walden. Boston: Houghton Mifflin, 1936.

449 _____, ed. The Works of Thoreau: Selected and
      Edited. Boston: Houghton Mifflin, 1937.

450 _____, ed. The Works of Thoreau. Boston: Hough-
      ton Mifflin, 1947. Cambridge edition.

451 CANTWELL, Robert. "Ralph Waldo Emerson and Henry
      David Thoreau," in Cantwell, Famous American Men
      of Letters. New York: Dodd, Mead, 1956, pp. 75-
      90. For teenagers.

452 CARBERG, Warren. "Thoreau's Fame Still Expands."
      Boston Post, July 27, 1947.

453 CARLEY, Peter King. "The Early Life and Thought of
      Frederick Henry Hedge, 1805-1850." Ph.D. diss.,
      Syracuse, 1973. DA, 34 (1974), 6558A.

454 CARPENTER, Frederic I. American Literature and the
      Dream. New York: Philosophical Library, 1955.
      Thoreau, passim.

455 _____. " 'The American Myth': Paradise (To Be)
      Regained." PMLA, 74 (December, 1959), 599-606.

456 _____. "American Transcendentalism in India:
      1961." Emerson Society Quarterly, 31 (1963), 59-62.

457 CARPENTER, Nan Cooke. "Louisa May Alcott and
      Thoreau's Flute." Huntington Library Quarterly, 24
      (November, 1960), 71-74. Two letters.

458 CARPER, Thomas R. "The Whole History of Thoreau's
      'My Prisons.' " Emerson Society Quarterly, 50 Sup-
      plement (1968), 35-38. On "Civil Disobedience."

459 CARROLL, Mary Suzanne. "Symbolic Patterns in Henry
      David Thoreau's A Week on the Concord and Merri-
      mack Rivers." Ph.D. diss., Indiana, 1975. DA,
      36 (1976), 5292A.

460 CARSON, Barbara H. "Orpheus in New England: Al-
      cott, Emerson, and Thoreau." Ph.D. diss., Johns
      Hopkins, 1968. DA, 29 (1968), 1533A.

461 _____. "An Orphic Hymn in Walden." Emerson So-
      ciety Quarterly, 20 (1974), 125-130.

462   CARSON, Clarence B.   "Henry David Thoreau," in The
      American Tradition.   Tokyo:  Kaibunsha, 1966, pp.
      29-30.

463   CARSON, H. T.   "An Eccentric Kinship:  Henry David
      Thoreau's 'A Plea for Captain John Brown.' "  South-
      ern Speech Journal, 27 (Winter, 1961), 151-155.

464   CARTER, Everett.  The American Idea:  The Literary
      Response to American Optimism.  Chapel Hill:  Uni-
      versity of North Carolina Press, 1977.  Thoreau,
      pp. 93-109 and passim.

465   CARTER, George F.  "Thoreau, the Great Transcendent-
      alist."  Literary Collector, 8 (October, 1904), 169-
      177.  Reprinted in Hobbies, 54 (August, 1949), 139-
      142.

466   CASTERET, Norbert.  Ten Years Under the Earth.
      Translated from French and edited by Barrows Mus-
      sey, with Preface by E. A. Martel.  New York:
      Greystone, 1938.

467   CASSERES, Benjamin de.  "Thoreau," in Casseres,
      Forty Immortals.  New York:  Lawren, 1926, pp.
      129-138.

468   CATLIN, G. E. G.  "Individualists and Anarchists,"
      in Catlin, The Story of the Political Philosophers.
      New York:  McGraw-Hill, 1939, pp. 405-431.

469   CAVELL, Stanley.  The Senses of Walden.  New York:
      Viking, 1972.

470   CESTRÉ, Charles.  "Thoreau et Emerson."  Revue
      Anglo-Américaine, 7 (February, 1930), 215-230.
      In French.

471   _____ .  "Thoreau et la dialectique."  Revue Anglo-
      Américaine, 7 (February, 1930), 230-233.  In French.

472   CHAMBERLIN, Joseph Edgar.  "Thoreau's Last Pencil."
      Magazine of History, 22 (May, 1916), 173-176.

473   _____ .  "Note on Thoreau," in Waxman, S. M., ed.,
      Nomads and Listeners.  New York:  Privately printed
      for the editor, 1937, pp. 114-117.

474   CHANDER, Jagdish, ed.   Perspectives in American
      Literature.  Ludhiana, India:  Lyall, 1969.  Contains
      seven essays on Thoreau.

475   _____, and Narindar S.  Pradhan, eds.  Studies in
      American Literature:  Essays in Honour of William
      Mulder.  New Delhi, India:  Oxford University
      Press, 1976.

476   CHANDRASEKHARAN, K. R.  "Thoreau's Literary Art
      and His Philosophy," in Mukherjee and Raghavachar-
      yulu, eds., Indian Essays (1969), pp. 41-54.

477   CHANG, Chung-nam.  "Confucian Influences on Tho-
      reau's Walden."  English Language and Literature,
      50 (1974), 47-68.  Korean publication; abstract of
      article in English.

478   CHANNING, William Ellery (the younger).   Thoreau:
      The Poet-Naturalist.  Boston:  Roberts Brothers,
      1873.  Revised and enlarged by Frank B. Sanborn.
      Boston:  Goodspeed, 1902.  Sanborn revision re-
      printed New York:  Biblo and Tannen, 1966.

479   _____.  Collected Poems, ed.  Walter Harding.
      Gainesville, Fla.:  1967.  Contains Channing's poems
      on Thoreau.

480   CHARI, V. K.  "The Question of Form in Thoreau's
      A Week on the Concord and Merrimack Rivers,"
      in Mukherjee and Raghavacharyulu, eds, Indian
      Essays (1969), pp. 99-112.

481   CHASE, Mary Ellen.  The Lovely Ambition, a novel.
      New York:  Norton, 1960.  Excerpt "The Parson and
      Thoreau," pp. 63-66.  Reprinted in Thoreau Society
      Bulletin, 74 (Winter, 1961), 5-6.

482   CHERUVELIL, Joseph M.  "The Influence of Indian
      Philosophy on Henry David Thoreau."  Ph. D. diss.,
      Mississippi, 1966.  Not completed.

483   CHESNICK, Eugene William.  "The Amplitude of Time:
      A Study of the Time-Sense of Walt Whitman."  Ph. D.
      diss., Washington University, 1968.  DA, 29 (1969),
      3969A-3970A.  Thoreau, passim.

484   CHRISMAN, L. H. "Lessening the Denominator," in
      John Ruskin, Preacher.   Nashville, Tenn.:   Abing-
      don, 1921, pp. 177-187.

485   CHRISTIE, John Aldrich.   "Henry David Thoreau, Trav-
      eler."   Ph. D. diss., Duke, 1956.

486   _____.   Thoreau as World Traveler.   New York:
      Columbia University Press, with the Co-operation
      of the American Geographical Society, 1965.   Tho-
      reau's reading of travel books; extensive bibliography
      of books read by Thoreau, pp. 311-333.

487   _____.   "Thoreau on Civil Resistance."   Emerson
      Society Quarterly, 54 (1969), 5-12.

488   CHRISTY, Arthur.   The Orient in American Transcen-
      dentalism:   A Study of Emerson, Thoreau, and Al-
      cott.   New York:   Columbia University Press, 1932;
      reissued, 1963.

489   _____, ed. with Notes.   The Transmigration of the
      Seven Brahmans:   A Translation from the Harivansa
      of Langlois, by Henry David Thoreau.   New York:
      Columbia University Press, 1932.

490   _____, ed.   "A Thoreau Fact-Book."   Colophon, 4
      (March, 1934), Part 16, 12pp.   Thoreau's reading;
      over 100 books on natural history, botany, etc.

491   CHUBB, E. W.   "Henry David Thoreau," in Chubb,
      Stories of Authors:   British and American.   New
      York:   Macmillan, 1926, pp. 297-302.

492   CLAPPER, Ronald E.   "The Development of Walden:
      A Genetic Text."   Ph. D. diss., California (Los
      Angeles), 1967.   DA, 28 (1968), 2643A.

493   CLARK, Harry Hayden.   "Changing Attitudes in Early
      American Literary Criticism," in Stovall, Floyd,
      ed., The Development of American Literary Criti-
      cism.   Chapel Hill:   University of North Carolina
      Press, 1955, pp. 15-73.   Includes Thoreau.

494   _____.   American Literature:   Poe Through Garland.
      New York:   Appleton-Century-Crofts, 1971.   Includes
      Thoreau, Melville, et al.

495 _____, ed. Transitions in American Literary His-
     tory. Durham, N. C.: Duke University Press, 1954.
     "The Rise of Transcendentalism, 1815-1860," Chapter
     V, pp. 245-314.

496 CLARKSON, John W. Jr. "Mentions of Emerson and
     Thoreau in the Letters of Franklin Benjamin San-
     born," in Myerson, ed., Studies (1978), pp. 387-420.

497 CLENDENNING, John. "Emerson, Thoreau, and Tran-
     scendentalism," in American Literary Scholarship, a
     Review of current scholarship. 1964, pp. 3-15.

498 CLERC, Charles. "The Now Thoreau: Caveat Emptor."
     Midwest Quarterly, 16 (1975), 371-388.

499 COBB, Robert Paul. "Society Versus Solitude: Studies
     in Ralph Waldo Emerson, Thoreau, Hawthorne, and
     Whitman." Ph. D. diss., Michigan, 1955.

500 _____. "Thoreau and 'The Wild.' " Emerson So-
     ciety Quarterly, 18 (1960), 5-7.

501 COCHNOWER, Mary E. "Henry David Thoreau and
     Stoicism." Ph. D. diss., Iowa, 1939.

502 COHEN, Benjamin Bernard. "The Perspective of an
     Old Master." Emerson Society Quarterly, 56 (1969),
     53-56.

503 COHEN, Hennig, ed. The American Culture: Ap-
     proaches to the Study of the United States. Boston:
     Houghton Mifflin, 1968. Thoreau, passim.

504 _____, ed. Landmarks of American Writing. New
     York and London: Basic, 1969. Also published
     Washington, D. C.: U. S. Information Agency, 1970.
     "Henry David Thoreau: Walden," by Walter Harding,
     pp. 134-143.

505 COHEN, Lance Nevin. "Contending for Humanity in the
     Technological Age: The Art and Argument of Norman
     Mailer." Ph. D. diss., Columbia, 1975. DA, 36
     (1975), 3709A. Thoreau, passim.

506 COLACURCIO, Michael Joseph. "A Better Mode of
     Evidence: The Transcendental Problem of Faith and

Spirit," in Cook, Reginald L. , ed. , Themes, Tones, and Motifs in the American Renaissance: A Symposium (1968), pp. 12-22. Also published in Emerson Society Quarterly, 54 (1969), 12-22.

507 COLEMAN, G. P. "Thoreau and His Critics." Dial, 40 (June 1, 1906), 352-356. Reprinted in Glick, ed. , Recognition (1969), pp. 161-171.

508 COLLINS, Christopher. "The Use of Observation: A Study of the Correspondential Vision in the Writings of Emerson, Thoreau, and Whitman." Ph. D. diss. , Columbia, 1964. DA, 26 (1965), 352.

509 COLLINS, Joseph, ed. The Doctor Looks at Biography: Psychological Studies of Life and Letters. New York: Doran, 1925. "Henry David Thoreau," excerpt from book by Léon Bazalgetti (1914 and 1924), pp. 79-88.

510 COLLINS, Thomas Lyle. "Thoreau's Coming of Age." Sewanee Review, 49 (January, 1941), 57-66.

511 COLLYER, Robert. "Thoreau," in Clear Grit. Boston: Beacon, 1913, pp. 294-297.

512 COLQUITT, Betsy F. "Thoreau's Poetics." American Transcendental Quarterly, 11 (1971), 74-81.

513 COLYER, Richard. "Thoreau's Color Symbols." PMLA, 86 (1971), 999-1008.

514 COMBELLACK, C. R. B. "Two Critics of Society." Pacific Spectator, 3 (August, 1949), 440-445.

515 COMMAGER, Henry Steele, and Allan Nevins, eds. The Heritage of America. Boston: Little, Brown, 1949. "Henry Thoreau Builds a Cabin at Walden Pond," excerpt from Walden, pp. 432-438.

516 CONCORD SAUNTERER, THE. Quarterly established in 1965, edited by Anne McGrath of the Thoreau Lyceum in Concord.

517 CONDRY, William. Thoreau. London: Witherly, 1954; New York: Philosophical Library, 1954. Reprinted New Delhi, India: Chand, 1962.

518        _____. "A Hundred Years of Walden. " Dublin Mag-
           azine, 31 (January-March, 1955), 42-46.

519    CONWAY, Moncure Daniel. Emerson at Home and
           Abroad. Boston: Osgood, 1882. Reprinted New
           York: Haskell House, 1968. Thoreau, passim.

520        _____. Autobiography. Boston: Houghton Mifflin,
           1904. Thoreau, pp. 142-143 and passim.

521        _____. A Century Ago with Thoreau. Berkeley
           Heights, State: Oriole, 1962. Reprinted excerpts
           from the Autobiography.

522    COOK, Reginald Lansing. "The Concord Saunterer:
           Including a Discussion of the Nature-Mysticism of
           Thoreau. " Ph. D. diss., Middlebury (Vermont) Col-
           lege, 1940. Published by Middlebury College Press,
           1940.

523        _____. "Thoreau in Perspective. " University of
           Kansas City Review, 14 (Winter, 1947), 117-125.
           Reprinted in Young, T. D., and R. E. Fine, eds.,
           American Literature: A Critical Survey. New York:
           American Book Co. , 1968, pp. 164-174.

524        _____. Passage to Walden. Boston: Houghton
           Mifflin, 1949. Revised and reprinted New York:
           Russell and Russell, 1966. Reprint edition adds
           key to references and citations.

525        _____. "From the Sinews of Walden, " excerpt from
           Passage to Walden, in Glick, ed., Recognition (1969),
           pp. 291-297.

526        _____. "Thoreau's Annotations and Corrections in
           the First Edition of Walden. " Thoreau Society Bulle-
           tin, 42 (Winter, 1953), 1-2.

527        _____. "Think of This, Yankees!" Massachusetts
           Review, 4 (1962), 44-52. Reprinted in Hicks, John
           H. , ed. , Thoreau in Our Season (1966), pp. 29-37.

528        _____. "Ancient Rites at Walden. " Emerson Society
           Quarterly, 39 (1965), 52-56.

529        _____. "An Encounter with Myth at Walden. " Amer-
           ican Transcendental Quarterly, 10 (1971), 39-42.

530 _____. "Looking for America: A Binocular Vision. "
Thoreau Journal Quarterly, 8 (1976), 10-17.

531 _____, ed. Themes, Tones, and Motifs in the
American Renaissance: A Symposium. Hartford,
Conn.: Transcendental, 1968. Also published in
Emerson Society Quarterly, 54 (1969).

532 COOK, Richard C. "Henry Thoreau's Poetic Imagery:
An Analysis of the Imagery of Walden. " M. A. Thesis, Maine, 1959.

533 _____. "Thoreau and His Imagery: The Anatomy of
an Imagination. " Thoreau Society Bulletin, 70 (Winter, 1960), 1-3.

534 COOKE, George Willis. "The Two Thoreaus." Independent, 48 (December 10, 1896), 1671-1672.

535 _____. An Historical and Biographical Introduction
to Accompany "The Dial. " Reprinted in numbers for
the Rowfant Club, 2 vols. Cleveland: Rowfant Club,
1902. Reprinted and edited by Kenneth Cameron,
American Transcendental Quarterly, 27 (1975), 1-122.

536 _____, ed. The Poets of Transcendentalism: An
Anthology. Boston: Houghton Mifflin, 1903. Reprinted Hartford, Conn.: Transcendental, 1971. Also
reprinted in American Transcendental Quarterly, 16
(1972), Parts 3 and 4.

537 COOKE, J. W. "Freedom in the Thought of Henry
David Thoreau. " Thoreau Society Bulletin, 105 (Fall,
1968), 1-3.

538 CORNER, Philip. "Thoreau, Charles Ives, and Contemporary Music," in Harding, et al. , eds. , Henry
David Thoreau: Studies (1972), pp. 53-81.

539 COSBEY, Robert C. "Thoreau at Work: The Writing
of 'Ktaadn. ' " Bulletin of the New York Public Library, 65 (January, 1961), 21-30.

540 COSMAN, Max. "Apropos of John Thoreau. " American
Literature, 12 (May, 1940), 241-243.

541 _____. "Thoreau and Nature. " Personalist, 21
(August, 1940), 289-293.

542          . "Thoreau and Staten Island." Staten Island
       Historian, 6 (January, March, 1943), 1-2, 7-8.

543          . "Thoreau Faced War." Personalist, 25
       (Winter, 1944), 73-76.

544          . "A Yankee in Canada." Canadian Historical
       Review, 25 (March, 1944), 33-37.

545    COSTA, Richard H. "Lowry's Forest Path: Echoes of
       Walden." Canadian Literature, 62 (1974), 61-68.

546    COURNOS, John. "Henry Thoreau--Hater of Shams."
       Century, 116 (June, 1928), 140-149. Reprinted in
       Cournos, A Modern Plutarch. London: Butterworth;
       Indianapolis: Bobbs-Merrill, 1928, pp. 59-69.

547          . "Gauguin and Thoreau: A Comparison."
       Bookman, 67 (July, 1928), 548-551. Reprinted in
       A Modern Plutarch (1928), pp. 70-77.

548    COUSER, G. Thomas. " 'The Old Manse, ' Walden,
       and the Hawthorne-Thoreau Relationship." Emerson
       Society Quarterly, 21 (1975), 11-20.

549          . "Thoreau's Cape Cod Pilgrimage." Ameri-
       can Transcendental Quarterly, 26 Supplement (1975),
       31-37.

550    COWAN, Michael H. City of the West: Emerson,
       America, and the Urban Metaphor. New Haven:
       Yale University Press, 1967. Thoreau, passim.

551    COWAN, Thomas D. "Six Poets of the Nineteenth-
       Century: Images of the Common Man in a Changing
       Society." Ph.D. diss., St. Louis, 1973. DA, 34
       (1974), 5903A-5904A.

552    COX, James M. "Autobiography and America," in Mil-
       ler, Joseph Hillis, ed., Aspects of Narrative. New
       York: Columbia University Press, 1971, pp. 143-172.

553    CRAIG, George D. "Literary Criticism in the Works
       of Henry David Thoreau." Ph.D. diss., Utah, 1952.

554    CRAWFORD, Bartholow V., ed. with Introduction, Bib-
       liography, and Notes. Henry David Thoreau: Repre-

sentative Selections. New York: American Book Co., 1934. American Writers series.

555 CRAWLEY, Thomas Edward, ed. Four Makers of the American Mind: Emerson, Thoreau, Whitman, and Melville. Durham, N. C.: Duke University Press, 1976. Thoreau, by James Lyndon Shanley, pp. 25-42. A Bicentennial Tribute from the Hampden-Sydney College Symposium (1976).

556 CRONKHITE, George Ferris. "Literature as Livelihood: The Attitude of Certain American Writers Toward Literature as a Profession from 1820 to the Civil War." Ph. D. diss., Harvard, 1948.

557 _____. "The Transcendental Railroad." New England Quarterly, 24 (September, 1951), 306-328. Railroad imagery in Emerson, Thoreau, and Hawthorne.

558 CROSBIE, Mary. "The Poet by His Pond." John O'London's Weekly, 56 (October 3, 1947), 621.

559 CROWELL, Reid. "Henry Thoreau at Walden Pond." Classmate, 55 (August, 1948), 3-4.

560 CRUICKSHANK, Helen, ed. with Notes. Thoreau on Birds. New York: McGraw-Hill, 1964. Based on work by Francis Henry Allen (1910, 1925).

561 CULHANE, Mary J. "Henry David Thoreau, Melville, Poe, and the Romantic Quest." Ph. D. diss., Minnesota, 1945.

562 CULVER, Kathleen Anne. "Mandala: The Deep Structure of Walden." Ph. D. diss., Florida, 1977. DA, 39 (1978), 284A. Mandala, or crossed circle.

563 CUMMINGS, Laurence A. "Thoreau Poems in Bixby Washington University Manuscripts." Emerson Society Quarterly, 26 (1962), 9-28.

564 CUMMINS, Roger W. "Thoreau and Isaac Newton Goodhue." Thoreau Society Bulletin, 123 (Spring, 1973), 2-3.

565 CURLE, Richard. Collecting American First Editions: Its Pitfalls and Its Pleasures. Indianapolis: Bobbs-

Merrill, 1930. Thoreau, pp. 77-78, 86-87, and passim.

566 CURTIS, Edith Raelker. A Season in Utopia: The Story of Brook Farm. New York: Nelson, 1961. Thoreau, passim.

567 DABBS, James McBride. "Thoreau--The Adventurer as Economist." Yale Review, 36 (Summer, 1947), 667-672.

568 DAHLBERG, Edward. "Thoreau and Walden," in Can These Bones Live? New York: Harcourt, Brace, 1941. Revised and reprinted with a new Preface by Herbert Read, New York: New Directions, 1960, pp. 8-18.

569 DALE, D. "Natural Mystics." American Catholic Quarterly, 39 (January, 1914), 167-173.

570 DANIELS, Stephen Lewis. "From Letter to Spirit: A Four-Fold Hermeneutic and Its Application to Selected American Poems." Ph.D. diss., Emory, 1974. DA, 35 (1974), 2935A.

571 DARROW, F. S. "The Transcendentalists and Theosophy." New Outlook, 11 (March, 1958), 8-18.

572 DAUGHERTY, James, ed. and Illustrated. Henry David Thoreau: A Man for Our Time. New York: Viking, 1967. Illustrations and selections from Thoreau chiefly for children.

573 D'AVANZO, Mario L. "Thoreau's Walden, Chapter 16." Explicator, 29 (1971), Item 41.

574 _____. "Fortitude and Nature in Thoreau's Cape Cod." Emerson Society Quarterly, 20 (1974), 131-138.

575 _____. "Thoreau's Brick Pillow." New England Quarterly, 50 (1977), 664-666.

576 _____. "How to Build a Chimney: Frost Gleans Thoreau." Thoreau Journal Quarterly, 9 (1977), 24-26.

577 DAVENPORT, E. B. "Thoreau in Vermont." <u>Vermont
Botanical Club Bulletin</u>, 3 (April, 1908), n. p.

578 DAVIDSON, Frank. "Thoreau's Contribution to Hawthorne's Mosses." <u>New England Quarterly</u>, 20 (December, 1947), 535-542.

579 _____. "Melville, Thoreau, and 'The Apple-Tree
Table.' " <u>American Literature</u>, 25 (January, 1954),
479-488.

580 _____. "Thoreau's Hound, Bay-Horse, and Turtle-
Dove." <u>New England Quarterly</u>, 27 (December,
1954), 521-524.

581 _____. "A Reading of <u>Walden</u>." <u>Emerson Society
Quarterly</u>, 18 (1960), 9-11.

582 _____. "Thoreau and David Starr Jordon." <u>Tho-
reau Society Bulletin</u>, 109 (Fall, 1969), 5-6.

583 DAVIES, John D. "Thoreau and the Ethics of Food."
<u>Vegetarian Messenger</u>, 44 (February, 1947), 40-41.

584 _____. "A Letter from England." <u>Thoreau Society
Bulletin</u>, 21 (Fall, 1947), 2-3.

585 _____. "On Reading Thoreau." <u>Thoreau Society
Bulletin</u>, 45 (Fall, 1953), 1-2.

586 DAVIS, Grace S. "Thoreau's Cats." <u>Cats Magazine</u>,
18 (September, 1961), 9-42. Selections from the
Journal.

587 DAVIS, Joseph Addison. "Rolling Home: The Open
Road as Myth and Symbol in American Literature,
1890-1940." Ph. D. diss., Michigan, 1974. <u>DA</u>,
35 (1975), 4509A. Thoreau, passim.

588 DEAMER, Robert Glen. "The American Dream: A
Study in the Beliefs, Possibilities, and Problems in
the American Dream as Dramatized in the Lives and
Writings of Major American Authors." Ph. D. diss.,
New Mexico, 1972. <u>DA</u>, 33 (1972), 5717A-5718A.

589 _____. "Thoreau: Walking Toward England," in
<u>The Westering Experience in American Literature</u>.

Bellingham:   Bureau for Faculty Research, Western
Washington University Press, 1977, pp. 85-93.

590   DE ARMOND, Fred.   "Thoreau and Schopenhauer:   An
      Imaginary Conversation. "   New England Quarterly,
      5 (January, 1932), 55-64.

591   DEDMOND, Francis B.   "Thoreau as Critic of Society. "
      Thoreau Society Bulletin, 34 (Winter, 1951), 1-3.

592   _____ .   "A Faint Clew in Ellery Channing's Quarrel
      with Ticknor and Fields. "   Thoreau Society Bulletin,
      39 (1952), 1.

593   _____ .   "William E. Channing on Thoreau:   An Un-
      published Satire. "   Modern Language Notes, 67
      (January, 1952), 50-52.

594   _____ .   "Economic Protest in Thoreau's Journal. "
      Studia Neophilologica (Uppsala, Sweden), 26 (1953-
      1954), 65-76.

595   _____ .   "A Check List of Mss. Relating to Thoreau
      in the Huntington Library, the Houghton Library of
      Harvard University, and the Berg Collection of the
      New York Public Library. "   Thoreau Society Bulle-
      tin, 43 (Spring, 1953), 3-4.

596   _____ .   "Thoreau and the Ethical Concept of Govern-
      ment. "   Personalist, 36 (Winter, 1955), 36-46.

597   _____ .   "A Footnote to Marcia Moss's A Catalog of
      Thoreau's Surveys. "   Thoreau Society Bulletin, 140
      (Summer, 1977), 7.

598   DEEVEY, Edward S. Jr.   "A Re-examination of Tho-
      reau's Walden. "   Quarterly Review of Biology, 17
      (March, 1942), 1-11.   Thoreau as a limnologist.

599   DE FALCO, Joseph M.   "From 'Civil Disobedience' to
      'A Plea for Captain John Brown. ' "   Topic, 6 (1966),
      43-49.   Reprinted as "Thoreau's Ethic and the 'Bloody
      Revolution, ' "   in New Perspectives in American
      Literature.   Washington, Pa. :   Washington and Jeffer-
      son College, 1966.

600   _____ .   " 'The Landlord': Thoreau's Emblematic

Technique. " Emerson Society Quarterly, 56 (1969), 23-32.

601  DEISS, Joseph Jay.  The Roman Years of Margaret Fuller: A Biography.  New York:  Crowell, 1969. Thoreau, passim.

602  DELIZIA, Michael.  "Dr. Nabokov and Mr. Thoreau. " Thoreau Society Bulletin, 142 (Winter, 1978), 1-2.

603  DE MOTT, Robert J.  " 'The Eccentric Orbit':  Dimensions of the Artistic Process in Henry David Thoreau's Major Writings. "  Ph. D. diss. , Kent State, 1969.  DA, 30 (1970), 5405A-5406A.

604  _____.  "Thoreau and 'Our Cabin':  A Note on Walden's Subtitle. "  Thoreau Journal Quarterly, 5 (1973), 19-24.

605  _____, and Sanford E. Marovitz, eds.  Artful Thunder:  Versions of the Romantic Tradition in American Literature in Honor of Howard P. Vincent.  Kent, Ohio:  Kent State University Press, 1975.

606  DENNIS, Carl Edward.  "The Poetry of Mind and Nature: A Study of the Idea of Nature in American Transcendental Poetry. "  Ph. D. diss. , California (Berkeley), 1966.  DA, 27 (1967), 2496A.

607  _____.  "The Balance of Walden. "  Thoreau Journal Quarterly, 2 (1970), 19.

608  _____.  "Correspondence in Thoreau's Nature Poetry. " Emerson Society Quarterly, 58 (1970), 101-109.

609  DERLETH, August William.  And You, Thoreau.  Norfolk, Conn. :  New Directions, 1943.  A collection of nature poems published as a tribute to Thoreau. See review in Poetry, 65 (March, 1945), 338-341.

610  _____.  Concord Rebel:  A Life of Henry David Thoreau.  Philadelphia:  Chilton, 1962.

611  DESAI, Rupin W.  "Biblical Light on Thoreau's Axe. " Thoreau Society Bulletin, 134 (Winter, 1976), 3-4.

612  DEVLIN, James.  "Henry Thoreau and Gilbert White:

Concord and Selborne. " Xavier University Studies, 11 (1972), 6-15.

613  DE VOTO, Bernard. The Year of Decision: 1846. Boston: Little, Brown, 1943. Thoreau, pp. 30-32 and passim.

614  DEWEY, John. "John Dewey on Thoreau. " Thoreau Society Bulletin, 30 (Winter, 1950), 1. First publication of a letter from Dewey to the Bulletin.

615  DIAS, E. J. "Daniel Ricketson and Henry Thoreau. " New England Quarterly, 26 (September, 1953), 388-396.

616  DICKENS, Robert S. "Henry David Thoreau: A Discussion of His Use of the Terms 'Nature' and 'nature. ' " Thoreau Society Bulletin, 71 (Spring, 1960), 1-3.

617  _____. "Thoreau and the Abdication of American Philosophy. " Emerson Society Quarterly, 22 (1961), 33-35.

618  _____. "Thoreau and the 'Other Great Tradition. ' " Emerson Society Quarterly, 29 (1962), 26-28.

619  _____. Thoreau, the Complete Individualist: His Relevance--and Lack of It--for Our Time. New York: Exposition, 1974.

620  DILLARD, Annie. "Thoreau and the Telegraph Harp. " Thoreau Society Bulletin, 125 (Fall, 1973), 1.

621  _____. Pilgrim at Tinker Creek. New York: Harper's Magazine Press, 1975. Reprinted New York: Bantam, 1975. Not about Thoreau; but a good modern companion to Walden.

622  DOMINA, Lyle D. "Frost and Thoreau: A Study in Affinities. " Ph. D. diss. , Missouri (Columbia), 1968. DA, 29 (1969), 2705A-2706A.

623  _____. "Conversation Folder Thick: The Technique of Thoreau's Art. " Aegis, 1 (1973), 21-27.

624  _____. "Thoreau and Frost: The Search for Reality. " Ball State University Forum, 19 (1978), 67-72.

625  DONALD, David.  Lincoln Reconsidered.  New York:
     Vintage, 1956.  Thoreau, passim.

626  DOWNS, Robert Bingham.  "The Individual Versus the
     State," in Downs, Books That Changed the World.
     Chicago:  American Library Association, 1956, pp.
     65-75.  Reprinted 1978, pp. 217-227.  On "Civil
     Disobedience."

627  _____.  "Terrible Power of the Meek," in Downs,
     Molders of the Modern Mind.  New York:  Barnes
     and Noble, 1961, pp. 259-262.

628  _____.  "Escape from Materialism," in Downs,
     Famous American Books.  New York:  Macmillan,
     1970, pp. 115-122.

629  _____.  "State Versus Individual," in Downs, Books
     That Changed America.  New York:  Macmillan, 1970,
     pp. 78-88.

630  DRAKE, William D.  "A Formal Study of Henry David
     Thoreau."  M. A. thesis, Iowa, 1948.

631  _____.  "Spiritual Ideals and Scientific Fact:  Tho-
     reau's Search for Reality."  Thoreau Society Booklet,
     No. 19 (1963), 8pp.

632  _____.  "The Depth of Walden:  Thoreau's Symbolism
     of the Divine in Nature."  Ph. D. diss., Arizona,
     1967.  DA, 28 (1967), 1393A-1394A.

633  DREISER, Theodore, ed.  Theodore Dreiser Presents
     the Living Thoughts of Thoreau.  New York:  Long-
     mans, Green, 1939.  Reprinted Greenwich, Conn.:
     Fawcett, 1963.

634  DRINNON, Richard.  "Thoreau's Politics of the Upright
     Man."  Massachusetts Review, 4 (1962), 126-138.
     Reprinted in Anarchy, 3 (April, 1963), 117-128.  Also
     reprinted in Hicks, John H., ed., Thoreau in Our
     Season (1966), pp. 154-168; and in Glick, ed., Recogni-
     tion (1969), pp. 365-381.

635  DUFFEY, Bernard.  Poetry in America:  Expression and
     Its Values in the Times of Bryant, Whitman, and
     Pound.  Durham, N. C.:  Duke University Press,
     1978.  Thoreau, passim.

636   DUNCAN, Jeffrey L. , ed. with Introduction. Thoreau:
        The Major Essays. New York: Dutton, 1972.
        Anthology contains "A Walk to Wachusett, " "Paradise
        (to Be) Regained, " "Walking, " "Wild Apples, " etc.

637   DUNTON, E. K. "The Old and New Estimate of Tho-
        reau. " The Dial, 33 (December 16, 1902), 464-466.

638   DU PREE, Robert Hickman. "From Analogy to Meta-
        phor to Wordplay: Thoreau's Shifting View of the
        Relationship Between Men and Nature. " Ph. D. diss. ,
        Auburn, 1975. DA, 36 (1976), 7419A.

639   DURDEN, Fred. "Thoreau and Frost: Birds of a
        Feather. " Thoreau Journal Quarterly, 9 (1977),
        28-32.

640   DUSSINGER, Gloria Roth. "The Romantic Concept of
        Self, Applied to the Works of Emerson, Whitman,
        Hawthorne, and Melville. " Ph. D. diss. , Lehigh,
        1973. DA, 34 (1974), 5963A. Thoreau, passim.

641   DUVALL, S. P. C. "Robert Frost's 'Directive' Out of
        Walden. " American Literature, 31 (1960), 482-488.

642   EARNEST, Ernest. "Thoreau and Little Rock. " Best
        Articles and Stories. November, 1949, pp. 42-43.

643   EASTWOOD, Dorothy, ed. Golden Thoughts from Tho-
        reau. London: John Lane, 1907.

644   EATON, Philip Walter. "The Middle Landscape: Tho-
        reau's Development in Style and Content. " Ph. D.
        diss. , Arizona State, 1970. DA, 32 (1971), 1467A.

645   EATON, Richard J. "Thoreau's Herbarium. " Man
        and Nature. December, 1972, pp. 2-5.

646   EATON, Walter Prichard. "Thoreau and Nature. "
        Thoreau Society Bulletin, 39 (Spring, 1952), 1-2.

647   ECKSTORM, Fanny Hardy. "The Death of Thoreau's
        Guide. " Atlantic, 93 (June, 1904), 736-746.

648   _____ . "Thoreau's Maine Woods. " Atlantic, 102
        (July, August, 1908), 16-18, 242-250. Reprinted in

Harding, ed. , A Century (1954), pp. 103-117.  Also
reprinted in Thoreau Society Bulletin, 51 (Spring,
1955), as "Notes on Thoreau's Maine Woods. "

649   EDDLEMAN, Floyd Eugene.  "Use of Lemprière's Classical Dictionary in Walden. " Emerson Society Quarterly, 43 (1966), 62-65.

650   EDEL, Leon.  Henry David Thoreau.  Minneapolis:
University of Minnesota Press, 1970.  Pamphlet
series.  Reprinted in Paul, Sherman, ed. , Six Classic American Writers, pp. 160-194.

651   _____. "Walden:  The Myth and the Mystery. "
American Scholar, 44 (1975), 272-281.

652   EDMAN, Irwin.  Fountain-Heads of Freedom.  New
York:  Reynal and Hitchcock, 1942.  Thoreau, pp.
149-153.

653   EIDSON, John Olin.  Charles Stearns Wheeler:  Friend
of Emerson.  Athens:  University of Georgia Press,
1951.  Reprinted in Emerson Society Quarterly, 52
(1968), 13-75.  Thoreau, passim.

654   _____. "Charles Stearns Wheeler:  Emerson's 'Good
Grecian. '" New England Quarterly, 27 (December,
1954), 472-483.

655   EIFERT, Virginia L.  "The Botanist Thoreau, " in
Eifert, Tall Trees and Far Horizons.  New York:
Dodd, Mead, 1965, pp. 239-256.  Does not include
material in the Journal.

656   EISELEY, Loren.  "Thoreau's Unfinished Business. "
Natural History, 87 (1977), 6-19.

657   EISENLOHR, Herman L.  "The Development of Henry
David Thoreau's Prose. "  Ph. D.  diss. , Pennsylvania,
1966.  DA, 27 (1966), 1334A-1335A.

658   ELLIGEN, Betty J.  "Henry David Thoreau:  His Literary Theory and Criticism. "  Ph. D.  diss. , Oklahoma, c. 1958.

659   ELLIS, Havelock.  "Thoreau, " in The New Spirit.  London:  George Bell, 1890.  Reprinted in Harding, ed. ,
A Century (1954), pp. 91-96.

660  ELMORE, A. E.  "Symmetry Out of Season: The Form
     of Walden. "  South Atlantic Bulletin, 37 (1972), 18-24.

661  EMERSON, Edward Waldo.  Henry Thoreau as Remem-
     bered by a Young Friend.  Boston:  Houghton Mifflin,
     1917.  Reprinted Concord, Mass.:  Thoreau Lyceum,
     1968.

662  _____.  "Centenary of Henry David Thoreau, 1817-
     1862. "  Bookman (London), 52 (June, 1917), 81-84.

663  EMERSON, Ralph Waldo.  "Thoreau. "  Atlantic, 10 (Au-
     gust, 1862), 239-249.  Has been frequently reprinted,
     as in the following:

     "Biographical Sketch, " prefixed to Vol. I, Walden
     Edition of Thoreau.  Boston:  Houghton Mifflin, 1906.

     Clark, Barrett Harper, ed.  Great Short Biographies
     of the World.  New York:  McBride, 1928, pp. 1315-
     1328.

     Wilson, Edmund, ed.  The Shock of Recognition.
     Garden City, N. Y.:  Doubleday, Doran, 1943, pp.
     208-228.

     Mayberry, George, ed.  Little Treasury of American
     Prose.  New York:  Scribner, 1949, pp. 135-156.

     Harding, Walter, ed. , A Century (1954), pp. 22-40.

     Weeks, Edward, and Emily Flint, eds.  Atlantic
     Monthly Jubilee.  Boston:  Little, Brown, 1957, pp.
     227-288.

     Eaton, Clement, ed.  The Leaven of Democracy.
     New York:  Braziller, 1963, pp. 365-374.

     Glick, Wendell, ed. , Recognition (1969), pp. 18-34.

663a ENDERLE, Robert C.  " 'Beans. '"  Thoreau Journal
     Quarterly, 4 (1972), 10-12.

664  ENSOR, Allison.  "Thoreau and the Bible--Preliminary
     Consideration. "  Emerson Society Quarterly, 33
     (1963), 65-70.

665 EPSTEIN, Perle. Individuals All: Profiles of Americans Who Defied the Establishment. New York: Crowell-Collier, 1972.

666 ERICKSON, Richard B. "Sounds of a New England Village." New England Galaxy (Sturbridge, Mass.), 9 (Winter, 1968), 3-9. Thoreau on sounds.

667 ERIKSON, Erik. Gandhi's Truth. New York: Norton, 1969. Thoreau, p. 129 and passim.

668 _____. "Youth, Fidelity, and Diversity," in Erikson, The Challenge of Youth. Garden City, N. Y.: Doubleday, 1963, pp. 1-28.

669 ERISMAN, Fred. "Thoreau and the Texas Colonel." Emerson Society Quarterly, 31 (1963), 48-49.

670 ERLICH, Michael Glenn. "Selected Anti-Slavery Speeches of Henry David Thoreau, 1848-1859: A Rhetorical Analysis." Ph. D. diss., Ohio State (Speech), 1970. DA, 31 (1971), 4929A-&930A.

671 _____. "Thoreau's 'Civil Disobedience': Strategy for Reform." Connecticut Review, 7 (1973), 100-110.

672 EULAU, Heinz. "Wayside Challenger--Some Remarks on the Politics of Henry David Thoreau." Antioch Review, 9 (Winter, 1949), 509-522.

673 EUROPE, special Thoreau issue: 45 (July-August, 1967), pp. 149-246. Contains 12 essays in French:

   Asselineau, R., "Un Narcisse Puritan," 149-157.
   Flak, M., "L'Homme de Concord," 158-162.
   Normand, J., "Les ironies de la Solitude," 162-169.
   Miller, H., "Henry David Thoreau," 169-177.
   Flak, M., "Thoreau et Les Francais," 177-185.
   Harding, W., "L'Influence de 'La Desobeissance Civile,'" 186-204.
   Thoreau, H. D., "Plaidoyer pour John Brown," 204-210.
   Simon, L., "De Desobeir au Crime D'Obeir," 210-219.
   Raudnitz, J. P., "Thoreau on L'Humus Retrouve," 220-224.
   Thoreau, H. D., Various brief extracts, 225-235.
   Vernet, L., "Apercu Bibliographique," 236-238.

_____. "Chronologie de la Vie d'Henry-David Thoreau, " 239-246.

674  EVANS, Francis Eileen Beary.  "The Genuine Word, the Unfolding Sentence:  Thoreau's Paths to Truths. " Ph. D. diss. , Purdue, 1976.  DA, 37 (1977), 6456A.

675  EVANS, Robert O.  "Thoreau's Poetry and the Prose Works. "  Emerson Society Quarterly, 56 (1969), 40-52.

676  EZEKIEL, Nissim.  "The Thoreau-Gandhi Snydrome: An Ambiguous Influence. "  Quest, 58 (1968), 21-26. Reprinted in Harding et al. , eds. , Henry David Thoreau:  Studies (1972), pp. 133-143.

677  FAIRBANKS, Jonathan.  "The Impact of the Wild on Henry David Thoreau, Jack London, and Robinson Jeffers. "  Ph. D. diss. , Otago (New Zealand), 1969.

678  _____. "Thoreau:  Speaker for Wildness. "  South Atlantic Quarterly, 70 (1971), 487-506.

679  FASEL, Ida.  "Emily Dickinson's Walden. "  Iowa English Yearbook, 7 (1962), 22-28.

680  FEDERMAN, Donald.  "Toward an Ecology of Place: Three Views of Cape Cod. "  Colby Library Quarterly, 13 (1977), 209-222.

681  FEIDELSON, Charles, Jr.  Symbolism and American Literature.  Chicago:  University of Chicago Press, 1953.  Thoreau, pp. 135-142.

682  FEIN, Richard J.  "Walden and the Village of the Mind. "  Ball State University Forum, 8 (Winter, 1967), 55-61.

683  FENDELMAN, Earl B.  "Toward a Third Voice:  Auto-biographical Form in Thoreau, Stein, Adams, and Mailer. "  Ph. D. diss. , Yale, 1971.  DA, 32 (1972), 6972A.

684  _____. "Toward Walden Pond:  The American Voice in Autobiography. "  Canadian Review of American Studies, 8 (1977), 11-25.

685   FENN, Mary Gail. "Thoreau's Easterbrook Country."
      Thoreau Society Booklet, No. 25 (1970).

686   _____. "Thoreau's Rivers." Thoreau Society Book-
      let, No. 27 (1973).

687   _____. "Susan Loring on Thoreau." Thoreau So-
      ciety Bulletin, 129 (Fall, 1974), 1.

688   _____. "Melvin: Friend of Thoreau." Thoreau So-
      ciety Bulletin, 132 (Summer, 1975), 4.

689   FERGENSON, Laraine Rita. "Wordsworth and Thoreau:
      A Study of the Relationship Between Man and Nature."
      Ph. D. diss., Columbia, 1970. DA, 32 (1971), 1468A.

690   _____. "Was Thoreau Re-reading Wordsworth in
      1851?" Thoreau Journal Quarterly, 5 (1973), 20-23.

691   FERGUSON, Alfred Royse. "Reflections on Transcen-
      dental Abolitionist Perfectionism in American Life,
      1830-1860: The Biography of a Fantasy." Ph. D.
      diss., Minnesota, 1971. DA, 32 (1971), 1420A-1421A.

692   FERGUSON, Malcolm. "An Excursion into Thoreau
      Country." Book Collector's Market, 3 (1978), 11-13.
      Refers to rare editions, out-of-prints, etc.

693   FERLAZZO, Paul J. "Thoreau's Sense of Natural
      Time." Thoreau Journal Quarterly, 4 (1972), 16-18.

694   FERTIG, Walter L. "John Sullivan Dwight's Prepublica-
      tion Notice of Walden." New England Quarterly, 30
      (March, 1957), 84-90.

695   FIEDLER, Leslie A. The Return of the Vanishing
      American. New York: Stein and Day, 1968. Tho-
      reau, pp. 104-106 and passim.

696   FIELDS, Ronald Milburn. "Four Concepts of an Organic
      Principle: Horatio Greenough, Henry David Thoreau,
      Walt Whitman, and Louis Sullivan." Ph. D. diss.,
      Ohio, 1968. DA, 29 (1969), 3929.

697   FIORINO. "An Approach to Henry David Thoreau."
      Lecture read at the Fourth Seminar in American
      Literature, in Rome, May 2, 1957, University of
      Catania.

698  FISCHER, Walter. "Henry David Thoreau (1817-1862)."
     Archiv (Germany), 186 (September, 1949), 28-48.

699  FITCH, George H. "Thoreau, the Pioneer Writer About
     Nature," in Fitch, Great Spiritual Writers of America.
     San Francisco: Elder, 1916, pp. 95-102.

700  FITZGERALD, Gabrielle Mary. "The Writer as Hero,
     the Writer as Contemplative: Thoreau's Divided
     Self-Image." Ph. D. diss., Northwestern, 1977.
     DA, 38 (1978), 4826A.

701  FLAK, Micheline. "L'homme de Concord." Europe,
     45 (July-August, 1967), 158-162. In French.

702  _____. "Thoreau et les Français." Europe, 45
     (July-August, 1967), 177-185. In French.

703  FLANAGAN, John T. "Thoreau in Minnesota." Minne-
     sota Historian, 16 (March, 1935), 35-46.

704  _____. "Henry Salt and His Life of Thoreau." New
     England Quarterly, 28 (June, 1955), 237-246.

705  FLECK, Richard F. "A Note on Thoreau's Mist Verse."
     Thoreau Journal Quarterly, 1 (1969), 1-5.

706  _____. "Evidence for Thoreau's 'Indian' Notebooks
     as Being a Source for His Journal. Thoreau Journal
     Quarterly, 1 (1969), 17-19.

707  _____. "Thoreau as Mythologist." Research Studies,
     40 (1972), 195-206.

708  _____. "Thoreau's Mythology in New England Sub-
     jects." Thoreau Journal Quarterly, 4 (1972), 1-9.

709  _____. "Manuscript Page from Thoreau's Indian
     Notebook." Concord Saunterer, 7 (Spring, 1972),
     1-9.

710  _____. "A Report on Irish Interest in Thoreau."
     Thoreau Journal Quarterly, 6 (1974), 21-27.

711  _____. Thoreau as Mythmaker and Fabulist." Ren-
     dezvous, 9 (1974), 23-32.

712 _____ . "Thoreau's Mythological Humor." Concord
Saunterer, 10 (1975), 1-7.

713 _____ . "Mythic Buds in Thoreau's Journals." Ariel,
7 (1976), 77-86.

714 _____ , ed. The Indians of Thoreau: Selections from
the Indian Notebooks. Albuquerque: Hummingbird,
1974.

715 _____ , ed. "Further Selections from the 'Indian
Notebooks.'" Thoreau Journal Quarterly, 9 (1977),
2-23.

716 FLETCHER, F. "Henry David Thoreau, Oriental."
Open Court, 44 (August, 1930), 510-512.

717 FLOAN, Howard R. "Emerson and Thoreau," in The
South in Northern Eyes, 1831-1861. Austin: University of Texas Press, 1958, pp. 51-70.

718 FOERSTER, Norman. "Henry David Thoreau: A Critical Sketch." Western Field, April, 1906, pp. 194-196.

719 _____ . "Thoreau as a Poet." Harvard Monthly,
October, 1909, pp. 18-22.

720 _____ . "Thoreau's Cabin at Walden Pond." Pittsburgh Dispatch, August 28, 1910.

721 _____ . "The Intellectual Heritage of Thoreau."
Texas Review, 2 (January, 1917), 192-212.

722 _____ . "Thoreau and 'The Wild.'" Dial, 63 (June
28, 1917), 8-12.

723 _____ . "Humanism of Thoreau." Nation, 105 (July
5, 1917), 9-12. Reprinted in Glick, ed., Recognition
(1969), pp. 214-225.

724 _____ . "Thoreau and Old Concord." Yale Review,
7 (January, 1918), 430-431.

725 _____ . "Thoreau as Artist." Sewanee Review, 29
(January, 1921), 2-13. Reprinted in Harding, ed.,
A Century (1954), pp. 123-135.

726    _____. Nature in American Literature. New York:
       Macmillan, 1923. Reprinted New York: Russell and
       Russell, 1958. Thoreau, pp. 69-142.

727    _____, and Robert P. Falk, eds. Eight American
       Writers: An Anthology. New York: Norton, 1963.
       "Henry David Thoreau," by Walter Harding, pp. 409-
       581. Consists of Introduction plus selected materials
       from Thoreau.

728    FOGARTY, Robert S. "A Utopian Literary Canon."
       New England Quarterly, 38 (1965), 386-391. Atti-
       tudes toward Hawthorne and Thoreau as expressed
       in the Circular of the Oneida Community, (1848).

729    FOLEY, Patrick Kevin. American Authors: 1795-1895.
       Boston: Publisher's Printing, 1897. Thoreau, passim.

730    FONE, Byrne R. S. "A Note on the Jones Very Edi-
       tions." American Notes and Queries, 6 (1968), 67-
       69.

731    FORD, Arthur Lewis Jr. "A Critical Study of the Poet-
       ry of Henry Thoreau." Ph. D. diss., Bowling Green,
       1963. DA, 25 (1964), 2980.

732    _____. "The Poetry of Henry David Thoreau."
       Emerson Society Quarterly, 61 (1970), 1-26. Also
       published as booklet, Hartford, Conn.: Transcenden-
       tal, 1970.

733    _____. A Critical Study of the Poetry of Henry Tho-
       reau. Ann Arbor: University of Michigan Micro-
       films, 1972.

734    FORD, Nick Aaron. "Henry David Thoreau: Abolition-
       ist." New England Quarterly, 19 (September, 1946),
       359-371.

735    FORD, Thomas W. "Thoreau and Lecturing." Mark
       Twain Quarterly, 17 (1973-1974), 8-13.

736    _____. "Thoreau's Cosmic Mosquito and Dickinson's
       Terrestrial Fly." New England Quarterly, 48 (1975),
       487-504.

737    FOSTER, Edward. The Civilized Wilderness. New

York and London: Macmillan, 1975. Thoreau, pp.
100-118.

738  FOSTER, Leslie D.  "Walden and Its Audiences: Trou-
bled Sleep, and Religious and Other Awakenings. "
Modern Language Review, 67 (1972), 756-762.

739  FRANCIS, Robert G.  "Two Brothers. "  Dalhousie Review, 9 (April, 1929), 48-52.

740  _____.  "Thoreau's Mask of Serenity. "  Forum, 106
(January, 1947), 72-77.

741  _____.  "Thoreau in Italy, " a poem, in Hicks, John
H., ed. , Thoreau in Our Season (1966), pp. 91-92.

742  _____.  "Thoreau on the Benevolence of Nature. "
Thoreau Society Bulletin, 140 (Summer, 1977), 1-3.

743  FRANK, Waldo David.  "France and Thoreau, " in In
the American Jungle.  New York:  Farrar, Straus,
1937, pp. 165-168.

744  FRANKLIN, Rosemary F.  "The Cabin by the Lake:
Pastoral Landscapes of Poe, Cooper, Hawthorne,
and Thoreau. "  Emerson Society Quarterly, 22
(1976), 59-69.

745  FREDERICK, Mary Purnele.  "The Idea of Retirement
into Nature:  Horace, Marvell, Thoreau. "  Ph. D.
diss. , California (Berkeley), 1977.  DA, 38 (1978),
4804A-4805A.

746  FRENCH, Allen.  Old Concord.  Boston:  Houghton
Mifflin, 1915.

747  FRENCH, William.  "Reminiscences of Thoreau. "
Thoreau Society Bulletin, 143 (Spring, 1978), 6-8.
Excerpt from previously unpublished 1902 article.
William French, brother of famed sculptor David
Chester French, September 1, 1902, read a paper
before the Chicago Literary Club on "Reminiscences
of Old Concord. "  Has never been published.

748  FRENIERE, Emil Abbott.  "Emerson and Parker Letters
in the Jackson Papers. "  Emerson Society Quarterly,
22 (1961), 46-48.

749 _____. "The Mountain Comes to Concord: Two New
Letters from Alcott and Thoreau." Thoreau Society
Bulletin, 75 (Spring, 1961), 2-3.

750 _____. "Henry David Thoreau: 1837-1847," 2 vols.
Ph. D. diss., Pennsylvania State, 1961. DA, 22
(1962), 4014-4015.

751 FRIESEN, Victor C. "Sensuousness in Thoreau's Approach to Nature." Thoreau Society Bulletin, 103
(Spring, 1968), 2.

752 _____. "Alexander Henry and Thoreau's Climb of
Mount Katahdin." Thoreau Society Bulletin, 123
(Spring, 1973), 5-6.

753 _____. "My Introduction to Thoreau." Thoreau
Society Bulletin, 127 (Spring, 1974), 7.

754 FROST, Robert, Reginald Cook, and J. Isaacs. "Thoreau's Walden." Listener, 52 (August 26, 1954),
319-320. Abstract of conversation on the 100th Anniversary of Walden; BBC broadcast.

755 FROST, Ruth Hallingby. "Thoreau's Worcester Associa-
tions." Worcester, Mass.: American Antiquarian
Society, 1943.

756 _____. "Theo Brown, Friend of Thoreau." Nature
Outlook, 2 (May, 1944), 15-19.

757 _____. "Thoreau's Worcester Friends." Nature
Outlook, 3 (May, 1945), 116-118; 4 (November, 1946),
16-18; 5 (May, 1947), 4-7, 33.

758 FRYE, Northrop. "Varieties of Literary Utopias."
Daedalus, 94 (Spring, 1965), 323-347. Comment on
Walden, passim.

759 FUSSELL, Edwin S. "The Red Face of Man," in Paul,
ed., Thoreau: A Collection (1962), pp. 142-160.
First publication here.

760 _____. "Henry David Thoreau," in Frontier: Ameri-
can Literature and the American West. Princeton,
N. J.: Princeton University Press, 1965, pp. 175-231.
Also contains "Thoreau's Unwritten Epic," pp. 327-

350, and "Indian Summer of the American West, pp. 327-396.

761  GABRIEL, Ralph H.  The Course of American Demo-
     cratic Thought.  New York:  Ronald, 1943.  "Emer-
     son and Thoreau, " pp. 39-51.

762  GAGNON, Ray.  "Thoreau:  Some Negative Considera-
     tions. "  Thoreau Society Bulletin, 121 (Fall, 1972),
     5-7.

763  GALE, Robert L.  Barron's Simplified Approach to
     Walden.  Woodbury, N. Y. :  Barron's Educational
     series, 1965.

764  GALGAN, Gerald Joseph.  "The Self and Society in the
     Thought of Henry David Thoreau. "  Ph. D. diss. ,
     Fordham, 1971.  DA, 32 (1971), 2131A-2132A.

765  GALLIGAN, Edward L.  "The Comedian at Walden Pond. "
     South Atlantic Quarterly, 69 (1970), 20-37.

766  GARATE, Justo.  "Thoreau and the Spanish Language:
     A Bibliography. "  Thoreau Society Booklet, No. 24
     (1970), 12pp.

767  GARBER, Frederick.  "Unity and Diversity in 'Walking.' "
     Emerson Society Quarterly, 56 (1969), 35-40.  Also
     printed in Stein, ed. , New Approaches:  A Symposium.
     Hartford, Conn. :  Transcendental, 1969, pp. 35-40.

768  _____.  Thoreau's Redemptive Imagination.  New
     York:  New York University Press, 1977.

769  GARRISON, Joseph Marion, Jr.  "John Burroughs as a
     Literary Critic:  A Study Emphasizing His Treatment
     of Emerson, Whitman, Thoreau, Carlyle, and Ar-
     nold. "  Ph. D. diss. , Duke, 1962.  DA, 23 (1963),
     3372-3373.

770  GATES, Michael.  "Walden:  Tantra Above Yantras. "
     Emerson Society Quarterly, 22 (1976), 14-23.

771  GELLER, L. D.  Between Concord and Plymouth:  The
     Transcendentalists and the Watsons.  Concord, Mass. :
     Thoreau Lyceum, 1973.  Catalog of Transcendental
     manuscripts in Pilgrim Hall in Plymouth.

772   GERSTENBERGER, Donna L.  "Walden:  The House
      That Henry Built."  Emerson Society Quarterly,  56
      (1969),  11-13.

773   GERSTER, Patrick G.   "Aesthetic Individualism:  Key
      to the Alienation of the American Intellectual--Studies
      in Ralph Waldo Emerson, Henry David Thoreau, and
      Walt Whitman."  Ph. D. diss.,  Minnesota (History),
      1970.  DA, 31 (1971), 4673A.

774   GIBBS, Jean.  "Dorothy Livesay and the Transcendental
      Tradition."  Humanities Association Bulletin (Canada),
      21 (1970),  24-39.

775   GIERASCH, Walter.  "Thoreau and Willa Cather."  Tho-
      reau Society Bulletin, 20 (Summer, 1947),  4.

776   GILLEY, Leonard.  "Transcendentalism in Walden."
      Prairie Schooner, 42 (1968), 204-207.

777   GILLIS, James Martin.   "Thoreau and the Urge to Self-
      Expression," in This Our Day.  Glen Rock, N. J.:
      Paulist, 1933, pp. 108-115.  Refers to Thoreau's
      Journal.

778   GILMAN, Albert, and Roger Brown.   "Personality and
      Style in Concord," in Simon and Parsons, eds.,
      Transcendentalism and Its Legacy (1966),  pp. 87-122.

779   GIMLIN, Joan S.   "Henry Thoreau and the American
      Indian."  Ph. D. diss.,  George Washington, 1973.
      DA, 35 (1974), 2221A-2222A.

780   GIRDLER, J.  "A Study of the Hound, Bay Horse, and
      Turtledove Allusion in Thoreau's Walden."  M. A. The-
      sis, Southern California, 1935.

781   GIRGUS, Sam B.  "The Mechanical Mind:  Thoreau and
      McLuhan on Freedom, Technology, and the Media."
      Thoreau Journal Quarterly, 9 (1977), 3-9.

782   GLAZIER, Lyle.  "Thoreau's Rebellious Lyric."  Emer-
      son Society Quarterly, 54 (1969), 27-30.

783   GLEASON, H. W.  "Winter Rambles in Thoreau's Coun-
      try."  National Geographic Magazine, 37 (February,
      1920),  165-180.

784 GLICK, Wendell P. "Thoreau and the 'Herald of Freedom.'" New England Quarterly, 22 (June, 1949), 193-204.

785 _____. "Henry David Thoreau and Radical Abolitionism: A Study of the Native Background of Thoreau's Social Philosophy." Ph.D. diss., Northwestern, 1950.

786 _____. "Three New Early Manuscripts by Thoreau." Huntington Library Quarterly, 15 (November, 1951), 59-72.

787 _____. "Yeats' Early Reading of Walden." Boston Public Library Quarterly, 5 (July, 1953), 164-166.

788 _____. "An Early Encounter with Joe Polis." Thoreau Journal Quarterly, 3 (1971), 12-15. Thoreau's Indian guide on his trip to Maine in 1857.

789 _____. "Thoreau's Use of His Sources." New England Quarterly, 44 (1971), 101-109. See article by Noverr (1971).

790 _____. "Thoreau Rejects an Emerson Text." Studies in Bibliography, 25 (1972), 213-216.

791 _____. "Go Tell It on the Mountain: Thoreau's Vocation as a Writer." Emerson Society Quarterly, 19 (1973), 161-169.

792 _____. "Thoreau as a Failed Poet." Lake Superior Journal (Duluth, Minn.), 2 (1976), 40-44.

793 _____. "Emerson, Thoreau, and Transcendentalism," a review of current scholarship, in American Literary Scholarship, 1976, pp. 3-14; 1977, pp. 3-16.

794 _____. "Scholarly Editing and Dealing with Uncertainties: Thoreau's 'Resistance to Civil Government.'" Analytical and Enumerative Bibliography, 2 (1978), 103-115.

795 _____, ed. with Preface. The Recognition of Henry David Thoreau: Selected Criticism Since 1848. Ann Arbor: University of Michigan Press, 1969. Contains 45 reprinted items.

796 _____, ed. with Introduction. Reform Papers. Princeton, N. J.: Princeton University Press, 1973.

797 GODDARD, Harold Clark. Studies in New England
Transcendentalism. New York: Columbia University
Press, 1908. Reprinted New York: Hillary House,
1960. Derived from "Studies in New England Tran-
cendentalism." Ph. D. diss., Columbia, 1908. Thoreau, pp. 63-81, and passim.

798 _____. Alphabet of the Imagination. Atlantic High-
lands, N. J.: Humanities, 1974. Posthumous publication of previously unpublished essays; Goddard died
1950.

799 GOHDES, Clarence L. F. "Henry Thoreau: Bachelor
of Arts." Classical Journal, 23 (February, 1928),
323-336.

800 _____. The Periodicals of American Transcendentalism. Durham, N. C.: Duke University Press,
1931.

801 GOLDBERG, M. A. "Egotisms: Ancient and Modern."
Colorado Quarterly, 10 (Winter, 1962), 285-295.

802 GOLLIN, Rita K. "The Place of Walden in The Undis-
covered Country." Thoreau Society Bulletin, 137
(Fall, 1976), 7-8. Refers to a scene in the novel by
William Dean Howells.

803 GOODWIN, James E. "1. Sergei Eisenstein's Ideologi-
cal Aesthetics: The Silent Films. 2. American
Autobiography and the Writing Life. 3. Transcendental Politics: Thoreau and John Brown." Ph. D.
diss., Rutgers, 1972. DA, 34 (1973), 2624A.

804 GORDON, John D. "A Thoreau Handbill." Bulletin of
the New York Public Library, 59 (May, 1955), 253-
258.

805 GORLEY, C. P. "Thoreau and the Land." Landscape
Architecture, 24 (April, 1934), 58-59.

806 GOUDIE, Andrea. "Exploring the Broad Margins:
Charles Ives' Interpretation of Thoreau." Midwest
Quarterly, 13 (1972), 309-317.

807 GOZZI, Raymond Danta. "Tropes and Figures: A Psychological Study of David Henry [sic] Thoreau." Ph. D. diss., New York, 1957. DA, 17 (1957), 1553.

808 _____. "Tropes and Figures: A Psychological Study of David Henry Thoreau." Thoreau Society Bulletin, 58 (Winter, 1957), 1-2. Summary of dissertation listed above; refers to Thoreau's reversal of names.

809 _____. "The Meaning of the 'Complemental' Verses in Walden." Emerson Society Quarterly, 35 (1964), 79-82.

810 _____. "Walden and a Carlyle Letter." Thoreau Society Bulletin, 118 (Winter, 1972), 4.

811 _____. "An Editorial Mishap by Thoreau in A Week? A Textual Note." Thoreau Society Bulletin, 119 (Spring, 1972), 6-7.

812 _____. "Some Aspects of Thoreau's Personality," in Harding, ed., A Profile (1971), pp. 150-171.

813 _____. "'Mother-Nature,'" in Harding, ed., A Profile (1971), pp. 172-187.

814 GRAHAM, D. B. "Dreiser and Thoreau: An Early Influence." Dreiser Newsletter, 7 (1976), 1-4.

815 GRANT, Douglas. Purpose and Place. London: Macmillan, 1965. Thoreau, passim.

816 GRAY, Leonard B. "Emerson and Thoreau." Unity, 4 (January-February, 1952), 88-92.

817 _____. "The Growth of Thoreau's Reputation." Thoreau Society Bulletin, 42 (Winter, 1953), 2-4.

818 GREEN, Eugene. "Reading Local History: Shattuck's History, Emerson's 'Discourse,' and Thoreau's Walden." New England Quarterly, 50 (1977), 303-314.

819 GREEN, Maud Honeyman. "Raritan Bay Union, Eagleswood, New Jersey." Proceedings of the New Jersey Historical Society, 68 (January, 1950), 1-20. Refers to land surveyed by Thoreau.

820    GREENE, David Mason.   The Frail Duration:   A Key to
       Symbolic Structure in Walden.   Humanities Monograph,
       Series I, No. 2.   San Diego, Calif. :   San Diego State
       College Publication, 1966.

821    GREWAL, Vanita.   "Thoreau as a Rebel, " in Maini,
       Darshan Singh, ed. , Variations on American Litera-
       ture.   New Delhi:   U. S. Educational Foundation in
       India, 1968, pp. 49-52.

822    GRIDLEY, Roy.   "Walden and Ruskin's 'The White-
       Thorn Blossom. '"   Emerson Society Quarterly, 26
       (1962), 31-34.

823    GRIFFIN, William J.   "Thoreau's Reactions to Horatio
       Greenough. "   New England Quarterly, 30 (December,
       1957), 509-512.

824    GRISCOM, Ludlow.   Birds of Concord.   Cambridge:
       Harvard University Press, 1949.   Based largely on
       Thoreau's Journal information concerning birds.

825    GROSS, Robert A.   " 'The Most Estimable Place in All
       the World':   A Debate on Progress in Nineteenth-
       Century Concord, " in Myerson, ed. , Studies (1978),
       pp. 1-16.

826    GRUBER, Christian P.   "The Education of Henry David
       Thoreau, Harvard, 1833-1837. "   Ph. D. diss. , Prince-
       ton, 1953.   DA, 14 (1954), 972.

827    GRUENERT, Charles F.   "Henry David Thoreau's Humor
       in Theory and Practice. "   Ph. D. diss. , Chicago,
       1957.

828    GUILFORD, Kelsey.   "The Thoreau Cultists. "   Chicago
       Tribune, December 1, 1946, p. 1.

829    GUILLET, Cephas.   "The Thoreau Family. "   Thoreau
       Society Bulletin, 19 (Spring, 1947), 3.

830    GUNN, Janet Varner.   "Autobiography and the Narrative
       Experience of Temporality as Depth. "   Soundings,
       60 (1977), 194-209.   Refers largely to Walden.

831    GUPTA, Rameshwar K.   "Thoreau's Water Privileges
       in Walden. "   Thoreau Journal Quarterly, 8 (1976),
       3-16.

832   GURA, Philip F. "Thoreau and John Josselyn." <u>New</u>
      <u>England Quarterly</u>, 48 (1975), 505-518.

833   _____. "Thoreau's Maine Woods Indians: More
      Representative Men." <u>American Literature</u>, 49
      (1977), 366-384.

834   GURNEY, Richard C. "The Worst of Thoreau." <u>Con-</u>
      <u>necticut Review</u>, 3 (1970), 68-71.

835   GUTHRIE, Harold N. "The Humor of Henry David Tho-
      reau." Ph. D. diss., Iowa, 1953.

836   H., C. C. "Walden Centenary." <u>New York Sun</u>, Sep-
      tember 6, 1947. p. 1.

837   HADDIN, Theodore. "The Changing Image of Henry
      Thoreau: The Emergence of the Literary Artist."
      Ph. D. diss., Michigan, 1968. <u>DA</u>, 30 (1969), 724A-
      725A.

838   _____. "Thoreau's Reputation Once More." <u>Tho-</u>
      <u>reau Journal Quarterly</u>, 4 (1972), 10-15.

839   _____. "Fire and Fire Imagery in Thoreau's Journal
      and <u>Walden</u>." <u>South Atlantic Bulletin</u>, 41 (1976), 78-
      89.

840   HAIGHT, Gordon S., ed. <u>Walden</u>. New York: Black,
      1942. Classics Club edition.

841   HALL, Ivan Roger. "Murdering the Time: A Study of
      the Temporal Order in Selected Works of Henry Tho-
      reau, Nathaniel Hawthorne, T. S. Eliot, and Ezra
      Pound." Ph. D. diss., Kent State, 1975. <u>DA</u>, 36
      (1976), 6099A.

842   HALPERIN, Irving. "Thoreau in Israel." <u>Thoreau</u>
      <u>Society Bulletin</u>, 94 (Winter, 1966), 1-2. <u>Also in</u>
      <u>University College Quarterly</u>, 12 (1967), 13-18.

843   HAMBY, James A. "Thoreau's Synthesizing Metaphor:
      Two Fishes with One Hook." <u>Bulletin of the Rocky</u>
      <u>Mountain Modern Language Association</u>, 27 (1973),
      17-22.

844   HAMILTON, Franklin Willard. "Henry David Thoreau's
      Ideas for Self Education of the Individual as Expressed
      in His Journal, 1837-1862." Ph. D. diss., Kansas
      (Education), 1961. DA, 22 (1962), 4004-4005.

845   _____, ed. with Introduction. Thoreau on the Art of
      Writing. Flint, Mich.: Walden, 1967. A collection
      of Thoreau's remarks on writing, style, etc.

846   HAMLIN, Talbot Faulkner. Greek Revival Architecture
      in America. London and New York: Oxford Univer-
      sity Press, 1944. Thoreau, passim.

847   HAND, Harry E. "Thoreau at One Hundred and Fifty."
      Hartford Review, 4 (1967), 52-55.

848   HANLEY, Katherine, C. S. J. "Walden: Forest Sonata."
      American Transcendental Quarterly, 1 (1969), 108-
      110.

849   HANSEN, Sister Regina, O. S. B. "The Conditions for
      Poetry: A Study of Thoreau's Challenge to Transcen-
      dentalism." American Benedictine Review, 28 (1977),
      188-200.

850   HANSON, Elizabeth Irene. "The Indian Metaphor in the
      American Renaissance." Ph. D. diss., Pennsylvania,
      1977. DA, 38 (1977), 1388A.

851   _____. "The Indian Metaphor in Henry David Tho-
      reau's A Week." Thoreau Journal Quarterly, 10
      (1978), 3-5.

852   HARDING, Brian R. "Transcendental Symbolism in the
      Work of Emerson, Thoreau, and Whitman." Ph. D.
      diss., Brown, 1971. DA, 32 (1972), 5789A.

853   _____. "Redskins and Transcendentalism: A Reading
      of A Week on the Concord and Merrimack Rivers."
      Research Studies, 40 (1972), 274-284.

854   _____. "Swedenborgian Spirit and Thoreauvian Sense:
      Another Look at Correspondence." Journal of Ameri-
      can Studies (Manchester), 8 (1974), 65-79.

855   HARDING, Walter R. "A Bibliography of Thoreau in
      Poetry, Fiction, and Drama." Bulletin of Bibliogra-
      phy, 18 (May-August, 1943), 15-18.

856 _____. "A Century of Thoreau." Audubon Magazine, 47 (March-April, 1945), 80-84.

857 _____. "Thoreau and Horace Greeley." Thoreau Society Bulletin, 11 (Spring, 1945), 1-2.

858 _____. "The Significance of Thoreau's Walden." Humanist, 5 (August, 1945), 115-121.

859 _____. "Thoreau: Pioneer of Civil Disobedience." Fellowship, 12 (July, 1946), 118-119, 131.

860 _____. "Thoreau." Word (Glasgow), 8 (October, 1946), 21.

861 _____. "Thoreau and the Negro." Negro History Bulletin, 10 (October, 1946), 5-6.

862 _____. "In Defense of Thoreau." Yankee, 11 (March, 1947), 26-27.

863 _____. "Gandhi and Thoreau." Thoreau Society Bulletin, 23 (Spring, 1948), 1-2.

864 _____. "A Checklist of Thoreau's Lectures." Bulletin New York Public Library. 70 (Fall, 1948), 78-87.

865 _____. "Uncle Charlie Comes to Concord." Nature Outlook, 7 (Fall, 1949), 7-9.

866 _____. "The Correspondence of Henry David Thoreau: 1836-1849." Ph. D. diss., Rutgers, 1950.

867 _____. "Thoreau and the Concord Lyceum." Thoreau Society Bulletin, 30 (Winter, 1950), 3-4.

868 _____. "The Correspondence of Sophia Thoreau and Marianne Dunbar." Thoreau Society Bulletin, 33 (Fall, 1950), 1-3.

869 _____. "Thoreau and the Worcester Ministers." Nature Outlook, 9 (Spring, 1951), 12-14, 23.

870 _____. "Thoreau on the Lecture Platform." New England Quarterly, 24 (September, 1951), 365-374.

871        _____. "Franklin B. Sanborn and Thoreau's Letters."
           Boston Public Library Quarterly, 3 (October, 1951),
           288-294.

872        _____. "The Francis H. Allen Papers: A Catalog."
           Thoreau Society Bulletin, 34 (Winter, 1951), 1-2.

873        _____. "James Russell Lowell and Thoreau's First
           Book." Thoreau Society Bulletin, 35 (Spring, 1951),
           1-4.

874        _____. "A Forgotten Review of Walden." Thoreau
           Society Bulletin, 39 (Winter, 1952), 2.

875        _____. "A Preliminary Checklist of the Editions of
           Walden." Thoreau Society Bulletin, 39 (Spring,
           1952), 2-3.

876        _____. "Thoreau at Fire Island." Thoreau Society
           Bulletin, 41 (Fall, 1952), 3.

877        _____. "Late Revisions in Thoreau's Walden."
           Secretary's News Sheet, Bibliographical Society of
           the University Press of Virginia, 25 (September,
           1962), 3.

878        _____. "A Centennial Check-list of the Editions of
           Henry David Thoreau's Walden." Secretary's News
           Sheet, Bibliographical Society of the University Press
           of Virginia, 28 (September, 1953), 1-32. Lists 133
           editions of Walden.

879        _____. "Two F. B. Sanborn Letters." American
           Literature, 25 (March, 1953), 230-234. Remarks on
           Thoreau, Harvard, and "Country Walking," edited by
           Ellery Channing for Emerson.

880        _____. "Thoreau's Feminine Foe." PMLA, 69
           (March, 1954), 110-116.

881        _____. "Thoreau's Professor Has His Say." Tho-
           reau Society Bulletin, 46 (Winter, 1954), 1-2.

882        _____. "Some Forgotten Reviews of Walden." Tho-
           reau Society Bulletin, 46 (Winter, 1954), 2-3.

883        _____. "A Century of Walden." Colorado Quarterly,
           3 (Autumn, 1954), 186-199.

884           .   A Centennial Check-List of the Editions of Henry David Thoreau's Walden.  Charlottesville: University Press of Virginia for the Bibliographical Society of the University of Virginia, 1954.

885           .   "The Francis H. Allen Papers in the Thoreau Society Archives: A Catalog Supplement."  Thoreau Society Bulletin, 50 (Winter, 1955), 2.

886           .   "Henry David Thoreau: A Check-List of His Correspondence."  Bulletin of the New York Public Library, 59 (May, 1955), 227-252.

887           .   "Thoreau as Seen by Fredrika Bremer." Thoreau Society Bulletin, 54 (Winter, 1956), 2.

888           .   "A Rare Thoreau Broadside."  Thoreau Society Bulletin, 54 (Winter, 1956), 2-3.  To announce John Brown memorial service in Concord.

889           .   "The Influence of Thoreau's Lecturing on His Writing."  Bulletin of New York Public Library, 60 (January, 1956), 74-80.

890           .   "Jack London and Thoreau."  Thoreau Society Bulletin, 57 (Fall, 1956), 1.

891           .   "A 'Lost' Thoreau Journal Found."  Thoreau Society Bulletin, 57 (Fall, 1956), 2-3.

892           .   "The Apple-Tree Table."  Boston Public Library Quarterly, 8 (1956), 213-215.

893           .   "Another Forgotten Review of Thoreau's Week."  Thoreau Society Bulletin, 59 (Spring, 1957), 2.

894           .   "Save Walden Committee Reports."  Thoreau Society Bulletin, 60 (Summer, 1957), 3-4.

895           .   "Thoreau's Library."  Thoreau Society Booklet, No. 11 (Spring, 1957), 102pp.  Also published as book, with Introduction. Charlottesville: University Press of Virginia, 1957.

896           .   "Thoreau and Timothy Dwight."  Boston Public Library Quarterly, 10 (April, 1958), 109-115.

897        .  "$32, 295 Worth of Thoreau Manuscripts. "
Thoreau Society Bulletin, 65 (Fall, 1958), 1-4.

898        .  "Thoreau and the Kalmucks:  A Newly Discovered Manuscript. "  New England Quarterly, 32
(March, 1959), 91-92.

899        .  "C. T. Jackson on Thoreau. "  Thoreau Society Bulletin, 67 (Summer, 1959), 3-4.

900        .  "Thoreau's Fame Abroad. "  Boston Public
Library Quarterly, 11 (August, 1959), 94-101.  Reprinted in Glick, ed. , Recognition (1969), pp. 315-323.

901        .  "Some Unfamiliar Glimpses of Thoreau. "
Thoreau Society Bulletin, 69 (Fall, 1959), 1-2.

902        .  A Thoreau Handbook.  New York:  New York
University Press, 1959.

903        .  "The Letters of Horace Mann, Jr. "  Thoreau
Society Booklet, No. 16 (Spring, 1960), 13pp.

904        .  "On Teaching Walden. "  Emerson Society
Quarterly, 18 (1960), 11-12.

905        .  "C. P. Snow and Thoreau. "  Thoreau Society
Bulletin, 70 (Winter, 1960), 3.

906        .  "Upton Sinclair on Thoreau. "  Thoreau Society Bulletin, 71 (Spring, 1960), 3.

907        .  "Thoreau in the Proceedings of the Boston
Society of Natural History. "  Thoreau Society Bulletin, 73 (Fall, 1960), 5.

908        .  "Hound, Bay Horse, and Turtledove, " in
Beebe, Maurice, ed. , Literary Symbolism.  San
Francisco:  Wadsworth, 1960, pp. 59-62.

909        .  "Thoreau and Mann on the Minnesota River,
June 1861. "  Minnesota History, 37 (1961), 225-228.
Letters by Horace Mann, Jr. , who accompanied Tho-
reau.

910        .  "A Lead Pencil Diploma. "  Thoreau Society
Bulletin, 74 (Winter, 1961), 7-8.

911 _____ . "An Early Thoreau Club." Thoreau Society
Bulletin, 77 (Fall, 1961), 3-4.

912 _____ . "The Centennial of Thoreau's Death." Thoreau Society Bulletin, 79 (Spring, 1962), 1-3.

913 _____ . "Five Ways of Looking at Walden." Massachusetts Review, 4 (1962), 149-162. Reprinted in
Hicks, John H. , ed. , Thoreau in Our Season (1966),
pp. 44-57.

914 _____ . " 'This Is a Beautiful World; But I Shall See
a Fairer. ' " American Heritage, 14 (December, 1962).

915 _____ . "Thoreau's Minnesota Journey: Two Documents." Thoreau Society Booklet, No. 18 (1962),
61pp.

916 _____ . "Thoreau and Kate Brady." American
Literature, 36 (November, 1964), 347-349.

917 _____ . "The Influence of Civil Disobedience."
Thoreau Society Booklet, No. 19 (1963), 15pp.

918 _____ . "Henry David Thoreau," in Foerster and
Falk, eds. , Eight American Writers (1963), pp.
409-581. Includes Introduction, plus selected writings
from Thoreau.

919 _____ . "Emerson, Thoreau, and Transcendentalism, "
a review of current scholarship, in American Literary Scholarship, 1963, pp. 3-16; 1965, pp. 3-14;
1966, pp. 3-11; 1973, pp. 3-14.

920 _____ . "A New Sophia Thoreau Letter." Thoreau
Society Bulletin, 87 (Spring, 1964), 4.

921 _____ . "A Source for a Walden Anecdote." Thoreau
Society Bulletin, 87 (Spring, 1964), 4. Refers to
Yeoman's Gazette, November 22, 1828; swamp-
bottom story in final chapter of Walden.

922 _____ . "The Camper in the Back Yard." Horizon,
6 (August, 1964), 32-39.

923 _____ . "Henry Thoreau and Ellen Sewall." South
Atlantic Quarterly, 64 (Winter, 1965), 100-109.

924          . The Days of Henry Thoreau:  A Biography.
New York:  Knopf, 1965.

925          . "The Thoreau Centennial. "  Thoreau Society
Booklet, No. 21 (1965), 119pp.

926          . "The Corruption of Walden.  "Thoreau Society Bulletin, 98 (Winter, 1967), 5-6.

927          . "Daniel Ricketson's Copy of Walden. "  Harvard Library Bulletin, 15 (1967), 401-411.  Relates
to two unknown caricatures of Thoreau, one reprinted.

928          . "Theodore Brown and Henry Thoreau. "
Thoreau Society Booklet, No. 23 (1968), 7pp.

929          . "John Shepard Keyes on Thoreau. "  Thoreau
Society Bulletin, 103 (Spring, 1968), 2-3.  Unpublished letter.

930          . "Thoreau at the Boston Music Hall. "  Thoreau Society Bulletin, 105 (Fall, 1968), 7.

931          . "Delugeous or Detergeous or    ?"  Certified
Editions of American Authors Newsletter, 1 (1968),
5-6.  Refers to a word in Thoreau's essay on
Carlyle (1847).

932          . "Henry David Thoreau:  Walden; or Life in
the Woods, " in Cohen, Hennig, ed. , Landmarks in
American Literature.  New York:  Basic, 1969, pp.
134-143.

933          . "Elizabeth Oakes Smith on Thoreau. "  Thoreau Society Bulletin, 110 (Winter, 1970), 2-3.

934          . "George Sturt and Thoreau. "  Thoreau Society Bulletin, 111 (Spring, 1970), 3-5.

935          . "Thoreau at the Oneida Community. "  Thoreau Society Bulletin, 115 (Spring, 1971), 3-5.  Reprinted excerpts from three reviews in the Oneida
weekly, The Circular, 1864.

936          . "Horace Greeley on Thoreau:  A Forgotten
Portrait. "  Thoreau Society Bulletin, 116 (Summer,
1971), 5-7.  Reprints Greeley's "The Bases of
Character. "

937 _____ . "The First Year's Sales of Thoreau's Walden." Thoreau Society Bulletin, 117 (Fall, 1971),
1-3.

938 _____ . "The Early Printing Records of Thoreau's
Books." American Transcendental Quarterly, 11
(1971), 44-59.

939 _____ . "The Thoreau Collector's Guide to Book
Prices." Thoreau Society Booklet, No. 26 (1971),
12pp.

940 _____ . "Thoreau and Ecology." Thoreau Society
Bulletin, 123 (Spring, 1973), 6.

941 _____ . "More Excerpts from the Alfred Hosmer
Letter Files." Thoreau Society Bulletin, 123 (Spring,
1973), 6-7.

942 _____ . "Thoreau on the Lecture Platform." Thoreau Society Bulletin, 125 (Fall, 1973), 6-7. Reprint of contemporary newspaper report.

943 _____ . "An Early Review of Thoreau's Week."
Thoreau Society Bulletin, 130 (Winter, 1975), 8.

944 _____ . "Concord by [Alfred] Munroe." Thoreau
Society Bulletin, 133 (Fall, 1975), 1-3.

945 _____ . "Was It Legal? Thoreau in Jail." American Heritage, 26 (1975), 36-37.

946 _____ . "Thoreau Scholarship Today." Thoreau Society Bulletin, 139 (Spring, 1977), 1-2.

947 _____ , ed. Thoreau Society Bulletin. Quarterly
established in 1941--to date. Bibliography of current
Thoreau scholarship in each issue. See compilation
of these bibliographies by Jean Cameron Advena.

948 _____ , ed. Thoreau: A Century of Criticism. Dallas: Southern Methodist University Press, 1954.

949 _____ , ed. Thoreau: Man of Concord. New York:
Holt, Rinehart, and Winston, 1960. Collection of
documents by contemporaries and near-contemporaries
of Thoreau.

950 _____, ed. with Introduction and Notes. The Vario-
        rum Walden. New York: Twayne, 1962.

951 _____, ed. with Notes. A Week on the Concord and
        Merrimack Rivers. New York: Holt, Rinehart, and
        Winston, 1963.

952 _____, ed. with Introduction. A Yankee in Canada:
        Anti-Slavery and Reform Papers. Montreal: Harvest
        House, 1963. Reprinted New York: Haskell House,
        1968. Facsimile of 1892 text.

953 _____, ed. "Sophia Thoreau's Scrapbook: From the
        Collection of George L. Davenport, Jr." Thoreau
        Society Booklet, No. 20 (1964), 66pp.

954 _____, ed. The Thoreau Centennial. Albany: State
        University of New York Press, 1965. Papers gath-
        ered by Lewis Leary in 1962.

955 _____, ed. with Introduction and Annotation. The
        Variorum Civil Disobedience. New York: Twayne,
        1967. Based on 1866 text.

956 _____, ed. A Bibliography of the Thoreau Society
        Bulletin Bibliographies, 1941-1969. Compiled by
        Jean Cameron Advena. Troy, N.Y.: Whitson, 1971.
        Has no index.

957 _____, ed. Henry David Thoreau: A Profile. New
        York: Hill and Wang, 1971. Reprinted criticism,
        plus original essays by Raymond D. Gozzi, pp. 150-
        187, and James Armstrong, pp. 222-243.

958 _____, ed. with Introduction. The Selected Works of
        Thoreau. Boston: Houghton Mifflin, 1975. Cam-
        bridge Editions series.

959 _____, ed. "A Catalog of the Thoreau Society Ar-
        chives in the Concord Free Public Library." Tho-
        reau Society Booklet, No. 29 (1978), 18pp.

960 _____, Donald S. Harrington, and Frederick T. Mc-
        Gill, Jr. "Panel Discussion on Thoreau," in Harding
        et al., eds., Studies (1972), pp. 82-102.

961 _____, and Carl Bode, eds. Correspondence of Hen-

ry David Thoreau.  New York:  New York University
Press, 1958.

962        , George Brenner, and Paul A. Doyle, eds.
        Henry David Thoreau:  Studies and Commentaries.
        Rutherford, N. J. :  Fairleigh Dickinson University
        Press, 1972.

963   HARMON, Roger J.  "Thoreau to His Publishers. "
        American Literature, 25 (January, 1954), 496-497.

964   HARPER, G. A.  "The Moon and Thoreau. "  Nature
        Study, 18 (November, 1922), 317-319.

965   HARRIS, Kenneth E.  "Thoreau's 'The Service': A
        Review of the Scholarship. "  American Transcen-
        dental Quarterly, 11 (1971), 60-63.

966   HARRISON, William Clinton.  "Thoreau as a Free-Lance
        Journalist. "  Ph. D. diss. , Texas A & M, 1976.  DA,
        37 (1977), 7750A.

967        .  "Thoreau on Thoughts and Thinking. "  Tho-
        reau Society Bulletin, 142 (Winter, 1978), 3.

968   HARTWICK, Harry.  "Henry David Thoreau," bibliog-
        raphy in revised/expanded form of Taylor, Walter
        Fuller, A History of American Letters (1936).  Re-
        printed as The Story of American Letters.  Chicago:
        Regnery, 1956, pp. 513-515.

969   HAUSMAN, L. A.  "Thoreau on Monadnock. "  Thoreau
        Society Bulletin, 25 (Fall, 1948), 2-3.

970   HAWTHORNE, Hildegarde.  Concord's Happy Rebel:
        Henry David Thoreau.  New York and Toronto:  Long-
        mans, Green, 1940.  For young people.

971   HAY, Stephen H.  "Rabindranath Tagore in America. "
        American Quarterly, 14 (Fall, 1962), 439-463.  In-
        cludes Emerson, Thoreau, and Whitman, and the
        modern interest in the Indian poet.

972   HAYDEN, Brad.  "Echoes of Walden in Trout Fishing in
        America. "  Thoreau Society Quarterly, 8 (1976), 21-
        26.

973  HAYDON, W. T. "Thoreau: Philosopher, Poet, Natu-
     ralist." Bookman (London), 52 (June, 1917), 84-87.
     Also in Living Age, 294 (August 4, 1917), 300-303.

974  HAYWARD, Adrian. "The White Pond Tree." Nature
     Outlook, 4 (November, 1945), 29-31.

975  HAZARD, Lucy L. "The Golden Age of Transcendental-
     ism," in The Frontier in American Literature. New
     York: Crowell, 1927. Reprinted New York: Ungar,
     1967, pp. 147-180.

976  HEDGES, Elaine R., and William L. Hedges, eds. Land
     and Imagination: The Rural Dream in America. Ro-
     chelle Park, N. J.: Hayden, 1979. Contains material
     by Emerson and Thoreau.

977  HENDRICK, George. "Henry David Thoreau and Gandhi:
     A Study of the Development of 'Civil Disobedience' and
     Satyagraha." Ph. D. diss., Texas (Austin), 1954.

978  _____. "The Influence of Thoreau's 'Civil Disobedi-
     ence' on Gandhi's Satyagraha." New England Quar-
     terly, 29 (December, 1956), 462-471.

979  _____. "Pages from Sophia Thoreau's Journal."
     Thoreau Society Bulletin, 61 (Fall, 1957), 1-2.

980  _____. "Thoreau, F. D. R., and 'Fear.'" Thoreau
     Society Bulletin, 62 (Winter, 1958), 2.

981  _____. "Thoreau's 'Civil Disobedience' in Gandhi's
     Indian Opinion." Emerson Society Quarterly, 14
     (1959), 19-20. Reprinted extracts.

982  _____. "Influence of Thoreau and Emerson on Gand-
     hi's Satyagraha." Gandhi Marg, 3 (June, 1959), 165-
     178.

983  _____. "William Sloane Kennedy Looks to Emerson
     and Thoreau." Emerson Society Quarterly, 26 (1962),
     28-31.

984  _____. "Thoughts on the Variorum Civil Disobedi-
     ence." Emerson Society Quarterly, 56 (1969), 60-62.
     Refers to edition by Harding, 1967.

985 _____. "Henry Salt's Biography of Thoreau," in
Schumann, Kuno, Wilhelm Hortman, and Armin P.
Frank, eds. Miscellanes Anglo-Americana: Fest-
schrift für Helmut Viebrock. Munich: Pressler,
1974, pp. 221-230.

986 _____. "Henry S. Salt, the Late Victorian Socialists,
and Thoreau." New England Quarterly, 50 (1977),
409-422.

987 _____. Henry Salt: Humanitarian Reformer and Man
of Letters. Urbana: University of Illinois Press,
1977. Thoreau, pp. 99-112.

988 _____, ed. American Renaissance: The History and
Literature of an Era. Berlin and Frankfurt: Diester-
weg, 1961. "Thoreau in the Twentieth Century," pp.
89-96.

989 _____, ed. with Introduction. Remembrances of Con-
cord and Thoreaus: Letters of Horace Hosmer to
Dr. S. A. Jones. Urbana: University of Illinois
Press, 1977.

990 _____, and Fritz Oehlschlaeger, eds. "Thoreau's
Letter of August 5, 1836, to Charles Wyatt Rice:
A New Text." Thoreau Society Bulletin, 145 (Fall,
1978), 5-6.

991 HENRY, F. "Henry David Thoreau and Bronson Alcott:
A Study of Relationships." Teachers College Journal,
14 (July, 1943), 126-128.

992 HENTOFF, Nathaniel, ed. with Introduction. Walden
and Other Writings. Garden City, N.Y.: International Collectors Library, 1970.

993 HERR, William A. "Thoreau: A Civil Disobedient?"
Ethics, 85 (1974), 87-91.

994 _____. "Thoreau on Violence." Thoreau Society
Bulletin, 131 (Spring, 1975), 2-4.

995 _____. "A More Perfect State: Thoreau's Concept
of Civil Government." Massachusetts Review, 16
(1975), 470-487.

996 HESFORD, Walter. "The 1860 Concord Cattle-Show:

An Official Account." Thoreau Society Bulletin, 132
(Summer, 1975), 6-7.

997        . "'Incessant Tragedies': A Reading of A
Week." English Literary History, 44 (1977), 515-
525.

998        , ed. "Alcott's Criticism of A Week." Resources for American Literary Study, 6 (1976), 81-
84. Thoreau's 1849 comment, complete.

999  HIBLER, Richard. "Thoreau and Epicurus." Thoreau
Society Bulletin, 129 (Fall, 1974), 1-3.

1000  HICKS, Granville. The Great Tradition: An Interpretation of American Literature Since the Civil War.
New York: Macmillan, 1933. Thoreau, pp. 9-10
and passim.

1001  HICKS, John Harland, ed. "Thoreau: A Centenary
Gathering." Massachusetts Review, 4 (Fall, 1962),
41-172. Contains articles by Theodore Baird, Leo-
nard Baskin, Carl Bode, Martin Buber, Gary Burr,
Trevor N. W. Bush, Reginald Cook, Jo Davidson,
Richard Drinnon, Walter Harding, Malvina Hoffman,
Stanley Edgar Hyman, Martin Luther King, Louise
Osgood Koopman, Joseph Langland, Paul Lauter,
Thomas P. McDonnell, Jawaharlal Nehru, William
Stuart Nelson, Dorothy Nyren, Mary P. Sherwood,
Leo Stoller, and Willard Uphaus. Also issued as
Hicks, ed., Thoreau Society Booklet, No. 17 (1962),
228pp.

1002        , ed. with Introduction. Thoreau in Our Season. Amherst: University of Massachusetts Press,
1966. Reprinted and original articles.

1003  HICKS, Philip Marshall. "The Development of the
Natural History Essay in American Literature."
Ph. D. diss., Pennsylvania, 1924. Thoreau, passim.

1004  HIGASHIYAMA, Mawoyoshi. "A Study of Henry David
Thoreau--Man and Nature." Thoreau Society Bulletin, 73 (Fall, 1960), 4-5.

1005        . "Thoreau--a Japanese View." English and
American Literature (Kwansei Gakuin University), 7
(October, 1962), 76-83.

1006 _____. "A Japanese View of Henry David Thoreau. "
Thoreau Journal Quarterly, 7 (1975), 25-29.

1007 HIGGINSON, Thomas Wentworth. Short Studies of
American Authors. Boston: Lee and Shepard,
1880. Reprinted New York: Dillingham, 1888.
Thoreau, pp. 22-31.

1008 _____. "Henry David Thoreau, " in Carlyle's
Laugh. Boston: Houghton Mifflin, 1909, pp. 65-74.

1009 _____. "Cape Cod: A Review. " Atlantic, 15
(March, 1865), 381. Reprinted in Harding, ed. ,
A Century (1954), pp. 41-43.

1010 _____. "Review of The Maine Woods. " Atlantic,
14 (September, 1864), 386-387. Reprinted in Glick,
ed. , Recognition (1969), pp. 34-37.

1011 HILDENBRAND, Christopher A. A Bibliography of
Scholarship About Henry David Thoreau, 1940-1967.
Fort Hays, Kan. : Fort Hays State College, 1967.
Bibliography series, No. 3.

1012 HILL, Douglas B. , Jr. "Getting to Walden: The
Strategies of Thoreau's Thought. " Ball State Uni-
versity Forum, 15 (1974), 14-26. Discussion of
Walden, "Ktaadn, " and "Civil Disobedience. "

1013 HILLWAY, Tyrus. "The Personality of Henry David
Thoreau. " College English, 6 (March, 1945), 328-
330.

1014 HIMELICK, Raymond. "Thoreau and Samuel Daniel. "
American Literature, 24 (May, 1952), 177-185.

1015 HINCKLEY, Edward B. "Thoreau and Beston: Two
Observers of Cape Cod. " New England Quarterly,
4 (April, 1931), 216-229. Cape Cod and Beston's
The Outermost House (New York, 1928).

1016 HIRSH, John C. "Henry David Thoreau, Dewitt Miller,
and Christian Bunsen's Outlines. " Papers of the
Bibliographic Society of America, 71 (1977), 351-
356.

1017 HOAGLAND, Clayton. "Edmund Sewall's Concord

Diary. "  Thoreau Society Bulletin, 53 (Fall, 1955),
1.

1018 _____ . "The Diary of Thoreau's 'Gentle Boy.'"
New England Quarterly, 28 (December, 1955), 473-
489.

1019 HOAR, George F.  Autobiography of Seventy Years.
New York:  Scribner, 1903.  Thoreau, pp. 70-72.

1020 HOBLITZELLE, Harrison.  "The War Against War in
the Nineteenth Century:  A Study of the Western
Backgrounds of Gandhian Thought. "  Ph. D.  diss. ,
Columbia, 1959.

1021 HOCH, David George.  "Theory of History in A Week:
Annals and Perennials. "  Emerson Society Quarterly,
56 (1969), 32-35.

1022 _____ . "Annals and Perennials:  A Study of Cosmo-
gonic Imagery in Thoreau. "  Ph. D.  diss. , Kent
State, 1969.  DA, 30 (1970), 5446A.

1023 _____ . "Thoreau's Source for the Story of the
King's Son. "  Thoreau Journal Quarterly, 2 (1970),
10-12.

1024 _____ . "Concord's Coat of Arms. "  Thoreau Society Bulletin, 110 (Winter, 1970), 1.

1025 _____ . "Thoreau's Use of The Hindoos. "  Thoreau
Society Bulletin, 114 (Winter, 1971), 1-2.

1026 _____ . "Ex Oriente Lux:  Thoreau's Allusion to
the Emblem of the Oriental Translator's Fund and
a Bibliography of the Fund's Publications Through
1854. "  Serif, 9 (1972), 25-30.

1027 _____ . "Walden, Yoga, and Creation, " in DeMott,
Robert J. , and Sanford E.  Marovitz, eds. , Artful
Thunder:  Versions of the Romantic Tradition in
American Literature in Honor of Howard P.  Vin-
cent.  Kent, Ohio:  Kent State University Press,
1975, pp. 85-102.

1028 HOCHFIELD, George, ed.  Selected Writings of The
American Transcendentalists.  New York:  New

American Library, 1966. Includes Thoreau's translation from the poetry of Anacreon, published in
The Dial, 3 (April, 1843), 351-356.

1029 HOCKS, Richard A. "Thoreau, Coleridge, and Bar-
field: Reflections on the Imagination and the Law
of Polarity." Centennial Review, 17 (1973), 175-
198. Primarily on Walden.

1030 HODGES, Robert R. "The Functional Satire of Thoreau's Hermit and Poet." Satire Newsletter, 8
(1971), 105-108. .

1031 HOELTJE, Hubert H. "Thoreau in Concord Town and
Church Records." New England Quarterly, 12 (June,
1939).

1032 _____. "Thoreau as Lecturer." New England
Quarterly, 19 (December, 1946), 485-494.

1033 _____. "Thoreau and the Concord Academy." New
England Quarterly, 21 (March, 1948), 103-109.

1034 _____. "Misconceptions in Current Thoreau Criticism." Philological Quarterly, 47 (1968), 563-570.

1035 HOEVELER, James K. "The Endless Cycle: Visual
Perception and Literary Expression in the Writings
of Henry David Thoreau." Ph. D. diss., Pittsburgh,
1973. DA, 35 (1974), 2270A.

1036 HOFFMAN, Daniel G. "Thoreau's 'Old Settler' and
Frost's Paul Bunyan." Journal of American
Folklore, 73 (July-September, 1960), 236-238.

1037 HOFFMAN, Michael J. "From Analogism to Transcendentalism: Thoreau, the Individual versus the In-
stitution," The Subversive Vision. Port Washington, N.Y.: Kennikat, 1972, pp. 46-58.

1038 _____. "Miller's Debt to Whitman, Emerson, Thoreau, et al.: Miller and the Apocalypse of Transcendentalism." Lost Generation Journal, 4 (1976),
18-21. Refers to Henry Miller.

1039 HOLDER, Alan. "The Writer as Loon: Witty Structure in Walden." Emerson Society Quarterly, 43
(1966), 73-77.

1040    HOLLAND, Joyce M.  "Pattern and Meaning in Tho-
        reau's A Week." Emerson Society Quarterly, 50
        Supplement, (1968), 48-55.

1041    HOLLIS, C. C.  "Thoreau and the State." Common-
        weal, 50 (September 9, 1949), 530-533.

1042    HOLMES, John Haynes.  "Thoreau's Civil Disobedi-
        ence." Christian Century, 66 (June 29, 1949), 787-
        789.

1043    HOLTZ, Nancy Ann.  "The Great Measures of Time:
        A Study of Cosmic Order in Nineteenth-Century
        American Thought." Ph. D. diss., University of
        Washington, 1977.  DA, 38 (1977), 3500A-3501A.

1044    HOMAN, John, Jr.  "Thoreau, the Emblem, and The
        Week." American Transcendental Quarterly, 1
        (1969), 104-108.

1045    _____.  "Henry David Thoreau as Self-Actualizer."
        Ph. D. diss., Southern Illinois (Carbondale), 1978.
        DA, 39 (1978), 2273A-2274A.

1046    HOSMER, Gladys E. H.  "Phineas Allen, Thoreau's
        Preceptor." Thoreau Society Bulletin, 59 (Spring,
        1957), 1-3.

1047    _____.  "The Save Walden Committee Report."
        Thoreau Society Bulletin, 62, 63, 64, 65 (Winter-
        Fall, 1958), 3, 1, 2-3, 5.

1048    _____.  "Mrs. Alcott Writes Mrs. Thoreau a Let-
        ter." Thoreau Society Bulletin, 69 (Fall, 1959), 1.

1049    _____.  "Remarks on Thoreau, Concord, and Wal-
        den." Thoreau Society Booklet, No. 19 (1963), 6pp.

1050    HOSMER, Joseph, et al.  "Thoreau Annex." Thoreau
        Society Booklet, No. 10 (Fall, 1955), 8pp.  Reprints
        1880 Annex to Concord Freeman, devoted to Thoreau.

        HOSMER, Mary see BROWN, Mary Hosmer

1051    HOUGH, Henry Beetle.  Thoreau of Walden: The Man
        and His Eventful Life.  New York: Simon and
        Schuster, 1956.

1052    HOURIHAN, Paul.  "The Inner Dynamics of the Emer-
        son-Thoreau Relationship. "  Ph. D. diss. , Boston,
        1966.  DA, 28 (1967), 1787A-1788A.

1053    HOUSTON, Howard R.  "Metaphors in Walden. "  Ph. D.
        diss. , Claremont, 1967.  DA, 29 (1968), 603A.

1054    HOUSTON, Walter Scott.  "An Index to the First Ten
        Years of Thoreau Society Publications. "  Thoreau
        Society Booklet, No. 8 (1953), 32pp.

1055    HOVDE, Carl F.  "The Writing of Henry David Tho-
        reau's A Week on the Concord and Merrimack
        Rivers:  A Study in Textual Materials and Tech-
        niques. "  Ph. D. diss. , Princeton, 1955.  DA, 16
        (1956), 1453-1454.

1056    _____.  "Nature into Art:  Thoreau's Use of His
        Journals in A Week. "  American Literature, 30
        (May, 1958), 165-184.

1057    _____.  "Literary Materials in Thoreau's A Week. "
        PMLA, 80 (March, 1965), 76-83.

1058    _____.  "Conception of Character in A Week, " in
        Harding, ed. , Thoreau Centennial (1965), pp. 5-15.

1059    HOVEY, Allen Beecher.  The Hidden Thoreau.  Beirut,
        Lebanon:  Catholic Press, 1966.

1060    HOVEY, Richard B.  "The Christian Gadfly:  A Lay
        Sermon on Thoreau. "  Education Forum, 23 (Jan-
        uary, 1959), 187-191.

1061    HOWARD, Rich.  "Thoreau as a Surveyor. "  Thoreau
        Society Bulletin, 139 (Spring, 1977), 5.

1062    HOWARTH, William L.  "Henry David Thoreau's
        Journal:  A Study of Transcendental Craftsmanship. "
        Ph. D. diss. , Virginia, 1967.  DA, 28 (1968),
        2647A-1648A.

1063    _____.  "Successor to Walden?  Thoreau's 'Moon-
        light--An Intended Course of Lectures. '"  Proof, 2
        (1972), 89-115.

1064    _____.  "Response by the Numbers. "  Thoreau So-

ciety Bulletin, 130 (Winter, 1975), 3-4. See article
by Bode, same issue, "A Problem in Arithmetic,"
p. 3.

1065 _____. "From Concord North Bridge: Thoreau
and the American Revolution." Thoreau Society
Bulletin, 134 (Winter, 1976), 1-2.

1066 _____, ed. Thoreau Gazetteer by Robert F. Stowell (1948). Reprinted Princeton, N. J. : Princeton
University Press, 1970.

1067 _____, ed. The Literary Manuscripts of Henry
David Thoreau. Columbus: Ohio State University
Press, 1974.

1068 HOWE, Anne. "Following Thoreau's Birchbark by
Cabin Cruiser." Thoreau Journal Quarterly, 10
(1978), 20-23.

1069 HOWE, W. D. "Henry David Thoreau." Reader, 5
(February, 1905), 372-376.

1070 HUBBARD, Elbert. Little Journeys to the Homes of
Great Philosophers. London: Owen, 1905. Re-
printed East Aurora, N. Y. : The Roycrofters, 1916.
Thoreau, pp. 391-429. Memorial edition.

1071 HUBBELL, George Shelton. "Walden Revisited: A
Grammar of Dissent." Sewanee Review, 37 (September, 1929), 283-294.

1072 HUBBELL, Jay B. Who Are the Major American
Writers? Durham, N. C. : Duke University Press,
1972. Thoreau, pp. 46-51 and passim.

1073 HUDSPETH, Robert N. "A Perennial Springtime:
Channing's Friendship with Emerson and Thoreau."
Emerson Society Quarterly, 54 (1969), 30-36.

1074 HUFFERT, Anton M. "Henry David Thoreau as a
Teacher, Lecturer, and Educational Thinker."
Ph. D. diss., New York University (Education),
1951.

1075 _____. "Alcott on Thoreau's Atlas of Concord."
Thoreau Society Bulletin, 56 (Summer, 1956), 1-2.

1076   HUGHES, Mildred P.  "Thoreau as Writer and Teacher
       of Writing. "  English Journal, 67 (1978), 33-35.

1077   HULL, Raymona E.  "Hawthorne Promotes Thoreau
       as Writer. "  Emerson Society Quarterly, 33 (1963),
       24-28.

1078   _____.  "Some Further Notes on Hawthorne and
       Thoreau. "  Thoreau Society Bulletin, 121 (Fall,
       1972), 7-8.  See article by Peple.

1079   HUME, Robert A.  "February, Thoreau, and Spring. "
       Rendezvous, 2 (1967), 23-26.

1080   HURD, Harry Elmore.  "Henry David Thoreau--A
       Pioneer in the Field of Education. "  Education, 49
       (February, 1929), 372-376.

1081   HUTCHINSON, William R.   " 'To Heaven in a Swing':
       The Transcendentalism of Cyrus Bartol. "  Harvard
       Theological Review, 56 (1963), 275-295.

1082   HUTH, Hans.  Nature and the Americans.  Berkeley:
       University of California Press, 1957.  Thoreau,
       passim.

1083   HYMAN, Stanley Edgar.  "Henry Thoreau in Our Time. "
       Atlantic, 178 (November, 1946), 137-146.  Reprinted
       in Harding, ed. , A Century (1954), pp. 171-186.
       Also in Hyman, The Promised End:  Essays and
       Reviews, 1942-1962.  Cleveland: World, 1963, pp.
       23-39.  Excerpt reprinted in Glick, ed. , Recogni-
       tion (1969), pp. 334-351.

1084   _____.  "Thoreau Once More. "  Massachusetts Re-
       view, 4 (1962), 163-170.  Reprinted in Hicks, John
       H. , ed. , Thoreau in Our Season (1966), pp. 169-176.

1085   INGE, M. Thomas.  "Thoreau's Humor in Walden. "
       Randolph-Macon College Magazine, 37 (March,
       1966), 34-44.

1086   _____.  "Thoreau's Enduring Laugh. "  Thoreau
       Journal Quarterly, 2 (1970), 1-9.

1087   INGERSOLL, E.  "American Naturalists. "  Mentor, 7
       (June 15, 1919), 5-7.

1088   IRIE, Yukio. "Why the Japanese People Find a Kin-
       ship with Emerson and Thoreau." Emerson Society
       Quarterly, 27 (1962), 13-16.

1089   IRWIN, John T. "The Symbol of the Hieroglyphics in
       the American Renaissance." American Quarterly,
       26 (1974), 103-126. Refers to Emerson, Hawthorne,
       Melville, and Thoreau.

1090   IVES, Charles Edward. Essays Before a Sonata.
       New York: Knickerbocker, 1920. Thoreau, pp. 54-
       60. Reprinted, revised, and edited by Howard Boat-
       wright. New York: Norton, 1962. Thoreau, pp. 51-
       69.

1091   JACKSON, Holbrook. "Thoreau," in Dreamers of
       Dreams: The Rise and Fall of Nineteenth-Century
       Idealism. London: Faber and Faber, 1948, pp. 211-
       251.

1092   JACOBS, Edward Craney. "Thoreau and Modern Psy-
       chology." Thoreau Society Bulletin, 127 (Spring,
       1974), 4-5.

1093   _____. "Notes upon Walden." Thoreau Society
       Bulletin, 140 (Summer, 1977), 6-7.

1094   _____, and Karen Jacobs. "Walden's End and II
       Peter 1: 19." Thoreau Journal Quarterly, 10
       (1978), 30-31.

1095   JACOBS, John Tobias. "The Western Journey: Ex-
       ploration, Education, and Autobiography, in Irving,
       Parkman, and Thoreau." Ph. D. diss., Notre Dame,
       1976. DA, 37 (1976), 3598A.

1096   JAMES, David L. "Movement and Growth in 'Walk-
       ing.'" Thoreau Journal Quarterly, 4 (1972), 16-21.

1097   JAMES, E. H. "Thoreau and the State." Word, 41
       (March, 1951), 56.

1098   JAPP, Alexander Hay (H. A. Page, pseud.). Thoreau:
       His Life and Aims. Boston: Osgood, 1877.

1099   _____. "Preface and Excerpts from Part II," from

Japp, Thoreau (1877), by H. A. Page, in Glick, ed.,
Recognition (1969), pp. 51-64.

1100   JAQUES, John F.   "The Discovery of 'Ktaadn':   A
       Study of Thoreau's The Maine Woods."   Ph. D. diss.,
       Columbia, 1970.   DA, 32 (1971), 3309A.

1101   _____.   " 'Ktaadn'--A Record of Thoreau's Youthful
       Crises."   Thoreau Journal Quarterly, 1 (1969), 1-6.

1102   JENKINS, James T.   "Thoreau, Mythology, Simplicity,
       and Self-Culture."   Thoreau Journal Quarterly, 4
       (1972), 1-15.

1103   JESKE, Jeffrey M.   "Walden and the Confucian Four
       Books."   American Transcendental Quarterly, 24
       Supplement 1 (1974), 29-33.

1104   JESWINE, Miriam Alice.   "Henry David Thoreau:
       Apprentice to the Hindu Sages."   Ph. D. diss.,
       Oregon, 1970.   DA, 32 (1971), 3254A-3255A.

1105   JOHNSON, Kenneth.   "The Last Eden:   The New World
       in American Nature Writing."   Ph. D. diss., New
       Mexico, 1971.   DA, 34 (1972), 3346A.

1106   JOHNSON, Linck Christopher.   " 'A Natural Harvest':
       The Writings of A Week with the Text of the First
       Draft."   Ph. D. diss., Princeton University, 1975.
       DA, 37 (1976), 969A.

1107   JOHNSON, Michael C.   "Thoreau on Drugs."   Thoreau
       Society Bulletin, 134 (Winter, 1976), 4.

1108   JOHNSON, Paul David.   "Thoreau's Redemptive Week."
       American Literature, 49 (1977), 22-23.

1109   JOHNSTON, Joanne.   "The Meaning of the Metaphor in
       Thoreau's Walden."   Thoreau Society Bulletin, 116
       (Summer, 1971), 3-4.

1110   JOHNSTON, Kenneth G.   "Thoreau's Star-Spangled
       Losses:   The Hound, Bay Horse, and Turtle Dove."
       Thoreau Journal Quarterly, 3 (1971), 10-20.

1111   _____.   "Journeys into the Interior:   Hemingway,
       Thoreau, and Mungo Park."   Forum (Houston), 10
       (1972), 27-31.

1112   JOHNSTONE, Christopher L. "Thoreau and Civil Dis-
       obedience: A Rhetorical Paradox. " Quarterly
       Journal of Speech, 60 (1974), 313-322.

1113   JONES, Buford. "A Thoreauvian Wordplay and Para-
       dise Lost. " Emerson Society Quarterly, 47 (1967),
       65-66.

1114   _____. " 'The Hall of Fantasy' and the Early Haw-
       thorne-Thoreau Relationship. " PMLA, 83 (1968),
       1429-1438.

1115   JONES, Howard Mumford. "Thoreau as Moralist. "
       Atlantic, 210 (September, 1962), 59-61. Reprinted
       in Jones, History and the Contemporary: Essays in
       Nineteenth-Century Literature. Madison: Univer-
       sity of Wisconsin Press, 1964, pp. 127-144.

1116   _____, reader. Walden. New Rochelle, N. Y.:
       Spoken Arts Records, 1962.

1117   JONES, Joseph. "Walden and Ultima Thule: A Twin
       Centennial. " University of Texas Library Chronicle,
       5 (Fall, 1954), 13-22.

1118   _____. Index to Walden with Notes, Maps, and
       Vocabulary Lists. Austin, Texas: Hemphill's,
       1955.

1119   _____. "Transcendental Grocery Bills: Thoreau's
       Walden and Some Aspects of American Vegetarianism. "
       University of Texas Studies in English, 36 (1957),
       141-154.

1120   _____. "Thoreau and Hong Kong. " Thoreau Society
       Bulletin, 97 (Fall, 1966), 1-2. Teaching Thoreau
       in the British Crown Colony.

1121   JONES, Samuel Arthur. Thoreau: A Glimpse. A
       paper read before the Unity Club, Ann Arbor, Michi-
       gan, December, 1889. Published in The Unitarian,
       5 (January, February, and March, 1890), 18-20,
       65-68, 124-128. Reprinted Ann Arbor: Privately
       printed for the author, 1890. Also reprinted Con-
       cord, Mass.: The Erudite Press, 1903. 32-page
       pamphlet.

1122          . "Thoreau and His Biographers. " Lippin-
         cott's Monthly Magazine, 48 (August, 1891), 224-
         228.

1123          . Bibliography of Henry David Thoreau.   New
         York:  De Vinne Press for the Rowfant Club of
         Cleveland, 1894.  80 pages, arranged chronological-
         ly.

1124          . "Thoreau's Incarceration. " Inlander, 9
         (1898), 96-113.  Reprinted in Thoreau Society Bul-
         letin, 4 (1943), 2-4.

1125          . "Thoreau as a Skulker. "  Thoreau Society
         Bulletin, 135 (Spring, 1976), 1-5.  Reprinted 1901
         unpublished article.

1126          , ed.  Pertaining to Thoreau:  A Gathering of
         Ten Significant Nineteenth-Century Opinions.  De-
         troit:  Edwin B. Hill, 1901.  Reprinted, with a new
         Preface by Kenneth W. Cameron, Hartford, Conn. :
         Transcendental, 1970.  Contains the following:

         Pp. 9-12.  Ripley, George.  "H. D. Thoreau's Book. "
         New York Tribune, June 13, 1849, and New York
         Weekly Tribune, June 16, 1849.

         Pp. 12-17.  Lowell, James Russell.  "A Week on
         the Concord and Merrimack Rivers. "  Massachusetts
         Quarterly Review, 3 (December, 1849), 40-51.

         Pp. 17-21.  Briggs, Charles Frederick.  "A Yankee
         Diogenes. "  Putnam's Monthly Magazine, 4 (October,
         1854), 443-448.

         Pp. 21-27.  Morton, Edwin.  "Thoreau and His
         Books. "  Harvard Magazine, 1 (January, 1855), 87-
         99.

         Pp. 27-31.  Anonymous.  "Town and Rural Humbugs. "
         Knickerbocker Magazine, 45 (March, 1855), 235-
         241.

         Pp. 31-35.  Anonymous.  "An American Diogenes. "
         Chambers' Journal, 8 (November 21, 1857), 330-
         332.

Pp. 35-37. Alcott, Amos Bronson. "The Forester."
Atlantic Monthly, 9 (April, 1862), 443-445.

Pp. 37-40. Higginson, Samuel Storrow. "Henry
David Thoreau." Harvard Magazine, 8 (May, 1862),
313-318.

Pp. 40-48. Weiss, John. "Thoreau." Christian
Examiner, 79 (July, 1865), 96-117.

Pp. 48-51. Williams, Henry. "Henry David Thoreau," in Memorials of the Class of 1837 of Harvard University. Boston: George H. Ellis, 1887,
pp. 37-43.

1127   JOY, Neill R. "Two Possible Analogues for 'The
Ponds' in Walden: Jonathan Carver and Wordsworth." Emerson Society Quarterly, 24 (1978),
197-205.

1128   KAHN, Sholom J. "Thoreau in Israel." Thoreau-
Society Bulletin, 85 (Fall, 1963), 1-2.

1129   KAISER, Leo Max. "Remarks on Thoreau's Translation of the Aeschylus' Prometheus." Classical
Weekly, 46 (January 5, 1953), 69-70.

1130   _____, ed. "Thoreau's Translation of 'The Seven
Against Thebes' (1843)." Emerson Society Quar-
terly, 17 (1959), 3-30. Also printed as booklet,
Hartford, Conn.: Transcendental, 1960.

1131   KAISER, Mary I. "'Conversing with the Sky': The
Imagery of Celestial Bodies in Thoreau's Poetry."
Thoreau Journal Quarterly, 9 (1977), 15-28.

1132   KAIYALA, Marguerite LaVoy. "The Poetic Development of Theodore Roethke in Relation to the Emer-
sonian-Thoreauvian Tradition of Nature." Ph. D.
diss., University of Washington, 1970. DA, 31
(1971), 3507A-3508A.

1133   KALMAN, David. "A Study of Thoreau." Thoreau
Society Bulletin, 22 (Winter, 1948), 1-3.

1134   KANE, Henry Bugbee. Thoreau's Walden: A Photo-

graphic Registrar. Edited with Introduction by
Brooks Atkinson. New York: Knopf, 1946. See
other works by Kane listed under Lunt, D. C.,
editor.

1135    KAPLAN, Harold. "Thoreau: The Walden of the
World," in Democratic Humanism and American
Literature. Chicago: University of Chicago Press,
1972, pp. 79-102.

1136    KARABATSOS, James. "A Concordance to Henry David
Thoreau's A Week on the Concord and Merrimack
Rivers." Ph. D. diss., Nebraska, 1970. DA, 31
(1971), 6012A.

1137    _____. "A Word Index to A Week on the Concord
and Merrimack Rivers." American Transcendental
Quarterly, 12 Supplement (1971), 1-99. Also in
book form, Hartford, Conn.: Transcendental, 1971.

1138    KASEGAWA, Koh. "Thoreau's 'Civil Disobedience.'"
Aoyama Journal of General Education, 2 (November,
1961), 45-61. Japanese publication in English.

1139    _____. "Thoreau's Walden: A Nature-Myth."
Studies in English Literature (Japan), 39 (November,
1963), 213-240.

1140    _____. "Emerson, Thoreau, Melville." Aoyama
Journal of General Education, 5 (November, 1964),
15-24.

1141    _____. "Thoreau, 'The Succession of Forest
Trees.'" Journal of College Literature (Tokyo),
9 (1966), 53-68.

1142    _____. "A Limnological Re-examination of Thoreau's
Walden." Studies in English and American Literature (Tokyo), 12 (1966), 1-7.

1143    _____. "Color in Nature: A View of 'Autumnal
Tints.'" Thoreau Journal Quarterly, 7 (1975),
20-24.

1144    KAUFMAN, L. R. "Thoreau's Philosophy of Life."
Columbia Literary Monthly, 8 (May, 1900), 241-247.

97                    Kazin

1145    KAZIN, Alfred. "Thoreau's Journals," in Harding,
        ed., A Century (1954), pp. 187-191. Also in Kazin,
        The Inmost Leaf. New York: Harcourt, Brace,
        1955, pp. 103-108.

1146    _____. "Dry Light and Hard Expressions." Atlan-
        tic, 200 (July, 1957), 74-76. Thoreau, passim;
        principally about Emerson's Journals.

1147    _____. "Thoreau's Lost Journal," in Kazin, Con-
        temporaries. Boston: Little, Brown, 1962, pp. 47-
        50.

1148    _____. "One Man's Communion with His World,"
        in The New York Times Book Review: "Opinions
        and Perspectives" Column, ed. with Introduction by
        Francis Brown. Boston: Houghton Mifflin, 1964,
        pp. 82-85.

1149    _____. "Thoreau and American Power." Atlantic,
        223 (May, 1969), 60-68.

1150    _____. "Writing in the Dark," in Harding et al.,
        eds., Henry David Thoreau: Studies (1972), pp.
        34-52.

1151    KEISER, Albert. "Thoreau's Manuscripts on the
        Indians." Journal of English and Germanic Philology,
        27 (April, 1928), 183-199.

1152    _____. "New Thoreau Material." Modern Language
        Notes, 44 (April, 1929), 253-254.

1153    _____. The Indian in American Literature. New
        York: Oxford University Press, 1933. "Thoreau,
        Friend of the Native," pp. 207-232.

1154    KELLER, Dean H. "Woodbury's Annotated Copy of
        Thoreau's Letters." Emerson Society Quarterly,
        43 (1966), 79-81. Refers to Charles J. Woodbury.

1155    KELLER, Karl. "'A Cheerful Elastic Wit': The
        Metaphysical Strain in Thoreau." Thoreau Journal
        Quarterly, 1 (1969), 1-17.

1156    KELLER, Michael Robert. "Henry David Thoreau:
        Mystic." Ph.D. diss., Ball State, 1977. DA, 38
        (1977), 263A-264A.

1157    KELLEY, Abner W. "Literary Theories About Pro-
        gram Music." PMLA, 52 (1937), 581-595. In-
        cludes remarks by Thoreau, Emerson, Poe, Lanier,
        et al.

1158    KELLEY, James Richard. "The Bloody Loam: The
        Indian as Viewed by Parkman and Thoreau." Ph. D.
        diss., State University of New York (Stony Brook),
        1976. DA 37 (1976), 1584A.

1159    KELLMAN, Steven G. "A Conspiracy Theory of Lit-
        erature: Thoreau and You." Georgia Review, 32
        (1978), 808-819.

1160    KENNEDY, D. E. "Thoreau in Old Dunatable."
        Granite State Magazine, 4 (December, 1907), 247-
        250.

1161    KENNEDY, William Sloane. "A New Estimate of
        Thoreau." The Penn Monthly, 11 (October, 1880),
        794-808. Reprinted in Glick, ed., Recognition
        (1969), pp. 90-106.

1162    _____. "Concord Recollections: Some Fresh
        Reminiscences of Emerson, Alcott, and Thoreau."
        Boston Evening Transcript, September 15, 1888.
        Reprinted in American Transcendental Quarterly,
        36 (1977), 43-45.

1163    KENT, Mrs. H. W. "A Catalog of the Thoreau Col-
        lection in the Concord Antiquarian Society." Tho-
        reau Society Bulletin, 47 (Spring, 1954), 2-3.

1164    KERN, Alexander C. "Thoreau Manuscripts at Har-
        vard." Thoreau Society Bulletin, 53 (Fall, 1955),
        1-2.

1165    _____. "American Studies and American Litera-
        ture: Approaches to the Study of Thoreau." College
        English, 27 (1966), 480-486.

1166    _____. "Thoreau's Sir Walter Raleigh." Certified
        Editions of American Authors Newsletter, 1 (1968),
        4-5.

1167    _____. "Church Scripture, Nature and Ethics in
        Thoreau's Religious Thought," in Falk, Robert, ed.,

Literature and Ideas in America:  Essays in Memory
of Harry Hayden Clark.  Athens:  Ohio University
Press, 1975, pp. 79-95.

1168    KERTESZ, Louise C.  "A Study of Thoreau as Myth
        Theorist and Myth Maker. "  Ph. D. diss. , Illinois
        (Urbana), 1970.  DA, 31 (1971), 6615A.

1169    KESTERSON, David Bert.  "Hawthorne and Nature:
        Thoreauvian Influence?"  English Language Notes,
        4 (March, 1967), 200-206.

1170    KESTNER, Joseph A.  "Thoreau and Kamo no Chòmei's
        Hut. "  American Transcendental Quarterly, 14 (1972),
        6.  Refers to medieval Japanese author who wrote
        "An Account of My Hut, " recording a withdrawal to
        two successively smaller huts for solitude, contem-
        plation, and asceticism.  Chòmei believed in no at-
        tachment to objects.

1171    KETCHAM, Ralph L.  "Some Thoughts on Buranelli's
        Case Against Thoreau. "  Ethics, 69 (April, 1959),
        206-208.

1172    KETTLER, Robert.  "The Quest for Harmony:  A
        Unifying Approach to Walden. "  Ball State Univer-
        sity Forum, 15 (1974), 3-13.

1173    KEYES, Langley Carleton.  Thoreau:  Voice in the
        Edgelands.  Chapel Hill:  University North Carolina
        Press, 1955.  Biography composed in a sonnet se-
        quence.

1174    KHER, Iñder Nath.  "Transcendental Aesthetics and
        Patterns of Consciousness. "  Canadian Review of
        American Studies, 6 (1975),  205-209.

1175    KILBOURNE, F. W.  "Thoreau and the White Moun-
        tains. "  Appalachia, 14 (June, 1919), 356-367.

1176    KIM, Kichung.  "Thoreau's Involvement with Nature:
        Thoreau and the Naturalist Tradition. "  Ph. D. diss.
        California (Berkeley), 1969.  DA, 30 (1969), 1985A.

1177    _____.  "Thoreau's Science and Teleology. "  Emer-
        son Society Quarterly, 18 (1972), 125-133.

1178        _____. "On Chuang Tzu and Thoreau." Literature
            East and West, 17 (1973), 275-281.

1179    KING, Bruce. "Thoreau's Walden." Etudes Anglaises,
            17 (July-September, 1964), 262-268.

1180        _____. "Emerson's Pupil." Venture (University
            of Karachi), 5 (1969), 112-122.

1181    KING, Joseph L. , ed. with Introduction. Walden.
            New York: Macmillan, 1929.

1182    KING, Martin Luther. "A Legacy of Creative Protest,"
            in Hicks, John H. , ed. , Thoreau in Our Season
            (1966), p. 13.

1183    KINGSLEY, M. E. "Outline Study of Thoreau's Wal-
            den." Education, 41 (March, 1921), 452-465.

1184    KIRCHNER, William H. "Henry David Thoreau as a
            Social Critic." Ph. D. diss. , Minnesota, 1938.

1185    KLEINE, Don W. " 'Civil Disobedience': The Way to
            Walden." Modern Language Notes, 75 (April,
            1960), 297-304.

1186    KLEINFIELD, Leonard F. A Henry David Thoreau
            Chronology. Forest Hills, N. Y. : Privately printed,
            1950. Pamphlet. Reprinted in American Transcen-
            dental Quarterly, 1 (1969), 113-117.

1187    KOHL, Kathleen A. "Morning, An Optimal Symbol in
            Walden." Thoreau Society Bulletin, 134 (Winter,
            1976), 2-3.

1188    KOLBENSCHLAG, M. Claire. "Thoreau and Crusoe:
            The Construction of an American Myth and Style."
            American Studies, 22 (1977), 229-246.

1189    KOOPMAN, Louise Osgood. "The Thoreau Romance."
            Massachusetts Review, 4 (1962), 61-67. Reprinted
            in Hicks, John H. , ed. , Thoreau in Our Season
            (1966), pp. 97-103.

1190    KOPP, Charles Calvin. "The Mysticism of Henry
            David Thoreau." Ph. D. diss. , Penn State, 1963.
            DA, 24 (1964), 5409A.

1191  KOSTER, Donald.  Transcendentalism in America.
      Boston:  Twayne, 1975.  Thoreau, pp. 48-56.

1192  KOVAR, Anton.  "Sophia Ford:  Thoreau's Feminine
      Foe."  Thoreau Journal Quarterly, 3 (1971), 22-23.

1193  KRAMER, Aaron.  "The Prophetic Tradition in American
      Poetry, 1835-1900."  Ph. D. diss., New York Uni-
      versity, 1967.  DA, 27 (1967), 3461A.

1194  _____.  "The Prophetic Tradition in American
      Poetry, 1835-1900.  Rutherford, N. J.:  Fairleigh
      Dickinson University Press, 1968.  Thoreau, passim.

1195  KRASTIN, Alexandra.  "He Took to the Woods 100
      Years Ago."  Saturday Evening Post, June 30,
      1945, pp. 26-27.

1196  KRIEGE, Jack W.  "Emerson's 'Thoreau' (last para-
      graph)."  Explicator, 31 (1972), item 38.

1197  KROB, Carol.  "Columbus of Concord:  A Week as a
      Voyage of Discovery."  Emerson Society Quarterly,
      21 (1975), 215-221.

1198  KRUTCH, Joseph Wood.  "Walden Revisited."  Nation,
      136 (May 3, 1933), 506-507.

1199  _____.  Henry David Thoreau.  New York:  Sloane,
      1948.

1200  _____.  "Thoreau and the Thoreauists," in Krutch,
      ed., Great American Nature Writing.  New York:
      Sloane, 1950.

1201  _____.  "A Kind of Pantheism."  Saturday Review
      of Literature, 23 (June 10, 1950), 7.

1202  _____.  "The Steady Fascination of Thoreau."  New
      York Times Book Review, May 20, 1951, pp. 1, 28.
      Reprinted in Glick, ed., Recognition (1969), pp. 297-
      301.

1203  _____.  "GBS Enters Heaven?"  Saturday Review
      of Literature, 25 (May 24, 1952), 19-21.  Where
      he converses with Thoreau.

1203a _____. "Introduction." In Wildness Is the Pre-
            servation of the World. Selections and photographs
            by Eliot Porter. San Francisco: Sierra Club,
            1962. Revised and reprinted New York: Ballantine,
            1974.

1204  _____. "Thoreau on 'Civil Disobedience.'" Ameri-
            can Scholar, 37 (1967), 15-18.

1205  KURTZ, Kenneth. "Style in Walden." Emerson So-
            ciety Quarterly, 60 (1970), 59-67.

1206  KWIAT, Joseph J. "Thoreau's Philosophical Appren-
            ticeship." New England Quarterly, 18 (1945), 51-
            69.

1207  LACEY, James F. "Henry David Thoreau in German
            Criticism, 1881-1965." Ph.D. diss., New York
            University, 1967. DA, 29 (1968), 901A.

1208  _____. "Thoreau in German Criticism: An Anno-
            tated Bibliography." Thoreau Society Bulletin, 105
            (Fall, 1968), 4-6.

1209  LA FORTE, Robert S. "The Political Thought of
            Henry David Thoreau: A Study in Paradox." Edu-
            cational Leader, 23 (July, 1959), 41-51.

1210  LAMBDIN, William. "Sounds in Walden." Colorado
            Quarterly, 18 (1969), 59-64.

1211  LAMBERT, Gary. "Rousseau and Thoreau: Their
            Concept of Nature." Ph.D. diss., Rice, 1968.
            DA, 30 (1969), 1988A.

1212  LANE, Laurist, Jr. "On the Organic Structure of
            Walden." College English, 21 (January, 1960),
            195-202. Reprinted in Young, Thomas Daniel, and
            Robert Edward Fine, eds., American Literature:
            A Critical Study. New York: American Book Co.,
            1968, pp. 187-198.

1213  _____. "Thoreau at Work: Four Versions of 'A
            Walk to Wachusett.'" Bulletin of New York Public
            Library, 69 (January, 1965), 3-16.

1214 _____. "Prose as Architecture: Thoreau and Theodore Winthrop on the Maine Woods." Canadian Association American Studies Bulletin, 2 (Spring, 1966), 17-24.

1215 _____. "Thoreau's Response to the Maine Woods." Emerson Society Quarterly, 47 (1967), 37-41.

1216 _____. " 'Civil Disobedience': A Bibliographic Note." Papers of the Bibliographic Society of America, 63 (1969), 295-296.

1217 _____. "Thoreau's Two Walks: Structure and Meaning." Thoreau Society Bulletin, 109 (Fall, 1969), 1-3. "A Walk to Wachusett" and "A Winter Walk" contrasted.

1218 _____. "Walden: The Second Year." Studies in Romanticism, 8 (1969), 183-192.

1219 _____. "Wordplay in Walden: Chapter I, paragraphs 1-3." Explicator, 29 (1970), item 35.

1220 _____. "Finding a Voice: Thoreau's Pentameters." Emerson Society Quarterly, 60 (1970), 67-72.

1221 _____. "Cape Cod--Thoreau's Sandy Pastoral." American Transcendental Quarterly, 11 (1971), 69-74.

1222 _____. "Thoreau's Autumnal Archetypal Hero: Captain John Brown." Ariel: A Review of English Literature, 6 (1975), 41-49.

1223 _____. "Thoreau's Autumnal Indian." Canadian Review of American Studies, 6 (1975), 228-236.

1224 _____. "Mountain Gloom and Yankee Poetry: Thoreau, Emerson, Frost." Dalhousie Review, 55 (1976), 612-630.

1225 _____. "Three Thoreaus (in One?)." Canadian Review of American Studies, 9 (1978), 201-208. Review article; See Marx, Leo, "The Two Thoreaus" (1978). Also refers to an article by Marco Cogno, in International Journal of Rumanian Studies (Amsterdam), 1 (1976), pp. 135-143; and to C. Webster

Wheelock, "Stancu's Barefoot in American Perspective." Miorita, 4 (1977), pp. 80-84.  Main reference is to Sayre, Thoreau and the American Indians (1977).

1226 _____, ed. with Introduction.  Approaches to Walden.  San Francisco: Wadsworth, 1961.  Collection
of reprinted critical essays.

1227 LANG, Berel.  "Thoreau and the Body Impolitic."
Colorado Quarterly, 18 (1969), 51-57.

1228 LANGLAND, Joseph.  "How It, So Help Me, Was!"
a poem, in Hicks, John H., ed., Thoreau in Our
Season (1966), pp. 38-39.

1229 LAPIN, Adam.  "On the 135th Anniversary of Henry
David Thoreau."  Worker, January 27, 1952, p. 7.

1230 LA ROSA, Ralph.  "David Henry Thoreau:  His American Humor."  Sewanee Review, 83 (1975), 602-622.

1231 LAUGHLIN, Clara.  "Two Famous Bachelors."  Book
Buyer, 25 (October, 1902), 241-247.

1232 LAUTER, Paul.  "Thoreau's Prophetic Testimony."
Massachusetts Review, 4 (1962), 111-123.  Re-
printed in Hicks, John H., ed., Thoreau in Our
Season (1966), pp. 80-90.

1233 LAWRENCE, Jerome, and Robert E. Lee.  The Night
Thoreau Spent in Jail, a play.  New York:  Hill
and Wang, 1970.  Serialized in Literary Cavalcade,
1971-1972; reprinted New York:  Bantam, 1972.

1234 LEACH, Joseph.  "Thoreau's Borrowings in Walden."
Notes and Queries, 184 (April 24, 1943), 269.

1235 LEARY, Lewis G.  "A Century of Walden."  Nation,
179 (August 7, 1954), 114-115.

1236 _____.  "Thoreau," in Stovall, ed., Eight American
Authors (1956), pp. 153-206; also in Woodress, James,
ed., Eight American Authors, revised edition (1971),
pp. 129-171.

1237 _____.  "Walden Goes Wandering:  The Transit of

Good Intentions." New England Quarterly, 32
(March, 1959), 3-30.

1238    _____. "A Man of Few Affairs: A Centenary Appreciation of Henry David Thoreau." Saturday Review of Literature, 45 (May 5, 1962), 12-13.

1239    _____. "The Thoreau Society Presidential Address."
Thoreau Society Bulletin, 80 (Summer, 1962),
1-3.

1240    _____. "In Wildness Is Thoreau," in Harding et
al., eds., Henry David Thoreau: Studies (1972),
17-24.

1241    _____. "'Now I Adventured': 1851 as a Watershed
Year in Thoreau's Career." Emerson Society Quarterly, 19 (1973), 141-148.

1242    _____. "Beyond the Brink of Fear: Thoreau's
Wilderness." Studies in the Literary Imagination,
7 (1974), 67-76.

1243    _____. American Literature: Study and Research
Guide. New York: St. Martin, 1976. Thoreau,
pp. 128-132.

1244    _____, ed. Articles on American Literature: 1900-
1950. Durham, N. C.: Duke University Press,
1954. Thoreau, pp. 287-293.

1245    _____, ed. American Literary Essays. New York:
Crowell, 1960. "Thoreau," by James Russell Lowell, pp. 96-102.

1246    _____, ed. The Teacher and American Literature.
Champaign, Ill.: National Council of Teachers of
English, 1965. Teaching Emerson and Thoreau,
passim.

1247    _____, ed. Articles on American Literature: 1950-
1967. Durham, N. C.: Duke University Press,
1968. Thoreau, pp. 515-531.

1248    LEBEAUX, Richard Mark. "Young Man Thoreau: A
Psychological Study of Henry David Thoreau's Pre-

Walden Life and Writings." Ph. D. diss., Boston,
1975. DA, 36 (1975), 1505A-1506A.

1249 _____. Young Man Thoreau. Amherst: University
of Massachusetts Press, 1977.

1250 LEBOWITZ, Martin. "The Condition of Life." Yale
Review, 64 (1974), 132-135. Review article on
James McIntoch's Thoreau as Romantic Naturalist
(1974) and Wendell Glick's edition of Reform Papers
(1973).

1251 LE BRUN, Mrs. Jean Munroe. "Henry Thoreau's
Mother." Boston Daily Advertiser, February 14,
1883.

1252 LEE, Lynn and Bile. "An Analysis of Thoreau's Hand-
writing." Thoreau Society Bulletin, 113 (Fall, 1970),
4-5.

1253 LEIDECKER, Kurt F. "That Sad Pagan Thoreau."
Visva-Bharati Quarterly, 29 (November, 1951 - January, 1952), 218-259.

1254 LEIGHTON, Walter L. "Henry Thoreau--An Estimate."
Arena, 30 (November, 1903), 128-198.

1255 _____. "French Philosophers and New England
Transcendentalists." Ph. D. diss., Virginia, 1908.

1256 _____. French Philosophers and New England
Transcendentalists. Charlottesville: University
Press of Virginia, 1908. Reprinted New York:
Greenwood, 1968. Thoreau, passim.

1257 LEISY, Ernest E. "Thoreau's Borrowings in Walden."
American Notes and Queries, 2 (November, 1942),
121.

1258 _____. "Thoreau and Ossian." New England Quarterly, 18 (March, 1945), 96-98.

1259 _____. "Francis Quarles and Henry David Thoreau." Modern Language Notes, 60 (May, 1945),
37-44.

1260 _____. "Sources of Thoreau's Borrowing in A
       Week." American Literature, 18 (March, 1946).

1261 LELIAERT, Richard Maurice. "Orestes A Brownson
       (1803-1876): Theological Perspectives on His Search
       for the Meaning of God, Christology, and the Devel-
       opment of Doctrine." Ph. D. diss., Graduate Theo-
       logical Union, 1974. DA, 35 (1974), 3108A. Tho-
       reau, Emerson et al., passim.

1262 LENNON, F. B. "The Voice of the Turtle." Thoreau
       Society Bulletin, 15 (Spring, 1946), 5-6.

1263 LENZ, Frederick P., III. "Henry David Thoreau:
       The Forgotten Poems." Concord Saunterer, 11
       (1976), 1-9.

1264 LERNER, Max. "Thoreau: No Hermit," in Ideas Are
       Weapons. New York: Viking, 1939, pp. 45-47. Re-
       printed in Paul, ed., Thoreau: A Collection (1962),
       pp. 20-22.

1265 LEVIERO, H. P. "Walden Pond Preserves Site Tho-
       reau Used as a Sanctuary." New York Herald Trib-
       une, August 31, 1947.

1266 LEWIS, R. W. B. The American Adam. Chicago:
       University of Chicago Press, 1955. Thoreau, pp.
       20-27 and passim.

1267 LEWIS, Sinclair. "One Man Revolution." Newsweek,
       10 (November 20, 1937), 33. Also in Saturday Re-
       view of Literature, 17 (December 11, 1937), 19.
       Reprinted in Harding, ed., A Century (1954), pp.
       148-149.

1268 _____. "Introduction to 'Four Days on the Webutuck
       River,'" in Lewis, Sinclair Lewis Reader. New
       York: Random House, 1953, pp. 168-170.

1269 LEWIS, Suzanne S. "Thoreau's Use of Sources in
       Cape Cod," in Myerson, ed., Studies (1978), pp.
       421-428.

1270 LIEBER, Todd Michael. "The Continuing Encounter:
       Studies of the American Romantic Hero." Ph. D.

diss., Case Western Reserve, 1969. <u>DA</u>, 30 (1970), 3911A.

1271 _____. <u>Endless Experiments</u>. Columbus: Ohio State University Press, 1973. "<u>Walden</u>: The Equivalent Response," pp. 41-74.

1272 LIGGERA, Joseph J. "Thoreau's Heroic Language." Ph. D. diss., Tufts, 1971. <u>DA</u>, 33 (1972), 2897A.

1273 LINSTROMBERG, Robin, and James Ballowe. "Thoreau and Etzler: Alternative Views of Economic Reform." <u>Midcontinent American Studies Journal</u>, 11 (1970), 20-29.

1274 LOMBARDO, Agostino. "L'arte di Henry David Thoreau." <u>Belfagor</u>, 14 (November 30, 1959), 674-685. In Italian.

1275 LONG, Larry Ray. "<u>Walden</u> and the Bible: A Study in Influence and Composition." Ph. D. diss., Ohio State, 1976. <u>DA</u>, 37 (1977), 7130A.

1276 _____. "The Bible and the Composition of <u>Walden</u>." in Myerson, ed., <u>Studies</u> (1979), pp. 309-354.

1277 LONGSTRETCH, T. Morris. "Our Most Famous Hill." <u>Christian Science Monitor</u>, 35 (November 5, 1943), 6.

1278 _____. "An Idyll Out of Season." <u>Christian Science Monitor</u>, 36 (March 4, 1944), 6.

1279 _____. "On Thoreau's Coldness." <u>Christian Science Monitor</u>, 36 (August 25, 1944), 6.

1280 _____. <u>Two Rivers Meet in Concord</u>. Philadelphia: Westminster, 1946.

1281 _____. <u>Henry Thoreau: American Rebel</u>. New York: Dodd, Mead, 1963. For young people.

1282 LOOMIS, C. Grant. "Thoreau and Zimmerman." <u>New England Quarterly</u>, 10 (December, 1937), 789-792. Refers to German writer (1728-1795) read by Thoreau in 1840.

1283    _____ . "Henry David Thoreau as Folklorist."
        Western Folklore, 16 (April, 1957), 90-106.

1284    LORCH, Fred W.  "Henry David Thoreau and the
        Organic Principle in Poetry."  Ph. D. diss., Iowa,
        1936.

1285    _____ . "Thoreau and the Organic Principle in Po-
        etry."  PMLA, 53 (March, 1938), 286-302.

1286    LOWANCE, Mason, Jr.  "From Edwards to Emerson
        to Thoreau:  A Re-valuation."  American Transcen-
        dental Quarterly, 18 (1973), 3-12.

1287    LOWELL, James Russell.  "Thoreau."  North Ameri-
        can Review, 101 (October, 1865), 597-608.  Re-
        printed in Lowell, My Study Window.  Boston:
        Houghton Mifflin, 1871.  Also reprinted in The Com-
        plete Writings of James Russell Lowell, 16 Vols.
        Boston:  Houghton Mifflin, 1904.  Vol. II, pp. 131-
        153.  Has been frequently reprinted, as in the fol-
        lowing:

        Payne, William Morton, ed.  American Literary
        Criticism.  New York:  Longmans, Green, 1904,
        pp. 167-182.

        Rhys, Ernest, ed.  Modern English Essays, 2 vols.
        New York:  Dutton, 1922.  Vol. I, pp. 101-121.

        Wilson, Edmund, ed.  The Shock of Recognition
        (1943), pp. 229-243.

        Warfel, Harry R., et al., eds.  The American
        Mind.  New York:  American Book Co., 1947, pp.
        735-739.

        Clark, William Smith, II, ed.  Essays, Poems, and
        Letters by James Russell Lowell.  New York:  Odys-
        sey, 1948, pp. 93-111.

        Harding, ed., A Century (1954), pp. 44-53.

        Howard, Leon, et al., eds.  The American Heritage,
        2 vols.  Boston:  Heath, 1955.  Vol. 2, pp. 80-86.

        Leary, ed., American Literary Essays (1960), pp.
        96-102.

Glick, ed. , Recognition (1969), pp. 38-46.

1288 LOWNES, Albert E. "Some Statistics About Thoreau's Week." Thoreau Society Bulletin, 66 (Winter, 1959), 1-2.

1289 _____. "Arthur Fifield and Thoreau's 'Civil Disobedience.'" Thoreau Society Bulletin, 86 (Winter 1964), 3. Refers to publication of Thoreau's essay in England.

1290 LUCAS, Alec. "Thoreau, Field Naturalist." University Toronto Quarterly, 23 (April, 1954), 227-232.

1291 LUDLOW, Robert. "Thoreau and the State." Commonweal, 50 (September 23, 1949), 581-582.

1292 LUDWIG, Richard M. "Bibliographical Supplement, II," in Spiller et al. , eds. , Literary History of the United States. Revised edition, New York: Macmillan, 1959, 1972.

1293 LUNT, Dudley Cammett, ed. Maine Woods. Illustrated by Henry Bugbee Kane. New York: Norton, 1950.

1294 _____, ed. with Notes. Introduction by Henry Beston. Cape Cod. Illustrated by Henry Bugbee Kane. New York: Norton, 1951.

1295 _____, ed. The Concord and Merrimack Rivers. Illustrated by Henry Bugbee Kane. Boston: Little, Brown, 1954.

1296 _____, ed. with Notes. The River: Selected Passages from the Journal. New York: Twayne, 1963. Passages on rivers and river travel.

1297 LYND, Straughton. "Henry Thoreau: The Admirable Radical." Liberation, February, 1963, pp. 21-36.

1298 _____. Intellectual Origins of American Radicalism. New York: Pantheon, 1968. Thoreau, passim.

1299 LYNN, Kenneth S. "Walden," in Lynn, Visions of America: Eleven Literary History Essays. Westport, Conn. : Greenwood, 1973, pp. 3-26.

1300 _____. "Adulthood in American Literature." Daedalus, 105 (1976), 52-54.

1301 LYON, Melvin E. "Walden Pond as a Symbol."
PMLA, 82 (May, 1967), 289-300.

1302 LYTTLE, David. "Thoreau's 'Diamond Body.'" Thoreau Journal Quarterly, 7 (1975), 18-29.

1303 MABIE, Hamilton W. "Thoreau, a Prophet of Nature."
Outlook, 80 (June 3, 1905), 278-282.

1304 _____. "A Theocritus of Cape Cod." Atlantic, 110
(August, 1912), 207-215.

1305 McALEER, John J. "The Therapeutic Vituperations of
Thoreau." American Transcendental Quarterly, 11
(1971), 81-87.

1306 _____, ed. "Artist and Citizen Thoreau: A Symposium." American Transcendental Quarterly, 11
(1971), 1-91. Also published as book, Hartford,
Conn.: Transcendental, 1971. Contents as follows:

Gandhi, Indira. "Verse Foreword," pp. 1-6.
Smith, George W., Jr. "Thoreau and Bacon:
The Idols of the Theatre," pp. 6-12.
Monteiro, George. "Thoreau's Defense of Man the
'Reading Animal,'" pp. 13-14.
McElrath, J. R. "Thoreau and James: Coincidence
in Angles of Vision?," pp. 14-15.
Stein, William B. "Thoreau's A Week and Om Cos-
mography," pp. 15-37.
Reed, Kenneth T. "Thoreauvian Echo in Uncle
Tom's Cabin?" pp. 37-38.
Ross, Donald, Jr. "Verbal Wit and Walden," pp.
38-44.
Harding, Walter. "The Early Printing Records of
Thoreau's Books," pp. 44-59.
Harris, Kenneth E. "Thoreau's 'The Service': A
Review of the Scholarship," pp. 60-63.
Neufeldt, Leonard. "'Extravagance' Through Econ-
omy: Thoreau's Walden," pp. 63-69.
Lane, Lauriat, Jr. "Cape Cod: Thoreau's Sandy
Pastoral," pp. 69-74.
Colquitt, Betsy F. "Thoreau's Poetics," pp. 74-81.

McAleer  see  listing above, pp. 81-87.
Basile, Joseph L.  "Technology and the Artist in
   A Week," pp. 87-91.

1307   McATEE, W. L.  "Adaptationist Naiveté."  Science
       Monthly, 48 (March, 1939), 253-255.

1308   McCARTHY, Paul E.  "Elements of Anatomy in Wal-
       den."  Ball State University Forum, 18 (1977), 67-
       78.

1309   McCLARY, Ben Harris.  "Burroughs to Whitman on
       Emerson:  An Unpublished Letter."  Emerson So-
       ciety Quarterly, 43 (1966), 67-68.

1310   McCORD, David Thompson Watson.  "Trout in the
       Milk," in McCord, In Sight of Sever:  Essays from
       Harvard.  Cambridge:  Harvard University Press,
       1963, pp. 268-271.

1311   McCORMICK, Edgar L.  "Thoreau and Higginson."
       Emerson Society Quarterly, 31 (1963), 75-78.

1312   McDONNELL, Thomas P.  "Walden Revisited," a
       poem, in Hicks, John H. , ed. , Thoreau in Our
       Season (1966), p. 67.

1313   McDOWELL, Robin S.  "Thoreau in the Current Scien-
       tific Literature."  Thoreau Society Bulletin, 143
       (Spring, 1978), 2.

1314   McELDERRY, Bruce R. , and M. J. Kelly.  "Two For-
       gotten Bits of Thoreauviana."  Thoreau Society
       Booklet, No. 14 (1959), 4pp.

1315   McELRATH, Joseph R. , Jr.  "Thoreau and James:
       Coincidence in Angles of Vision."  American Tran-
       scendental Quarterly, 11 (1971), 14-15.

1316   _____.  "Sawyer's Tribute to Thoreau."  American
       Transcendental Quarterly, 14 (1972), 54-66.

1317   _____.  "Nora C. Franklin on Holmes and Thoreau."
       Thoreau Journal Quarterly, 5 (1973), 17-19.

1318   _____.  "Practical Editions:  Henry David Thoreau's
       Walden."  Proof, 4 (1975), 175-182.

1319        _____ . "The First Two Volumes of the Writings
           of Henry David Thoreau:   A Review Article. "  Proof,
           4 (1975),  215-235.

1320        _____ , ed.  "Thoreau Symposium. "  Emerson So-
           ciety Quarterly,  19 (1973),  131-198.   Contents as
           follows:

           Porte, Joel.  "Henry David Thoreau:   Society and
              Solitude, "  pp. 131-140.
           Leary, Lewis.  "Now I Adventured:   1851 as a
              Watershed Year in Thoreau's Career, "  pp. 141-
              148.
           Boudreau, Gordon V.   " 'Remember thy Creator':
              Thoreau and St. Augustine, "  pp. 149-160.
           Glick, Wendell.  "Go Tell It on the Mountain:   Tho-
              reau's Vocation as a Writer, "  pp. 161-169.
           Rose, Edward J.  "The American Scholar Incarnate, "
              pp. 170-178.
           Albrecht, Robert C.  "Conflict and Resolution:
              'Slavery in Massachusetts, ' "  pp. 179-188.
           Williams, Paul O.  "Thoreau's Growth as a Tran-
              scendental Poet, "  pp. 189-198.

1321    McGEHEE, Judson D.  "The Nature Essay as a Lit-
           erary Genre:   An Intrinsic Study of the Works of
           Six English and American Nature Writers. "  Ph. D.
           diss. , University of Michigan, 1958.   DA, 19 (1958),
           1388-1389.   Includes Henry David Thoreau, John
           Burroughs, John Muir, W. H. Hudson, William Bee-
           be, and Donald Peattie.

1322    McGILL, Frederick T. , Jr.  "Thoreau and College
           Discipline. "  New England Quarterly,  15 (June,
           1942),  349-353.

1323        _____ . Channing of Concord:  A Life of William
           Ellery Channing, II.  New Brunswick, N. J. :   Rut-
           gers University Press, 1967.   Thoreau, passim.

1324    McGUIRE, Errol M.  "Answer to D. H. Lawrence:
           Thoreau's Vision of the Whole Man. "  Thoreau
           Journal Quarterly,  10 (1978),  14-24.

1325    McINERNEY, Peter Francis.  "Edenist Literary States-
           manship and The Writings of Henry Thoreau. "  Ph. D.
           diss. , Johns Hopkins, 1977.   DA, 38 (1977), 1392A.

1326 McINTOSH, James H. "Thoreau's Shifting Stance To-
wards Nature: A Study in Romanticism." Ph. D.
diss., Yale, 1966. <u>DA</u>, 28 (1967), 236A.

1327 _____. <u>Thoreau as Romantic Naturalist: His Shifting Stance Toward Nature</u>. Ithaca, N. Y.: Cornell
University Press, 1974.

1328 MacKAYE, Benton. "Thoreau on Ktaadn." <u>Living
Wilderness</u>, 9 (September, 1944), 3-6.

1329 MacKAYE, James, ed. with Introduction. <u>Thoreau,
Philosopher of Freedom: Writings on Liberty</u>.
New York: Vanguard, 1930.

1330 McKEE, Christopher. "Thoreau: A Week on Mt.
Washington and in Tuckerman Ravine." <u>Appalachia</u>,
30 (December, 1954), 169-183.

1331 _____. "Thoreau's First Visit to the White Mountains." <u>Appalachia</u>, 31 (December, 1956), 199-209.

1332 MacLACHLAN, C. H. "Vivekananda and Thoreau."
<u>Vedanta and the West</u> (Hollywood, Calif.), 188 (Nov-
ember-December, 1967), 18-36.

1333 McLAUGHLIN, E. T. "Thoreau and Gandhi: The
Date." <u>Emerson Society Quarterly</u>, 43 (1966), 65-
66.

1334 McLEAN, Albert F., Jr. "Four Letters by Thoreau."
<u>Emerson Society Quarterly</u>, 48 (1967), 73-81.

1335 _____. "Addenda to the Thoreau Correspondence."
<u>Bulletin of the New York Public Library</u>, 71 (April,
1967), 265-267.

1336 _____. "Thoreau's True Meridian: Natural Fact
and Metaphor." <u>American Quarterly</u>, 20 (1968),
567-579.

1337 MacLEAN, Robert L. "Walden: An Eastern Interpretation." <u>Thoreau Society Bulletin</u>, 125 (Fall, 1973),
4. Abstract of M. A. thesis.

1338 MacLEISH, Archibald, reader. "Civil Disobedience."
Caedmon Records, TC 1263, 1968.

1339  MacMECHAN, Archibald M.  "Thoreau," in Trent et
      al., eds., Cambridge History of American Litera-
      ture (1944), Vol. II, pp. 1-15.  Reprinted in Glick,
      ed., Recognition (1969), pp. 198-214.

1340  MacSHANE, Frank.  "Walden and Yoga."  New England
      Quarterly, 37 (September, 1964), 322-342.

1341  McWILLIAMS, Wilson Carey.  The Idea of Fraternity
      in America.  Berkeley:  University of California
      Press, 1973.  "Emerson and Thoreau," pp. 280-300.

1342  MACY, John Albert.  The Spirit of American Litera-
      ture.  New York:  Boni and Liveright, 1908.  Re-
      printed New York:  Doubleday, 1913.  Thoreau, pp.
      171-188.

1343  _____.  "Thoreau," excerpt from The Spirit of
      American Literature (1908), in Glick, ed., Recog-
      nition (1969), pp. 172-184.

1344  _____, ed.  American Writers on American Litera-
      ture.  New York:  Liveright, 1931.  "Thoreau,"
      by Gilbert Seldes, pp. 164-176.

1345  MADDEN, Edward H.  Civil Disobedience and Moral
      Law in Nineteenth Century American Philosophy.
      Seattle:  University of Washington Press, 1968.
      Thoreau, pp. 90-91; Emerson, pp. 85-95.  Section on
      Emerson better than that on Thoreau.

1346  MADISON, Charles A.  "Henry David Thoreau:  Tran-
      scendental Individualist."  Ethics, 54 (January,
      1944), 110-123.  Reprinted in Madison, Critics and
      Crusaders:  A Century of American Protest.  New
      York:  Holt, 1947, pp. 174-193.

1347  MAGNUS, John Lawrence, Jr.  "Thoreau's Poetic
      Cosmos and Its Relation to Tradition:  A Study of
      His Reading and His Writings, 1837-1854."  Ph. D.
      diss., Johns Hopkins, 1964.  DA, (1965), 2219.

1348  MAIDEN, Emory V., Jr.  "Cape Cod:  Thoreau's
      Handling of the Sublime and the Picturesque."  Ph.D.
      diss., Virginia, 1971.  DA, 32 (1972), 4571A.

1349  MAJUMBAR, R.  "Virginia Woolf and Thoreau."  Tho-
      reau Society Bulletin, 109 (Fall, 1969), 4-5.

1350  MANN, Thomas.  "Nietzsche in the Light of Modern
      Experience."  Commentary, 5 (January, 1948), 18.

1351  MANNING, Clarence A.  "Thoreau and Tolstoi."  New
      England Quarterly, 16 (June, 1943), 234-243.

1352  MARBLE, Annie Russell.  "Where Thoreau Worked
      and Wandered."  Critic, 40 (June, 1902), 509-516.

1353  _____.  Thoreau:  His Home, Friends, and Books.
      New York:  Crowell, 1902.

1354  MARCUS, Mordecai.  "Walden as a Possible Source
      for Stephen Spender's 'The Express.'"  Thoreau
      Society Bulletin, 75 (Spring, 1961), 1.

1355  _____.  "Eugene O'Neill's Debt to Thoreau in A
      Touch of the Poet."  Journal of English and Ger-
      manic Philology, 62 (April, 1963), 270-279.

1356  MARKEN, Ronald.  "'From Within Outward':  Thoreau,
      Whitman, and Wright on Domestic Architecture."
      Wascana Review, 11 (1976), 21-36.

1357  MARKS, Barry A.  "Retrospective Narrative in Nine-
      teenth-Century American Fiction."  College English,
      31 (1970), 366-375.  Studies Thoreau, Whitman, and
      Ishmael of Moby-Dick.

1358  MARKS, Jason.  "Thoreau's Literary Style."  Literary
      Review, 17 (1974), 227-237.

1359  MAROVITZ, Stanford E.  "Emerson, Thoreau, and the
      Phenomenon of Jimmy Carter."  Kyushu American
      Literature (Fukuoka, Japan), 19 (1978), 54-64.

1360  MARSHALL, James M.  "The Heroic Adventure in 'A
      Winter Walk.'"  Emerson Society Quarterly, 56
      (1969), 16-23.

1361  MARTIN, James J.  Men Against the State.  DeKalb,
      Ill.:  Adrian Allen, 1953.

1362  MARTIN, John Stephen.  "The 'Mirage' of the Sublime
      in Walden."  Thoreau Journal Quarterly, 8 (1976),
      3-15.

1363  MARTINEZ-ESTRADA, Ezequiel. "Taking Sides with
      Nature. " Review, 17 (1976), 32-34.

1364  MARX, Leo. "Walden as Transcendental Pastoral. "
      Emerson Society Quarterly, 18 (1960), 16-17.

1365  _____. "Thoreau's Excursions. " Yale Review, 51
      (Spring, 1962), 363-369.

1366  _____. The Machine in the Garden, and the Pas-
      toral Ideal in America. New York: Oxford Uni-
      versity Press, 1964. Thoreau, pp. 242-265.

1367  _____. "The Two Thoreaus. " New York Review
      of Books, 26 (October, 1978), 37-44. Review
      article; see article by Lauriat Lane (1978).

1368  _____, ed. with Introduction. Excursions. New
      York: Corinth, 1962.

1369  MATHEWS, J. C. "Thoreau's Reading of Dante. "
      Italica, 27 (June, 1950), 77-81.

1370  MATHEWSON, Rufus W. , Jr. "Thoreau and Chekhov:
      A Note on 'The Steppe. '" Ulbandus Review (Colum-
      bia University), 1 (1977), 28-40.

1371  MATHY, Francis. "The Three Johns: Portraits of
      Emerson, Thoreau, Hawthorne, and Holmes. "
      English Language and Literature Studies (Hiroshima),
      10 (1973), 163-181.

1372  MATLOCK, James H. "The Alta California's Lady
      Correspondent. " New York Historical Society Quar-
      terly, 58 (1974), 280-303.

1373  _____. "Early Reviews of Walden by the Alta Cali-
      fornia and Its 'Lady Correspondent. '" Thoreau
      Society Bulletin, 131 (Spring, 1975), 1-2.

1374  MATTFIELD, Mary S. "The Week: The 'Way In' to
      Walden. " College English Association, 30 (October,
      1967), 12-13.

1375  _____. "Emendation for Thoreau's Poem No. 189. "
      CEA Critic, 33 (October, 1970), 10-12. Refers to
      Carl Bode, ed. , Thoreau's Poems.

1376    MATTHEWS, Kenneth. "Making the Earth Say Beans:
        Thoreau's Bean-Field." Thoreau Society Bulletin,
        143 (1978), 5-6.

1377    MATTHIESSEN, Francis O. American Renaissance.
        London and New York: Oxford University Press,
        1941. Reissued in paperback, 1967. Thoreau, pp.
        76-119 and 166-175.

1378    MAXFIELD-MILLER, Elizabeth. "Elizabeth Hoar of
        Concord and Thoreau." Thoreau Society Bulletin,
        106 (Winter, 1969), 1-3.

1379    MAYER, Frederick. The Great Teachers. New York:
        Citadel, 1967. Thoreau, pp. 259-272.

1380    MAZZINI, Carla. "Epiphany in Two Poems by Tho-
        reau." Thoreau Journal Quarterly, 5 (1973), 23-
        25.

1381    _____. "Serenade Within the Mind: A Study of
        Epiphany in Selected Works of Henry David Thoreau."
        Ph. D. diss., North Carolina (Chapel Hill), 1977.
        DA, 39 (1978), 287A.

1382    MEAD, D. S., ed. Great English and American Es-
        says. New York: Rinehart, 1950. "Life Without
        Principle." pp. 95-111. With comment.

1383    MEESE, Elizabeth A. "Transcendental Vision: A
        History of the Doctrine of Correspondence and Its
        Role in American Transcendentalism." Ph. D. diss.,
        Wayne State, 1972. DA, 33 (1972), 6319A-6320A.

1384    MEIGS, Peveril. "The Cove Names of Walden."
        Thoreau Society Bulletin, 104 (Summer, 1968), 5-7.

1385    MELTZER, Milton, ed. with Introduction. Thoreau:
        People, Principles, Politics. New York: Hill and
        Wang, 1963. Selections from Thoreau's works ar-
        ranged topically.

1386    _____, and Walter Harding, eds. A Thoreau Pro-
        file. New York: Crowell. 1962. Reprinted Con-
        cord, Mass.: Thoreau Foundation, 1970. Biogra-
        phical profile using passages by Thoreau and his
        contemporaries; contains many illustrations.

1387  MENCKEN, H. L.  The American Language.  New
      York: Knopf, 1936.  Thoreau, passim.

1388  MENGER, W. H.  "Thoreau's Walden Manuscript."
      Trace, 4 (August, 1961), 209-215.

1389  MERIDITH, Robert.  "A Maine-iac in Search of Tradi-
      tion."  Colby Library Quarterly, 7 (1965), 27-29.

1390  METCALF, Henry Aiken, ed. with Introduction by
      Franklin B. Sanborn.  Sir Walter Raleigh.  Boston:
      Bibliophile Society, 1905.  Essay based on Tho-
      reau's lecture on Raleigh, Concord, February, 1843.

1391  METZGER, Charles Reid.  "The Transcendental Esthet-
      ics in America:  Essays on Emerson, Greenough,
      Thoreau, and Whitman."  Ph. D. diss., University
      of Washington, 1953.  DA, 14 (1954), 1214-1215.

1392  _____.  "Thoreau on Science."  Annals of Science,
      12 (September, 1956), 206-211.

1393  _____.  Thoreau and Whitman:  A Study of Their
      Esthetics.  Seattle:  University of Washington Press,
      1961.

1394  MEYER, Michael C.  "Several More Lives to Live:
      Thoreau's Political Reputation in America, 1920-
      1970."  Ph. D. diss., Connecticut, 1973.  DA, 35
      (1974), 1113A.

1395  _____.  Several More Lives to Live:  Thoreau's
      Political Reputation in America.  Westport, Conn.:
      Greenwood, 1977.  Contributions to America Studies,
      No. 29.

1396  MICHAELS, W. B.  "Walden's False Bottoms," in
      Weber, Samuel, and Henry Sussman, eds., Glyph:
      Johns Hopkins Textual Studies, Vol. I (1977), pp.
      132-149.

1397  MICHAELSON, L. W.  "The Man Who Burned the
      Woods."  English Record, 20 (1970), 72-75.

1398  MICHAUD, Régis.  "Henry David Thoreau."  Vie des
      Peuples, 14 (August, 1924), 27-44.

1399    MIDDLEBROOK, Samuel M. "Henry David Thoreau,"
        in Mason, Gabriel Richard, ed., Great American
        Liberals. Boston: Starr King, 1956.

1400    MILLER, F. DeWolfe. "Thoreau's Walden, Chapter
        I, Paragraph 63." Explicator, 32 (1973), Item 10.

1401    MILLER, Henry. "Preface," in Life Without Princi-
        ple: Three Essays by Henry David Thoreau. Stan-
        ford, Calif.: Stanford University Press, 1946.
        Reprinted in Harding, ed., A Century (1954), pp.
        162-170.

1402        _____. "Henry David Thoreau," in Stand Still Like
        the Hummingbird. New York: New Directions,
        1962, pp. 111-118. Similar to "Preface" in 1946
        edition of Three Essays.

1403    MILLER, Lewis H., Jr. "Bounding Walden." Tho-
        reau Journal Quarterly, 5 (1973), 25-29.

1404        _____. "The Artist as Surveyor in Walden and The
        Maine Woods." Emerson Society Quarterly, 21
        (1975), 76-81.

1405        _____. "Thoreau's Telegraphy." American Tran-
        scendental Quarterly, 26 Supplement (1975), 14-18.

1406    MILLER, Perry. "From Jonathan Edwards to Emer-
        son." New England Quarterly, 13 (December, 1940),
        589-617. Reprinted with important changes in
        Miller, Errand into the Wilderness. Cambridge:
        Harvard University Press, 1956, pp. 184-203.

1407        _____. "One Night in Concord Jail." Reporter,
        18 (January 23, 1958), 48.

1408        _____. "Thoreau in the Context of International
        Romanticism." Thoreau Society Bulletin, 72 (Fall,
        1960), 1-4. Expanded version with same title in
        New England Quarterly, 34 (June, 1961), 147-159.
        Reprinted in Miller, Nature's Nation (1967), pp. 175-
        183.

1409        _____. "New England's Transcendentalism: Native
        or Imported?" Lecture given at Rice University,
        Winter 1962-1963. Reprinted in Camden, Carroll,

ed. , Literary Views:  Critical and Historical Essays.  Chicago:  University of Chicago Press,
1964.

1410 _____ . Nature's Nation.  Cambridge:  Harvard
University Press, 1967.  Reprints 1961 expanded
article and "An American Language, " pp. 208-240.
Posthumous publication.

1411 _____ , ed. with Introduction.  The Transcendentalists:  An Anthology.  Cambridge:  Harvard University Press, 1950.  Thoreau, pp. 324, 396, and
passim.  Contains good bibliography, pp. 505-510.

1412 _____ , ed.  The American Transcendentalists:  Their
Prose and Poetry.  New York:  Doubleday/Anchor,
1957.  Shorter than 1950 item, but contains some
new material.  Thoreau, pp. 69, 143, 230, and
passim.

1413 _____ , ed. with Notes and Commentary.  Conscious-
ness in Concord:  The Text of Thoreau's Hitherto
Lost Journal (1840-1841).  Boston:  Houghton Mifflin,
1958.

1414 _____ , ed. with Afterword.  Walden, or Life in
the Woods and on the Duty of Civil Disobedience.
New York:  New American Library, 1960.

1415 MILLER, William Lee.  Of Thee, Nevertheless, I Sing.
New York:  Harcourt Brace Jovanovich, 1976.
Thoreau, pp. 265-271.  Studies Thoreau as a man
claiming to be more righteous than his neighbors.

1416 MILLICHAP, Joseph R.  "Plato's Allegory of the Cave
and the Vision of Walden. "  English Language
Notes, 7 (1970), 274-282.

1417 MINNEGERODE, Meade.  The Fabulous Forties:  1840-
1850.  New York:  1924.  Thoreau, passim.

1418 MOGAN, Joseph J. Jr.  "Thoreau's Style in Walden. "
Emerson Society Quarterly 50 Supplement (1968), 2-5.

1419 MOHANTY, Jatindra Mohan.  "Walden :  Style Con-
sidered as Vision of Life. "  Literary Criterion
(India), 7 (1966), 78-85.

1420    MOLDENHAUER, Joseph J.  "Images of Circularity in
        Thoreau's Prose."  Texas Studies in Literature and
        Language, 1 (Summer, 1959), 245-263.

1421    _____.  "A Recently Discovered Addition to the
        Thoreau Correspondence."  Thoreau Society Bulletin,
        84 (Summer, 1963), 4.

1422    _____.  "A New Manuscript Fragment by Thoreau."
        Emerson Society Quarterly, 33 (1963), 17-21.

1423    _____.  "The Extra-Vagrant:  Paradox in Walden."
        Graduate Journal, 6 (1964), 132-146.  Reprinted in
        Harding, ed., Thoreau Centennial (1965), pp. 16-30.
        Also in Ruland, Richard, ed., Twentieth Century
        Interpretations of Walden (1968), pp. 73-84; and in
        Glick, ed., Recognition (1969), pp. 351-365.

1424    _____.  "Rhetoric of Walden."  Thoreau Society
        Bulletin, 91 (Spring, 1965), 3.

1425    _____.  "Thoreau to Blake:  Four Letters Re-
        Edited."  Texas Studies in Literature and Language,
        8 (Spring, 1966), 43-62.

1426    _____.  "The Rhetoric of Walden."  Ph. D. diss.,
        Columbia, 1964.  DA, 28 (1967), 638A.

1427    _____.  "The Rhetorical Function of Proverbs in
        Walden."  Journal of American Folklore, 80 (April-
        June, 1967), 151-159.

1428    _____.  "On the Editing of The Maine Woods."
        Thoreau Journal Quarterly, 4 (1972), 15-20.  See
        item below.

1429    _____, ed. with Preface.  The Merrill Studies in
        Walden.  Columbus, Ohio:  Merrill, 1971.  Re-
        printed criticism.

1430    _____, ed. with new Introduction.  The Maine
        Woods.  Princeton, N. J.:  Princeton University
        Press, 1972.  Original publication, New York:
        Norton, 1950.

1431    _____, ed. with Introduction.  Illustrated Maine
        Woods:  With Photographs from the Gleason Collec-

tion.  Princeton, N. J.:  Princeton University Press, 1974.

1432 _____, Edwin Moser, and Alexander Kern, eds. Early Essays and Miscellanies. Princeton, N. J.: Princeton University Press, 1975.

1433 MOLLER, Mary Elkins. "Thoreau, Womankind, and Sexuality." Emerson Society Quarterly, 22 (1976), 123-148.

1434 _____. "'You Must First Have Lived': Thoreau and the Problem of Death." Emerson Society Quarterly, 23 (1977), 226-239.

1435 MOLONEY, Michael F. "Thoreau: Christian Malgré-Lui," in Gardiner, Harold C., ed., American Classics Reconsidered. New York: Scribner, 1958, pp. 193-209.

1436 MONDALE, R. Lester. "Henry David Thoreau and the Naturalizing of Religion." Unity, 137 (March-April, 1951), 14-17.

1437 MONTEIRO, George. "Redemption Through Nature: A Recurring Theme in Thoreau, Frost, and Richard Wilbur." American Quarterly, 20 (1968), 795-809.

1438 _____. "'Delugeous' or 'Detergeous'? A Contextual Argument." Certified Editions of American Authors Newsletter, 2 (1969), 45. See also similar article by Harding (1968).

1439 _____. "Thoreau's Defense of Man, the 'Reading Animal.'" American Transcendental Quarterly, 11 (1971), 13-14.

1440 MOORE, John Brooks. "Crèvecoeur and Thoreau." Papers of the Michigan Academy of Science, Arts, and Letters, 5 (1926), 309-333.

1441 _____. "Thoreau Rejects Emerson." American Literature, 4 (November, 1932), 241-256.

1442 MORDELL, Albert. "Roosevelt and Thoreau." Saturday Review of Literature, 30 (September 13, 1947), 23.

1443    MORE, Paul Elmer. "A Hermit's Notes on Thoreau."
        Atlantic, 87 (June, 1901), 857-864. Also in More,
        Shelburne Essays: First Series. New York: Put-
        nam, 1904, pp. 1-21. Reprinted in the following
        publications:

        Bowman, James Cloyd, et al., eds., Essays for
        College English: First Series, 2 vols. Boston:
        Heath, 1915, 1918, pp. 152-167.

        Harding, ed., A Century (1954), pp. 97-102.

        Excerpt in More, Shelburne Essays on American
        Literature. Selected from the 11 series of Shel-
        burne essays (1904-1921), and edited by Daniel
        Aaron. New York: Harcourt, Brace, 1963, pp.
        199-212. Published posthumously; More died in
        1937.

        Glick, ed., Recognition (1969), pp. 155-161.

1444    _____. "Thoreau and German Romanticism." Na-
        tion, 83 (November 8, 15, 1906), 388-390, 411-412.

1445    _____. "Thoreau's Journal," in More, Shelburne
        Essays: Fifth Series. New York: Houghton Miff-
        lin, 1908, pp. 106-131. Reprinted in More, Selected
        Shelburne Essays. New York: Oxford University
        Press, 1935, pp. 97-117. Also in Aaron, Daniel,
        ed., Shelburne Essays on American Literature
        (1963), pp. 213-229.

1446    MORGAN, Charles. "Walden and Beyond." London
        Times, November 8, 1947, p. 3.

1447    MORRIS, Wright. Territory Ahead. New York: Har-
        court, Brace, 1958. "To the Woods: Henry Tho-
        reau," pp. 39-50.

1448    _____. Earthly Delights, Unearthly Adornments.
        New York: Harper and Row, 1978. Thoreau, pas-
        sim.

1449    MORRISON, Helen Barber. "Thoreau and the New
        York Tribune: A Checklist." Part I, Thoreau So-
        ciety Bulletin, 77 (Fall, 1961), 1-2; Part II, Tho-
        reau Society Bulletin, 82 (Winter, 1963), 1-2.

1450 _____, ed. Thoreau Today: Selections from His
Writings. Introduction by Odell Shepard. New
York: Comet, 1957.

1451 MOSELEY, Caroline. "Some Observations on the
Thoreau Family's Sheet Music." Thoreau Society
Bulletin, 142 (Winter, 1978), 3-4.

1452 MOSER, Edwin. "Thoreau's Theme Grades." Thoreau Society Bulletin, 91 (Spring, 1965), 1-2.

1453 _____. "The Order of Fragments of Thoreau's
Essay on [Milton's] 'L'Allegro' and 'Il Penseroso.'"
Thoreau Society Bulletin, 101 (Fall, 1967), 1-2.

1454 MOSHER, Harold F., Jr. "The Absurd in Thoreau's
Walden." Thoreau Journal Quarterly, 3 (1971),
1-9.

1455 MOSS, Marcia, ed. "An Indenture for John Thoreau's
Store." Thoreau Society Bulletin, 129 (Fall, 1974),
7-8.

1456 _____, ed. "A Catalog of Thoreau's Surveys in
the Concord Free Public Library." Thoreau Society
Booklet, No. 28 (1976), 13pp.

1457 MOSS, Sidney P. "'Cock-a-Doodle-Doo!' and Some
Legends in Melville Scholarship." American Literature, 40 (May, 1968), 192-210.

1458 MOTT, Wesley Theodore. "Emerson and Thoreau as
Heirs to the Tradition of New England Puritanism."
Ph.D. diss., Boston University Graduate School,
1975. DA, 35 (1975), 7916A.

1459 _____. "John Brown in Concord." New England
Galaxy, 19 (1977), 25-31.

1460 _____. "Thoreau and Lowell on 'Vacation': The
Maine Woods and 'A Moosehead Journal.'" Thoreau Journal Quarterly, 10 (1978), 14-24.

1461 MOULTON, Charles Wells, ed. Library of Literary
Criticism of English and American Authors, 8 Vols.
Buffalo, N.Y.: Moulton 1901. Thoreau, Vol. 6,
pp. 267-278. Reprinted New York: Ungar, 1966,
in 4-vol. set, edited by Martin Tucker.

1462 MOYNE, Ernest J. "Thoreau and Emerson: Their
Interest in Finland." Neuphilologische Mitteilungen
(Helsinki), 70 (1969), 738-750. Relates to Peter
Kalm, a Swedish-Finnish scientist and traveler who
visited America in the eighteenth century. Thoreau
read Kalm's Travels in North America, believed to
have influenced Thoreau's journal writing.

1463 MUELLER, Roger Chester. "The Orient in American
Transcendental Periodicals, 1835-1886." Ph. D.
diss., Minnesota, 1968. DA, 29 (1969), 2681A.

1464 _____. "Transcendental Periodicals and the Orient."
Emerson Society Quarterly, 57 (1969), 52-57.

1465 _____. "Thoreau's Selections from Chinese Four
Books for The Dial." Thoreau Journal Quarterly,
4 (1972), 1-8.

1466 _____. "A Significant Buddhist Translation by
Thoreau." Thoreau Society Bulletin, 138 (Winter,
1977), 1-2.

1467 _____. "Thoreau and the Art of Motorcycle Main-
tenance: Transcendentalism in Our Time." Thoreau Journal Quarterly, 9 (1977), 10-17.

1468 MUKHERJEE, S., and D. V. K. Raghavacharyulu, eds.
Indian Essays in American Literature: Papers in
Honor of Robert E. Spiller. Bombay: Popular
Prakashan, 1969. "Thoreau's Literary Art and
His Philosophy," by K. R. Chandrasekharan, pp. 41-
54.

1469 MUMFORD, Lewis. The Golden Day. New York:
Boni and Liveright, 1926. "Thoreau, the Dawn,"
pp. 107-120. Excerpt reprinted in Glick, ed.,
Recognition (1969), pp. 247-255; excerpt also reprinted in Mumford, Interpretations and Forecasts
1922-1972. New York: Harcourt Brace Jovanovich, 1973, pp. 35-50.

1470 _____. "Renewal of the Landscape," in Mumford,
The Brown Decades (1931). Revised edition New
York: Dover, 1966, pp. 59-106.

1471 MUNSON, Gorham B. "Dionysian in Concord." Outlook, 149 (August 29, 1928), 690-692.

1472 _____. "The Lesson of Thoreau." Thinker, 3
     (March, 1931), 3, 7-27.

1473 MURET, Maurice. "Un poète-naturalist Américain."
     La Revue, 42 (August 15, September 1, 1902), 428-
     436, 572-580. In French.

1474 MURRAY, Donald M. "Thoreau's Indians and His
     Developing Art of Characterization." Emerson So-
     ciety Quarterly, 21 (1975), 222-229.

1475 _____. "Thoreau and the Example of the Muskrat."
     Thoreau Journal Quarterly, 10 (1978), 3-12.

1476 MURRAY, James G. Henry David Thoreau. New
     York: Washington Square, 1968. Great American
     Thinkers series.

1477 MYERS, Douglas. "The Bean-Field and the Method
     of Nature." Thoreau Journal Quarterly, 4 (1971),
     1-9.

1478 MYERS, Jay Arthur. "Henry David Thoreau," in
     Fighters of Fate. Baltimore: Williams and Wilkins,
     1927, pp. 118-139.

1479 MYERSON, Joel. "A History of The Dial (1840-1844)."
     Ph. D. diss., Northwestern, 1971. DA, 32 (1971),
     4573A. First complete study of The Dial and its
     contributors; 647pp.

1480 _____. "A Margaret Fuller Addition to Thoreau's
     Library." Thoreau Society Bulletin, 123 (Spring,
     1973), 3.

1481 _____. "Thoreau and The Dial: A Survey of the
     Contemporary Press." Thoreau Journal Quarterly,
     5 (1973), 4-7.

1482 _____. "More Apropos of John Thoreau." Ameri-
     can Literature, 45 (1973), 104-116.

1483 _____. "Transcendentalism and Unitarianism in
     1840: A New Letter by Christopher P. Cranch."
     College Language Association Journal, 16 (1973),
     366-368.

1484 _____ . "Eight Lowell Letters from Concord in
1838." Illinois Quarterly, 38 (1975), 20-42.

1485 _____ . "Emerson's 'Thoreau': A New Edition from
Manuscript," in Myerson, ed., Studies (1979), pp.
17-92.

1486 _____ , ed. Studies in the American Renaissance.
Boston: Twayne, 1977, 1978, 1979.

1487 NAIR, Pyarelal. Thoreau, Tolstoy, and Gandhi. Cal-
cutta: Banerji, 1958. In English.

1488 NARASIMHAIAH, C. D. "Where Thoreau and Gandhi
Differed." Thoreau Journal Quarterly, 7 (1975),
11-20.

1489 NASH, Roderick. Wilderness and the American Mind.
New Haven: Yale University Press, 1967. Thoreau,
pp. 84-95.

1490 NATHAN, Rhoda B. "The Soul at White Heat: Meta-
physical Tradition in Thoreau's Journal and Dickinson's Poetry." Ph. D. diss., City University of
New York, 1972. DA, 33 (1973), 6925A.

1491 _____ . "'This Delicious Solitude': Thoreau's Metaphysics and the Journey of the Self." Thoreau
Journal Quarterly, 10 (1978), 3-8.

1492 NELSON, Carl. "Sound Knowledge in Walden." Thoreau Journal Quarterly, 2 (1970), 1-6.

1493 NELSON, Truman. "Shores of Strife." New York
Times Magazine, April 27, 1958, pp. 78-79. Refers
to desecration and pollution of Walden Pond.

1494 _____ . "Walden on Trial." Nation, 187 (July 19,
1958), 30-33. Also in Western Humanities Review,
12 (1958), 307-311.

1495 _____ . "Thoreau and John Brown," in Hicks, John
H., ed., Thoreau in Our Season (1966), pp. 134-153.

1496 NELSON, William Stuart. "Thoreau and American
Non-Violent Resistance." Massachusetts Review,

4 (1962), 56-60.  Reprinted in Hicks, John H. , ed. ,
Thoreau in Our Season (1966), 14-18.

1497 _____ . "Thoreau and the Current Non-Violent
Struggle for Integration. " Thoreau Society Bulletin,
88 (Summer, 1964), 1-3.

1498 NETTLES, Elsa.  "'A Frugal Splendour':  Thoreau and
James and the Principles of Economy. "  Colby Library Quarterly, 12 (1976), 5-13.

1499 NEUFELDT, Leonard N.  "The Wild Apple Tree:  Possibilities of the Self in Thoreau. "  Ph. D. diss. ,
Illinois, 1966.  DA, 27 (1967), 4261A.

1500 _____ . "The Severity of the Ideal:  Emerson's
'Thoreau. '"  Emerson Society Quarterly, 58 (1970),
77-84.

1501 _____ . "'Extravagance' Through Economy:  Thoreau's Walden. "  American Transcendental Quarterly, 11 (1971), 63-69.

1502 NEVINSON, Henry Wood.  "Nature's Priest and Rebel
(Thoreau), " in Essays in Freedom and Rebellion.
New Haven:  Yale University Press, 1921, pp. 108-
114.

1503 NEWCOMER, Lee Robert.  "Classical Mythology in the
American Renaissance. "  Ph. D. diss. , Utah, 1971.
DA, 31 (1971), 4730A.

1504 NICHOLS, Charles E.  "Thoreau on the Citizen and
His Government. "  Phylon, 13 (1952), 19-24.

1505 NICHOLS, William W.  "Science and the Development
of Thoreau's Art. "  Ph. D. diss. , Missouri, 1966.
DA, 27 (1967), 3056A-3057A.

1506 _____ . "Science and the Art of Walden:  Experi-
ment and Structure. "  Emerson Society Quarterly,
50 supplement (1968), 77-84.

1507 _____ . "Individualism and Autobiographical Art:
Frederick Douglass and Henry Thoreau. "  College
Language Association Journal, 16 (1972), 145-158.
Refers to Douglass, a Maryland slave  who escaped

to Massachusetts and later to England; wrote My
Bondage and My Freedom, 1855. New edition printed New York: Arno, 1968.

1508   NICKOLS, John. "Thoreau and the Pig." Thoreau
       Society Bulletin, 77 (Fall, 1961), 1.

1509   NITKIN, Nathaniel. "Wild, the Mountain of Thoreau."
       New England Galaxy, 9 (Fall, 1967), 35-43.

1510   NORMAN, Charles. To A Different Drum: The Story
       of Henry David Thoreau. New York: Harper,
       1954. For young people.

1511   NORMAND, Jean. "Thoreau et Hawthorne à Concord
       --Les ironies de la solitude." Europe, 45 (July-
       August, 1967), 162-169. In French.

1512   NORTH, Sterling. Thoreau of Walden Pond. Illustrated
       by Harve Stein. Boston: Houghton Mifflin, 1959.
       Children's biography.

1513   NOVERR, Douglas Arthur. "Thoreau's Letter to
       Charles Sumner, July 16, 1860: An Addendum and
       Correction." Thoreau Society Bulletin, 107 (Spring,
       1969), 2.

1514   _____. "Thoreau's July 16, 1860 Letter to Charles
       Sumner: An Additional Note." Thoreau Society
       Bulletin, 110 (Winter, 1970), 2. See item above.

1515   _____. "Further Observations on Thoreau's Use of
       the Coat-of-Arms Symbol." Thoreau Society Bulle-
       tin, 113 (Fall, 1970), 1-2.

1516   _____. "A Note on Hildenbrand's Bibliography."
       Thoreau Journal Quarterly, 3 (1971), 7-11.

1517   _____. "A Note on Wendell Glick's 'Thoreau's Use
       of His Sources.'" New England Quarterly, 44
       (1971), 475-477.

1518   _____. "The Divining of Walden." Thoreau Journal
       Quarterly, 4 (1972), 9-14.

1519   _____. "Thoreau's Development as an Observer and
       Critic of American Society." Ph. D. diss., Miami
       (Ohio), 1972. DA, 34 (1973), 282A-283A.

1520    NYREN, Dorothy. "The Concord Academic Debating
        Society." Massachusetts Review, 4 (1962), 81-84.
        Reprinted in Hicks, John H., ed., Thoreau in Our
        Season (1966), pp. 93-96.

1521    OANDASAN, William. "Eternal Youth." Thoreau
        Journal Quarterly, 8 (1976), 2-6.

1522    O'DONNELL, Charles Robert. "The Mind of the
        Artist: Cooper, Thoreau, Hawthorne, and Mel-
        ville." Ph. D. diss., Syracuse, 1957. DA, 17
        (1957), 1752.

1523    OEHLSCHLAEGER, Fritz H. "Toward the Making of
        Thoreau's Modern Reputation: Correspondence of
        Dr. Samuel Arthur Jones and Alfred W. Hosmer."
        Ph. D. diss., Illinois (Urbana-Champaign), 1977.
        DA, 38 (1977), 3502A.

1524    _____. "The Thoreau Collection of Ernest W. Vic-
        kers." Thoreau Society Bulletin, 140 (Summer,
        1977), 7-8.

1525    _____. "More on the Composite Portrait of Tho-
        reau." Thoreau Society Bulletin, 142 (Winter,
        1978), 4-5.

1526    _____. "An Early English Response to Walden."
        Thoreau Society Bulletin, 143 (Spring, 1978), 1-2.

1527    OEHSER, Paul H. "Pioneers in Conservation." Na-
        ture Magazine, 38 (April, 1945), 188-190.

1528    _____. "The Word 'Ecology.'" Science, 129 (April
        17, 1959), 992. Thoreau's use of the word eight
        years before presumably coined.

1529    _____. "Thoreau: Exponent of Silence." Thoreau
        Society Bulletin, 72 (Summer, 1960), 1-2.

1530    OHLHOFF, Klaus. "A Meaning of the Word 'Walden.'"
        Thoreau Society Bulletin, 140 (Summer, 1977), 4.

1531    OLIVER, Egbert S. "A Second Look at 'Bartleby.'"
        College English, 6 (May, 1945), 431-439.

1532 _____ . "Melville's Picture of Emerson and Thoreau in The Confidence-Man." College English, 8 (November, 1946), 61-72.

1533 _____ . "Thoreau Finds the Dawn in Asia." Korean Survey, 2 (November, 1953), 6, 7, 10. Also in New Outlook, 6 (December, 1953), 8-13. Reprinted in Nagar, Ram, ed., Studies in American Literature. New Delhi: Eurasia, 1965, pp. 33-39.

1534 _____ . "Thoreau and the Puritan Tradition." Emerson Society Quarterly, 44 (1966), 79-86.

1535 _____ . "My Introduction to Thoreau." Thoreau Society Bulletin, 125 (Fall, 1973), 3-4.

1536 OLSON, Steve. "The Unanswered Question." Thoreau Journal Quarterly, 4 (1972), 22-26.

1537 ONG, Walter. "Personalism and the Wilderness." Kenyon Review, 21 (Spring, 1959), 297-304.

1538 ORRICK, Donald and Allan, eds. Designs of Famous Utopias. New York: Rinehart, 1959. "Walden Two," by B. F. Skinner, pp. 55-62, condensed.

1539 ORTH, Ralph H. "A Volume from Thoreau's Library." Thoreau Society Bulletin, 87 (Spring, 1964), 1.

1540 _____ . "Emerson, Thoreau, and Transcendentalism," a review of current scholarship. American Literary Scholarship, 1972. Pp. 3-17.

1541 OSTRANDER, G. M. "Emerson, Thoreau, and John Brown." Mississippi Valley Historical Review, 39 (March, 1953), 713-726.

1542 PACKER, Barbara Lee. "Emerson's Apocalypse of Mind." Ph. D. diss., Yale, 1973. DA, 34 (1974), 7241A.

1543/4 PADOVER, Saul K. "The American as Anarchist: Henry David Thoreau," in Padover, The Genius of America: Men Whose Ideas Shaped Our Civilization. New York: McGraw-Hill, 1960, pp. 196-205.

PAGE, H. A. see JAPP, Alexander Hay

1545 PAINE, Barbara B. "Harvard's Botanical Treasures."
The Herbarist, 26 (1960), 19-23. Thoreau's herbarium.

1546 _____. "Thoreau's Wildflowers: A 100-Year Record." Audubon Magazine, 63 (July, 1961), 194-197.

1547 PALMER, Joseph. David Henry Thoreau. Chapel Hill,
N. C.: Privately printed for Raymond Adams, 1929.

1548 PANNILL, H. Burnell. "Bronson Alcott: Emerson's
'Tedious Archangel,'" in Henry, Stuart C., ed.,
A Miscellany of American Christianity: Essays in
Honor of H. Shelton Smith. Durham, N. C.: Duke
University Press, 1963, pp. 225-247. Thoreau,
passim.

1549 PARKER, Hershel. "Melville's Satire of Emerson and
Thoreau: An Evaluation of the Evidence." American Transcendental Quarterly, 7 (1970), 61-67.

1550 PARRINGTON, Vernon Louis. Main Currents in American Thought, 3 vols. New York: Harcourt, Brace,
and World, 1927-1930. Reissued in one-volume
edition, c. 1949. "Henry Thoreau, Transcendental
Economist," Vol. II, pp. 400-413. Excerpt reprinted
in Glick, ed., Recognition (1969), pp. 255-268.

1551 PARSONS, Thornton H. "Thoreau, Frost, and the
American Humorist Tradition." Emerson Society
Quarterly, 33 (1963), 33-43.

1552 PARSONS, Vesta M. "Thoreau's The Maine Woods:
An Essay in Appreciation." Husson Review, 1
(1967-1968), 17-27.

1553 PATTEE, Fred Louis. A History of American Literature. Boston: Silver Burdett, 1896. Revised and
Reissued New York: Century, 1909, 1915. Thoreau, pp. 221-227.

1554 _____. Side-Lights on American Literature. New
York: Century, 1922. Thoreau, passim.

1555 _____. The First Century of American Literature,
1770-1870. New York and London: Appleton-

Century, 1935. Thoreau, passim; "Romanticism, "
pp. 285-298.

1556    PAUL, Sherman. "The Wise Silence: Sound as the
Agency of Correspondence in Thoreau. " New England Quarterly, 22 (December, 1949), 511-527.

1557    _____. "Resolution at Walden. " Accent, 13 (Spring,
1953), 101-113. Reprinted in Feidelson, Charles,
and Paul Brodtkorb, eds. , Interpretations of American Literature. N. Y. : Oxford, 1959, pp. 161-175.
Also reprinted in Young, Thomas Daniel, and Robert
Edward Fine, eds. , American Literature: A Critical
Survey. New York: American Book Co. , 1968, pp.
199-212; and in Browne, Ray B. , and Martin Light,
eds. , Approaches to American Literature. New York:
Crowell, 1965, pp. 164-177.

1558    _____. "Thoreau's 'The Landlord': 'Sublimely
Trivial for the Good of Men. '" Journal of English
and Germanic Philology, 54 (October, 1955), 587-
590. Reprinted in Studies by Members of the English Department in Memory of John Jay Parry. Urbana: University of Illinois Press, 1955, pp. 127-
130.

1559    _____. The Shores of America: Thoreau's Inward
Exploration. Urbana: University of Illinois Press,
1958.

1560    _____. "Thoreau's Walden, " in Paul, Repossessing
and Renewing. Baton Rouge: Louisiana State University Press, 1976, pp. 14-56.

1561    _____, ed. with Introduction. Walden and Civil
Disobedience. Boston: Houghton Mifflin, 1957.
Riverside edition.

1562    _____, ed. with Introduction. Thoreau: A Collection of Critical Essays. Englewood Cliffs: Prentice-Hall, 1962. Reprinted twentieth-century criticism.

1563    _____, ed. Six Classic American Writers: An
Introduction. Minneapolis: University of Minnesota
Press, 1971. "Henry David Thoreau, " by Leon
Edel, pp. 160-194.

1564    PAUNCH, 24 (1965), 1-50. Issue devoted to Thoreau
        and the unconventional. Articles include Efron,
        Arthur, pp. 1-18; Thompson, Wade C., pp. 18-25;
        Callahan, Robert D., pp. 27-39; and Widmer, Kings-
        ley, pp. 40-50.

1565    PAVILIONIS, Rolandas. "Thoreau and Self-Determina-
        tion of Personality." Problemos, 2 (1973), 40-49.
        In Italian; abstract in English.

1566    PAYNE, William Morton. Leading American Essayists.
        New York: Holt, 1910. Reprinted Freeport, N. Y.:
        Books for Libraries, 1968. "Thoreau," pp. 241-316.

1567    PEACH, Linden. "Earth Household: A 20th-Century
        Walden?" Anglo-Welsh Review, 25 (1975), 108-114.

1568    PEAIRS, Edith. "The Hound, the Bay Horse, and the
        Turtle-Dove: A Study of Thoreau and Voltaire."
        PMLA, 52 (September, 1937), 863-869.

1569    PEARSON, Norman Holmes, ed. with Introduction.
        Walden, or Life in the Woods and "On the Duty of
        Civil Disobedience." New York: Holt, Rinehart,
        and Winston, 1948. Rinehart edition.

1570    PEATTIE, Donald Cross. "Is Thoreau a Modern?"
        North American Review, 245 (Spring, 1938), 159-
        169.

1571    PEBWORTH, Ted-Larry. "Evelyn's Lay Fields, Dig-
        by's Vital Spirits, and Thoreau's Beans." Thoreau
        Society Bulletin, 101 (Winter, 1968), 6-7.

1572    PECKHAM, Morse. "Toward a Theory of Romanti-
        cism." PMLA, 66 (1951), 5-23.

1573    _____. "Toward a Theory of Romanticism: II.
        Reconsiderations." Studies in Romanticism, 1
        (1961), 1-8.

1574    _____. Beyond the Tragic Vision. New York:
        Braziller, 1962. Discusses Transcendentalism and
        related authors, passim.

1575    PEDERSON, Lee A. "Thoreau's Source of the Motto
        in 'Civil Disobedience.'" Thoreau Society Bulletin,
        67 (Spring, 1959), 3.

1576 _____. "Thoreau's Rhetoric and Carew's Lines."
Thoreau Society Bulletin, 82 (Winter, 1963), 1.

1577 _____. "Americanisms in Thoreau's Journal."
American Literature, 37 (May, 1965), 167-184.

1578 PEPLE, Edward C., Jr. "The Personal and Literary
Relationship of Hawthorne and Thoreau." Ph.D.
diss., Virginia, 1970. DA, 31 (1971), 4730A.

1579 _____. "The Background of the Hawthorne-Thoreau
Relationship." Resources for American Literary
Study, 1 (1971), 104-112.

1580 _____. "Hawthorne on Thoreau: 1853-1857." Thoreau Society Bulletin, 119 (Spring, 1972), 1-3.

1581 _____. "Thoreau and Donatello." Thoreau Journal
Quarterly, 5 (1973), 22-25.

1582 PERRY, J. B. "Was Thoreau a Lover of Nature?"
Critic, 42 (August, 1903), 152.

1583 PFEFFER, Arthur S. "The Instauration of Spirit:
Transcendentalism and Francis Bacon." Ph.D.
diss., City University of New York, 1967. DA,
28 (1968), 5065A-5066A.

1584 PHELPS, William Lyon. "Thoreau," in Howells,
James, Bryant, and Other Essays. New York:
Macmillan, 1924.

1585 PHILLIPS, Emmett L. "A Study of Aesthetic Distance
in Thoreau's Walden." Ph.D. diss., Oklahoma,
1969. DA, 30 (1970), 3953A.

1586 PICKARD, John B. "The Religion of 'Higher Laws.'"
Emerson Society Quarterly, 39 (1965), 68-72.

1587 POCHMANN, Henry A. "Early Poets--Thoreau," in
Pochmann, German Culture in America: 1600-1900.
Madison: University of Wisconsin Press, 1957, pp.
432-436.

1588 _____, and Gay Wilson Allen. Introduction to
Masters of American Literature. Carbondale:
Southern Illinois University Press, 1969. Thoreau,

pp. 79-84. Based on introductory material in Pochmann and Allen, eds. , Masters of American Literature: Anthology, 2 vols. New York: Macmillan,
1949.

1589   POGER, Sidney Boris. "Thoreau: Two Modes of Discourse." Ph. D. diss., Columbia, 1965. DA, 26
(1966), 4671-4672.

1590   _____. "Thoreau as Yankee in Canada." American
Transcendental Quarterly, 14 (1972), 174-177.

1591   _____. "Yeats as Azed: A Possible Source in
Thoreau." Thoreau Journal Quarterly, 5 (1973),
13-15.

1592   POIRIER, Richard. "Self and Environment," in Poirier,
A World Elsewhere: The Place of Style in American
Literature. New York: Oxford University Press,
1966, pp. 3-49; Thoreau, passim.

1593   _____. "The Performing Self," in Brower, Reuben
A. , ed. , Twentieth-Century Literature in Retrospect.
Cambridge: Harvard University Press, 1971, pp.
87-109. Harvard English Studies, No. 2.

1594   POLAK, Henry S. L. "Gandhi and Thoreau." Thoreau
Society Bulletin, 45 (Winter, 1953), 3-4.

1595   POLLEY, Robert L. , ed. "America the Beautiful in
the Words of Henry David Thoreau, by the Editors
of Country Beautiful." Waukesha, Wis. : Country
Beautiful Foundation, 1966. Illustrated.

1596   PONTIN, John F. "Henry David Thoreau/Henry S.
Salt." Thoreau Journal Quarterly, 7 (1975), 3-11.

1597   POPS, Martin Leonard. "An Analysis of Thoreau's
Cape Cod." Bulletin of the New York Public Library,
67 (September, 1963), 419-430.

1598   PORTE, Joel. "Emerson and Thoreau: Transcendentalists in Conflict." Ph. D. diss., Harvard, 1962.

1599   _____. "Thoreau on Love: A Lexicon of Hate,"
2 parts. University of Kansas City Review, 31

(December, 1964, and March, 1965), 111-116, 191-
194.

1600            . Emerson and Thoreau:  Transcendentalists
          in Conflict. Middletown, Conn.: Wesleyan Uni-
          versity Press, 1966.

1601            . "Emerson, Thoreau, and the Double Con-
          sciousness." New England Quarterly, 41 (1968),
          40-50.

1602            . "Transcendental Antics," in Levin, Harry,
          ed., Veins of Humor. Cambridge:  Harvard Uni-
          versity Press, 1972, pp. 167-183.

1603            . "Henry Thoreau and the Reverend Poluplois-
          boios Thalassa," in Bruccoli, M. J., ed., The
          Chief Glory of Every People:  Essays on Classic
          American Writers. Carbondale:  Southern Illinois
          University Press, 1973, pp. 191-210.

1604            . "Henry Thoreau:  Society and Solitude."
          Emerson Society Quarterly, 19 (1973), 131-140.

1605            . " 'God Himself Culminates in the Present
          Moment': Thoughts on Thoreau's Faith." Thoreau
          Society Bulletin, 144 (Summer, 1978), 1-4.

1606   PORTER, Lawrence Charles.  "Transcendentalism:
          A Self-Portrait." New England Quarterly, 35
          (March, 1962), 27-47.

1607            . "New England Transcendentalism:  A Self-
          Portrait." Ph.D. diss., Michigan, 1964. DA, 26
          (1965), 372.

1608   POTTER, Harriet Smith, comp.  "A Checklist of
          Books in the Julian Willis Abernethy Library of
          American Literature." Middlebury College Bulletin,
          25 (October, 1930). Thoreau, pp. 200-211.

1609   POULET, Georges.  "Timelessness and Romanticism."
          Journal of the History of Ideas, 15 (1954), 3-22.
          Thoreau, passim.

1610            . Studies in Human Time, translated from
          French by Elliott Coleman. Baltimore:  Johns Hop-
          kins University Press, 1956. Thoreau, passim.

1611    POWERS, Christine.  "Unerring Nature."  <u>Thoreau</u>
        <u>Journal Quarterly</u>, 4 (1972), 19-21.

1612    POWYS, Llewellyn.  "Thoreau:  A Disparagment."
        <u>Bookman</u> (London), 69 (April, 1929), 163-165.
        <u>Reprinted</u> in Harding, ed., <u>A Century</u> (1954), pp.
        140-145.

1613    PREDMORE, R. L.  "Unamuno and Thoreau."  <u>Com</u>-
        <u>parative Literature Studies</u>, 6 (1969), 33-44.

1614    PRITCHARD, John Paul.  "Cato in Concord."  <u>Clas</u>-
        <u>sical World</u>, 36 (October 5, 1942), 3-4.

1615    _____.  Return to the Fountains.  Durham:  Duke
        University Press, 1942.  Reprinted New York:
        Octagon, 1966.  "Henry David Thoreau," pp. 61-67.

1616    _____.  <u>Criticism in America</u>.  Norman:  Oklaho-
        ma University Press, 1956.  Thoreau, pp. 54-59.

1617    PULOS, C. E.  "The Foreign Observer in <u>Walden</u>."
        <u>English Language Notes</u>, 7 (1969), 51-53.

1618    _____.  "<u>Walden</u> and Emerson's 'The Sphinx.'"
        <u>American Transcendental Quarterly</u>, 1 (1969), 7-11.

1619    QUICK, Donald G.  "Thoreau as Limnologist."  <u>Tho</u>-
        <u>reau Journal Quarterly</u>, 4 (1972), 13-20.

1620    QUINN, Arthur Hobson, ed.  <u>The Literature of the</u>
        <u>American People:  An Historical and Critical Sur</u>-
        <u>vey</u>.  New York:  Appleton, 1915.  Reissued, 1951.
        "The Establishment of a National Literature," by
        Arthur Hobson Quinn, pp. 175-568.  Includes Emer-
        son, Hawthorne, Melville, Thoreau, and Whitman;
        Thoreau discussed in "Idealistic Revolt and Re-
        form," pp. 262-275.

1621    QUINN, James P.  "Thoreau and Berrigan:  Seekers
        of the Lost Paradise."  <u>Thoreau Society Bulletin</u>,
        127 (Spring, 1974), 2-3.  Refers to the social
        critic, author of <u>No Bars to Mankind</u> (1970) and <u>The</u>
        <u>Trial of the Catonsville Nine</u> (1970).

1622  RAHV, Philip, ed. Literature in America: An Anthol-
      ogy of Literary Criticism. New York: Meridian,
      1957. "Concerning Walt Whitman, " by Henry David
      Thoreau, pp. 148-149.

1623  RAILTON, Stephen. "Thoreau's 'Resurrection of Vir-
      tue!'" American Quarterly, 24 (1972), 210-227.

1624  RAMSAY, C. T. "Pilgrimage to the Haunts of Tho-
      reau. " New England Magazine, 50 (November,
      December, 1913), 371-383, 434-441; 52 (April,
      1914), 67-71.

1625  RAO, E. N. "Thoreau and Gandhi. " Aryan Path,
      37 (August, 1966), 361-364.

1626  RAUDNITZ, J. P. "Thoreau ou l'humus retrouvé. "
      Europe, 45 (July-August, 1967), 220-224. In
      French.

1627  RAY, Gordon N. , Foreword, and C. Waller Barrett,
      Introduction. The American Writer in England.
      Charlottesville: University Press of Virginia, 1969.

1628  RAYAPATI, Jacob P. Rao. "Early American Interest
      in Vedic Literature and Vedantic Philosophy. " Ph.D.
      diss. , Pennsylvania, 1970. DA, 32 (1971), 397A.

1629  _____. Early American Interest in Vedanta. New
      York: Asia Publishing House, 1973. "Early Vedic
      Readings by American Transcendentalists, " pp. 93-
      106.

1630  RAYMOND, Walter, ed. Walden. London: Dent;
      New York: Dutton, 1908. Everyman's Library
      edition.

1631  RAYSOR, Thomas M. "The Love Story of Thoreau. "
      Studies in Philology, 23 (October, 1926), 457-463.
      Refers to letters by Ellen Sewell to two of her
      daughters.

1632  READY, George Russell. "Thoreau's Influence on One
      Life, " in Harding et al. , eds. , Henry David Tho-
      reau: Studies (1972), pp. 144-149.

1633  REAVER, J. Russell. "Mythology in Emerson's

Poems." Emerson Society Quarterly, 39 (1965),
56-63. Refers to Thoreau also.

1634 _____. "Thoreau's Ways with Proverbs." American Transcendental Quarterly, 1 (1969), 2-7.

1635 REED, Kenneth T. "Thoreauvian Echo in Uncle Tom's
Cabin?" American Transcendental Quarterly, 11
(1971), 37-38.

1636 REES, John O. "Et in Arcadia Thoreau." Emerson
Society Quarterly, 23 (1977), 240-243. Refers to
"Economy."

1637 REGER, William. "Beyond Metaphor." Criticism,
12 (1970), 333-344.

1638 REUBEN, Paul P. "Thoreau in B. O. Flowers'
Arena." Thoreau Society Bulletin, 117 (Fall, 1971),
5-6. Refers to magazine published 1889-1909.

1639 REYNOLDS, R. C., and J. S. Sherwin. "Variant
Punctuations in Two Editions of Walden." Thoreau
Society Bulletin, 74 (Summer, 1961), 1-5.

1640 RHOADS, Kenneth W. "Thoreau: The Ear and the
Music." American Literature, 46 (1974), 313-328.

1641 RIBBENS, Dennis Neil. "The Reading Interests of
Thoreau, Hawthorne, and Lanier." Ph. D. diss.,
Wisconsin, 1969. DA, 31 (1970), 777A.

1642 RICHARDSON, R. D., Jr. Myth and Literature in the
American Renaissance. Bloomington: Indiana University Press, 1978. Thoreau, pp. 90-137.

1643 RICKETSON, Anna and Walton, eds. Daniel Ricketson
and His Friends. Boston: Houghton Mifflin, 1902.
Thoreau, pp. 11-14 and passim.

1644 RICKETT, Arthur. "Henry David Thoreau," in The
Vagabond in Literature. London: Dent; New York:
Dutton, 1906, pp. 89-114.

1645 RIPLEY, George. "A Week on the Concord and Merrimack Rivers: A Review." New York Tribune,
June 13, 1849. Reprinted in Harding, ed., A Century (1954), pp. 3-7.

1646 RITCHELL, Rella. "Thoreau, Poet, and Philosopher."
Thoreau Society Bulletin, 41 (Fall, 1952), 2-3.

1647 ROBBINS, Deborah. "The Ascetic Winter and Excre-
mental Spring of Walden." Emerson Society Quarterly, 24 (1978), 77-82.

1648 ROBBINS, J. Albert, ed. American Literary Manuscripts: A Checklist of Holdings in Academic,
Historical, and Public Libraries, Museums, and
Authors' Homes in the U.S. (1960). Revised and
reprinted Athens: University of Georgia Press,
1977.

1649 ROBBINS, Roland Wells. Discovery at Walden. Illustrated. Introduction by Walter Harding. Stone-
ham, Mass.: Published by the author, 1947.

1650 _____. "House Hunting for Henry David Thoreau."
Thoreau Society Bulletin, 92 (Summer, 1965), 1-2.

1651 _____, and Evan Jones. Hidden America. New
York: Knopf, 1959. Thoreau, pp. 16-35. Thoreau's
hut site.

1652 ROBERTS, Harry, ed. with Prefatory Note. Life and
Friendship: Selections from Thoreau's Essays and
Diaries. London: Anthony Treherne. 1904.

1653 ROBINSON, E. Arthur. "Thoreau's Buried Short
Story." Studies in Short Fiction, 1 (Fall, 1963),
16-20. Refers to "Baker Farm" chapter in Walden.

1654 ROBINSON, Kenneth Allen. Thoreau and the Wild
Appetite. Hanover, N.H.: Westholm, 1957. Booklet on Thoreau's dieting views and habits. Also
published as Thoreau Society Booklet, No. 12 (1957),
29pp.

1655 ROCKER, Rudolf. Pioneers of American Freedom.
Los Angeles: Rocker, 1949. Thoreau, passim.

1656 RODABAUGH, Delmer. "Thoreau's 'Smoke.'" Explicator, 17 (April, 1959), Item 47.

1657 ROHMAN, David Gordon. "An Annotated Edition of
Henry David Thoreau's Walden." Ph.D. diss.,
Syracuse, 1960. DA, 22 (1961), 249.

1658        . "Second Growth in Walden." Papers Michigan Academy Science, Arts, and Letters, 47 (1962),
565-570.

1659        . "Walden I and Walden II." Papers Michigan Academy Science, Arts, and Letters. 48 (1963),
639-648.

1660        . "Thoreau's Transcendental Stewardship."
Emerson Society Quarterly, 44 (1966), 72-77. Refers to Thoreau's own affairs.

1661    ROSA, Alfred F. "A Study of Transcendentalism in
Salem with Special Reference to Nathaniel Hawthorne." Ph.D. diss., Massachusetts, 1970. DA,
32 (1971), 1485A.

1662        . "Charles Ives: Music, Transcendentalism,
and Politics." New England Quarterly, 44 (1971),
433-443.

1663    ROSE, Edward J. " 'A World with Full and Fair Pro-
portions': The Aesthetics and Politics of Vision,"
in Taylor, J. Golden, ed., The Western Thoreau
Centenary: Selected Papers (1963), pp. 45-63. Also
published as part of Thoreau Society Booklet, No.
19 (1963), 18pp.

1664        . "The Wit and Wisdom of Thoreau's 'Higher
Laws.'" Queen's Quarterly, 69 (Winter, 1963),
555-567.

1665        . "The American Scholar Incarnate." Emerson Society Quarterly, 19 (1973), 170-178. Relates
Thoreau to the Emerson essay.

1666    ROSE, Vattel T. "A Critical Review of the Ideas of
Henry David Thoreau." Ph.D. diss., Minnesota,
1971. DA, 33 (1972), 1694A-1695A.

1667    ROSELIEP, Raymond. Flute over Walden: Thoreau-
haiku. West Lafayette, Ind.: Sparrow, 1976.

1668    ROSENFELD, Alvin H. "Emerson and Whitman:
Their Personal and Literary Relationships." Ph.D.
diss., Brown, 1967. DA, 28 (1968), 3197A. Thoreau, passim.

1669    ROSENTHAL, Bernard. "Nature's Slighting Hand:
        The Idea of Nature in American Writing, 1820-
        1860." Ph.D. diss., Illinois, 1968. DA, 29
        (1969), 2226A.

1670    _____. "Thoreau's Book of Leaves." Emerson
        Society Quarterly, 56 (1969), 7-11. On "Autumnal
        Tints."

1671    ROSS, Donald, Jr. "The Style of Thoreau's Walden."
        Ph.D. diss., Michigan, 1967. DA, 28 (1968),
        5069A.

1672    _____. "Hawthorne and Thoreau on 'Cottage Archi-
        tecture.'" American Transcendental Quarterly, 1
        (1969), 100-101.

1673    _____. "Composition as a Stylistic Feature."
        Style, 4 (1970), 1-10.

1674    _____. "Verbal Wit and Walden." American Tran-
        scendental Quarterly, 11 (1971), 38-44.

1675    _____. "Emerson and Thoreau: A Comparison of
        Prose Styles." Language and Style, 6 (1973), 185-
        195.

1676    ROSS, Francis D. "Rhetorical Procedure in Thoreau's
        'Battle of the Ants.'" College Communication and
        Composition, 16 (1965), 14-18.

1677    ROSS, Morton L. "Thoreau and Mailer: The Mission
        of the Rooster." Western Humanities Review, 25
        (1971), 47-56.

1678    ROURKE, Constance M. American Humor: A Study
        of the National Character. New York: Harcourt,
        Brace, and World, 1931. Reprinted New York:
        Doubleday/Anchor, 1953. Thoreau, pp. 135-137.

1679    RUBINSTEIN, Annette T. "Emerson, Thoreau, and
        Jacksonian Democracy." Zeitschrift für Anglistik
        und Amerikanistik (East Berlin), 24 (1976), 199-212.

1680    RUITENBECK, Hendrik. The Individual and the Crowd:
        A Study of Identity in America. New York: New
        American Library, 1964. Thoreau, p. 15 and passim.

1681   RUKEYSER, Muriel. "Thoreau and Poetry," in Har-
       ding et al., eds., Henry David Thoreau: Studies
       (1972), pp. 103-116.

1682   RULAND, Richard. The Re-Discovery of American
       Literature: Premises of Critical Taste, 1900-1940.
       Cambridge: Harvard University Press, 1967. Tho-
       reau, pp. 42-46 and passim.

1683   _____. "The Search for Walden." Emerson So-
       ciety Quarterly, 23 (1977), 188-200. Review-essay
       of Glick's Recognition (1969).

1684   _____, ed. with Introduction. Twentieth Century
       Interpretations of Walden: A Collection of Critical
       Essays. Englewood Cliffs, N. J.: Prentice-Hall,
       1968. Reprinted criticism.

1685   RUSSELL, Elias Harlow. "A Bit of Unpublished Cor-
       respondence Between Henry Thoreau and Isaac T.
       Hecker." Atlantic, 90 (September, 1902), 370-376.
       Reprinted in Proceedings of the American Antiquarian
       Society, 15 (1904), 58-69.

1686   _____. Thoreau's Maternal Grandfather: Asa Dun-
       bar. Worcester, Mass.: Davis, 1908.

1687   _____. "Thoreau's Maternal Grandfather." Pro-
       ceedings of the American Antiquarian Society, 19
       (1909), 66-76. Based on item above.

1688   RUSSELL, Frank Alden (Ted Malone, pseud.). "Henry
       David Thoreau," in American Pilgrimage. New
       York: Dodd, Mead, 1942, pp. 199-215.

1689   RUSSELL, Jason Almus. "Thoreau: The Interpreter
       of the Real Indian." Queen's Quarterly (Kingston,
       Ontario), 35 (August, 1927), 37-48.

1690   RYAN, George E. "Shanties and Shiftlessness: The
       Immigrant Irish of Henry Thoreau." Eire-Ireland:
       A Journal of Irish Studies, 13 (1978), 54-78.

1691   SAALBACH, Robert P. "Thoreau and Civil Disobe-
       dience." Ball State University Forum, 13 (1972),
       18-24.

1692    SACKMAN, Douglas.  "The Original of Melville's
        'Apple-Tree Table.'"  American Literature, 11
        (1940), 448-451.

1693    SADER, Marion, ed.  Comprehensive Index to Little
        Magazines:  1890-1970, 8 vols.  Millwood, N.Y.:
        Kraus, Thompson Organization, 1976.  Thoreau,
        Vol. 8, pp. 4513-4516.  Lists reviews and articles;
        especially good for listings of reviews.

1694    ST. ARMAND, Barton Levi.  "Thoreau Comes to
        Brown."  Books at Brown, 22 (1968), 121-141.

1695    SALOMON, Louis B.  "The Practical Thoreau."  Col-
        lege English, 17 (January, 1956), 229-232.

1696    _____.  "The Straight-Cut Ditch:  Thoreau on Edu-
        cation."  American Quarterly, 14 (Spring, 1962),
        19-36.

1697    SALT, Henry Stephens.  Life and Writing of Henry
        David Thoreau.  London:  Richard Bentley and
        Son, 1890.  Revised to a shorter version, 1896.
        Reprinted facsimile short version (1896) New York:
        Haskell House, 1968.  Also reprinted Hamden,
        Conn.:  Archon, 1968.  Contains bibliography by
        John P. Anderson (1896).

1698    _____.  "Thoreau and Richard Jefferies."  Nature
        Notes, 11 (February, 1900), 22-23.

1699    _____.  "Thoreau and Gilbert White."  New Age,
        November 15, 1900.

1700    _____.  "Henry David Thoreau and the Humane
        Study of Natural History."  Humane Review, Octo-
        ber, 1903.  Pp. 220-229.

1701    _____.  "Gandhi and Thoreau."  Nation and Athen-
        aeum, 46 (March 1, 1930), 728.

1702    _____, and Franklin B. Sanborn, eds. with Preface.
        Poems of Nature by Henry David Thoreau.  Boston:
        Houghton Mifflin, 1895.

1703    SAMPSON, H. Grant.  "Structure in the Poetry of
        Thoreau."  Costerus, 6 (1972), 137-154.

1704    SAMS, Henry W. , ed.  Autobiography of Brook Farm.
        Englewood Cliffs, N. J.:  Prentice-Hall, 1958.  Col-
        lection of materials on the subject; Thoreau, passim.

1705    SANAVIO, Piero.  "Nota su Henry David Thoreau. "
        Lettres Modernes, 8 (April, 1958), 218-225.  In
        Spanish.

1706    SANBORN, Franklin B.  Henry David Thoreau.  Bos-
        ton:  Houghton Mifflin, 1882.

1707    _____.  "The Emerson-Thoreau Correspondence. "
        Atlantic, 69 (May, 1892), 557-596.

1708    _____.  "Thoreau and His English Friend, Thomas
        Cholmondelay. "  Atlantic, 72 (December, 1893),
        741-756.

1709    _____.  The Personality of Thoreau.  Boston:  Good-
        speed, 1901.  Reprinted Folcroft, Pa.:  Folcroft,
        1969.

1710    _____.  "Emerson, Thoreau, Channing. "  Spring-
        field Republican, July 2, 1902, p. 14.

1711    _____.  The First and Last Journeys of Thoreau.
        Boston:  Printed for members of the Bibliophile
        Society, 1905.

1712    _____.  "Thoreau and Ellery Channing. "  Critic,
        47 (November, 1905), 444-451.

1713    _____.  "Thoreau in Twenty Volumes. "  The Dial,
        41 (October 16, 1906), 232-234.

1714    _____.  "Thoreau in His Journals. "  The Dial, 42
        (February 16, 1907), 107-111.

1715    _____.  Hawthorne and His Friends:  Reminiscence
        and Tribute.  Cedar Rapids, Iowa:  Torch, 1908.
        Pamphlet.  Reprinted in American Transcendental
        Quarterly, 9 Supplement (1971), 5-24.  Thoreau,
        passim.

1716    _____.  Recollections of Seventy Years, 2 vols.
        Boston:  Badger, 1909.

1717          . "Thoreau and Confucius." <u>Nation</u>, 90
        (May 12, 1910), 481.

1718          . The Life of Henry David Thoreau, Including
        Many Essays Hitherto Unpublished and Some Account
        of His Family and Friends. Boston:  Houghton Miff-
        lin, 1917.  American Men of Letters series.  Fac-
        simile reprint, Detroit:  Gale, 1968.

1719          , ed.  <u>Familiar Letters</u>.  Boston:  Houghton
        Mifflin, 1894.

1720          , ed.  <u>The Service</u>.  Boston:  Houghton Miff-
        lin, 1902.  Written in July, 1840; was not published
        until this date, 1902.

1721          , ed.  <u>The Writings of Henry David Thoreau</u>,
        20 vols.  Boston:  Houghton Mifflin, 1906, 1916.
        Standard Walden edition.  Reprinted New York:
        AMS, 1968.  Vol. VI, <u>Familiar Letters</u>, ed. F. B.
        Sanborn; Vols. VII-XX, <u>Journals, 1837-1861</u>, ed.
        Bradford Torrey and Francis H. Allen.

1722          , ed.  <u>Walden</u>.  Boston:  Printed for members
        of the Bibliophile Society, 1909.

1723  SANBORN, John Newell.  "Thoreau in Emerson's 'For-
        bearance.'"  <u>Thoreau Journal Quarterly</u>, 9 (1977),
        22-23.

1724  SANFORD, Charles L.  "Classics of American Reform
        Literature."  <u>American Quarterly</u>, 10 (Fall, 1958),
        295-311.

1725          . "Emerson, Thoreau, and the Hereditary
        Duality."  <u>Emerson Society Quarterly</u>, 54 (1969),
        36-43.

1726  SANFORD, John.  <u>View From This Wilderness:  Amer-
        ican Literature as History</u>.  Foreword by Paul
        Mariani.  Santa Barbara, Calif.:  Capra, 1977.
        Thoreau, p. 90.

1727  SARMA, Sreekrishna.  "A Short Study of Oriental In-
        fluence on Henry David Thoreau."  <u>Jahrbuch für
        Amerikastudien</u>, 1 (1956), 76-92.  Emphasis on
        <u>Walden</u>.

1728  SATTELMEYER, Robert D., Jr.  "David A. Wasson's
      Elegy on Thoreau."  Thoreau Society Bulletin, 123
      (Spring, 1973), 3-4.

1729  _____.  "Away from Concord:  The Travel Writings
      of Henry Thoreau."  Ph. D. diss., New Mexico,
      1975.  DA, 36 (1976), 6690A-6691A.

1730  _____.  "Walden Comes to the Concord Town Li-
      brary."  Thoreau Society Bulletin, 139 (Spring,
      1977), 5.

1731  SAUNDERS, Judith Prichard.  "A Majority of One:
      Literary Subversion in Walden."  Ph. D. diss.,
      California (San Diego), 1975.

1732  _____.  "Economic Metaphor Redefined:  The Tran-
      scendentalist Capitalist at Walden."  American
      Transcendental Quarterly, 36 (1977), 4-7.

1733  _____.  "Thoreau's Walden."  Explicator, 36 (1978),
      item 4.

1734  SAYLOR, Vivian Louise.  "'Sounds':  An American
      Romantic Conversation."  Thoreau Journal Quarterly,
      10 (1978), 26-28.

1735  SAYRE, Robert F.  Thoreau and the American Indians.
      Princeton, N. J.:  Princeton University Press, 1977.
      See review by Lauriat Lane.

1736  SCANLON, Lawrence E.  "Thoreau's Parable of Baker
      Farm."  Emerson Society Quarterly, 47 (1967), 19-
      21.

1737  SCHAMBERGER, J. Edward.  "Grapes of Gladness:
      A Misconception of Walden."  American Transcen-
      dental Quarterly, 13 (1972), 15-16.  Discussion
      based on a booklet by Marshal V. Hartranft, issued
      in 1939, as an answer to Steinbeck's The Grapes of
      Wrath.

1738  SCHEIK, William J.  "The House of Nature in Tho-
      reau's A Week."  Emerson Society Quarterly, 20
      (1974), 111-116.

1739  SCHIFFMAN, Joseph.  "Walden and 'Civil Disobedience':

Critical Analyses. " <u>Emerson Society Quarterly,</u>
56 (1969), 57-60.

1740    SCHILLER, Andrew. "Thoreau and Whitman: The
Record of a Pilgrimage. " <u>New England Quarterly,</u>
28 (June, 1955), 186-197.

1741    SCHNEIDER, Herbert W. "Spiritual Solitude, " in <u>A</u>
<u>History of American Philosophy.</u> New York: Co-
lumbia University Press, 1946, pp. 289-293.

1742    _____. "American Transcendentalism's Escape
from Phenomenology, " in Simon and Parsons, eds. ,
<u>Transcendentalism and Its Legacy</u> (1966), pp. 215-
228.

1743    SCHNEIDER, Richard J. "The Balanced Vision: Thoreau's Observations of Nature. " Ph. D. diss. , California (Santa Barbara), 1973. <u>DA,</u> 34 (1974),
5929A.

1744    _____. "Reflections in Walden Pond: Thoreau's
Optics. " <u>Emerson Society Quarterly,</u> 21 (1975),
65-75.

1745    SCHNITTKIND, Henry Thomas, and D. A. Schnittkind
(Henry Thomas and Dana Lee Thomas, pseud. ). "Thoreau's Adventures into the Simple Life, " in Schnittkind
and Schnittkind, <u>Living Adventures in Philosophy.</u> New
York: Hanover House, 1954, pp. 230-239.

1746    SCHOENBERGER, H. W. "Henry David Thoreau, "
in Hunt, Percival, et al. , eds. , <u>Some Writers of</u>
<u>Older New England.</u> Pittsburgh: University of
Pittsburgh Press, 1928, pp. 41-47.

1747    SCHOFIELD, Edmund. "The Will of H. G. O. Blake. "
<u>Thoreau Society Bulletin,</u> 67 (Summer, 1959), 2-3.
Refers to Harrison Gray Otis Blake, Thoreau's
most devoted follower; inheritor of Thoreau's manuscript journals.

1748    _____. "Errors in Robert Stowell's A Thoreau
<u>Gazetteer.</u>" <u>Thoreau Society Bulletin,</u> 119 (Spring,
1972), 4. See Stowell listing (1948).

1749    SCHULTZ, Howard. "A Fragment of a Jacobean Song

in Thoreau's Walden." Modern Language Notes, 63
(April, 1948), 271-272.

1750 SCHUSTER, E. M. "Native American Anarchism."
Smith College Studies in History, 17 (October, 1931,
and July, 1932), pp. 5 and 202.

1751 SCHWABER, Paul. "Thoreau's Development in Walden." Criticism, 5 (Winter, 1963), 64-77.

1752 SCHWARTZ, James M. "Excursions 'Around' and
'Into' Nature: Thoreau's 'A Walk to Wachusett' and
'A Winter Walk.'" Thoreau Journal Quarterly, 10
(1978), 14-19.

1753 SCHWARTZMAN, Jack. "Walking Westward," in Harding et al., eds., Henry David Thoreau: Studies
(1972), pp. 150-153.

1754 SCOTT, Winfield Townley. "Walden Pond in the Nu-
clear Age." New York Times Magazine, May 6,
1962, pp. 34-35 and passim.

1755 SCUDDER, Townsend. Concord: American Town.
Boston: Little, Brown, 1947. Thoreau, passim.

1756 SEABURG, Alan. "Min Thoreau." Thoreau Society
Bulletin, 101 (Fall, 1967), 7-8.

1757 _____. "Thoreau's Favorite Farmer (Edmund Hosmer)." Thoreau Society Bulletin, 102 (Winter,
1968), 1-4.

1758 _____. "A Thoreau Document." Thoreau Society
Bulletin, 109 (Fall, 1969), 5.

1759 SEEFURTH, Nathaniel H. Thoreau: A View from
Emeritus. Chicago: Seefurth Foundation, 1968.
Pamphlet. Reprinted in Emerson Society Quarterly,
54 Supplement (1969), 2-18.

1760 _____. "How Relevant Is Thoreau Today?" American Transcendental Quarterly, 32 (1976), 10-13.

1761 SEELYE, John R. "Some Green Thoughts on a Green
Theme," in White, G. A., and C. Newman, eds.,
Literature in Revolution. Chicago: Northwestern
University Press, 1972, pp. 576-638.

1762  _____ . "Frightfully Thoreau." American Quarter-
      ly, 29 (1977), 222-229. Review article on Reform
      Papers, edited by Wendell Glick (1973); and Illus-
      trated Walden, edited by James Lyndon Shanley
      (1973).

1763  SEIB, Charles. "My Introduction to Thoreau." Tho-
      reau Society Bulletin, 127 (Spring, 1974), 4.

1764  SELDES, Gilbert V. "Thoreau," in Macy, John A.,
      ed., American Writers on American Literature
      (1931), pp. 164-176. Reprinted in Glick, ed., Rec-
      ognition (1969), pp. 268-280.

1765  SENNETT, Richard. The Uses of Disorder. New
      York: Knopf, 1970. Thoreau, passim.

1766  SEYBOLD, Ethel L. "Henry David Thoreau and the
      Classics." Ph. D. diss., Yale, 1947.

1767  _____ . Thoreau: The Quest and the Classics.
      New Haven: Yale University Press, 1951. Re-
      printed Hamden, Conn.: Shoestring, 1969.

1768  SHANLEY, James Lyndon. "A Study of the Making of
      Walden." Huntington Library Quarterly, 14 (Feb-
      ruary, 1951), 147-170.

1769  _____ . The Making of Walden, with the Text of the
      First Version. Chicago: University of Chicago
      Press, 1957.

1770  _____ . "Thoreau's Geese and Yeats' Swans."
      American Literature, 30 (November, 1958), 361-
      364.

1771  _____ . "The Pleasures of Walden." Thoreau So-
      ciety Booklet, No. 15 (1960), 6pp.

1772  _____ . "Rationale of the Intentions of the Editors
      of Thoreau's Journals." Center for Editions of
      American Authors Newsletter, 3 (1970), 24-25.

1773  _____ . "Thoreau: His 'Lover's Quarrel with the
      World,'" in Crawley, Thomas, ed., Four Makers
      of the American Mind: Emerson, Thoreau, Whit-
      man, and Melville. Durham, N.C.: Duke Univer-

sity Press, 1976, pp. 25-42.  The Hampden-Sydney
College Symposium given as a Bicentennial Tribute
to Thoreau et al.

1774 _____, ed. with Historical Introduction, Textual
Introduction, Textual Notes, and Variants.  Walden,
in The Writings of Thoreau.  Princeton, N. J. :
Princeton University Press, 1971.

1775 _____, ed.  The Illustrated Walden with Photographs
from the Gleason Collection.  Princeton, N. J. :
Princeton University Press, 1973.

1776 SHARMA, Mohan Lal.  "Cholmondeley's Gift for Thoreau:  An Indian Pearl to the U. S. "  Journal of
the Ohio Folklore Society, 3 (1968), 61-89.

1777 _____.  "The 'Oriental Estate, ' especially the
Bhagavad-Gita in American Literature. "  Forum
(Houston), 7 (1969), 4-11.

1778 SHARP, Dallas Lore.  "Pilgrim from Dubuque, " in
Hills of Hingham.  Boston:  Houghton Mifflin, 1916,
Sharp, pp. 109-120.

1779 SHARP, William.  "Fascinating Henry Thoreau. "
American Transcendental Quarterly, 36 (1977), 9-
10.

1780 SHEAR, Walter Lewis.  "Thoreau's Imagery and Symbolism. "  Ph. D. diss. , Wisconsin, 1960.  DA,
22 (1961), 860-861.

1781 SHEPARD, Odell.  "The Paradox of Thoreau. "  Scribner's Magazine, 68 (September, 1920), 335-342.
Reprinted in Glick, ed. , Recognition (1969), pp. 232-
237.

1782 _____.  "Thoreau and Columella:  A Comment. "
New England Quarterly, 11 (September, 1938), 605-
606.  Refers to article by Francis L. Utley.

1783 _____.  "Unconsciousness in Cambridge:  The Edi-
ting of Thoreau's 'Lost Journal. ' "  Emerson Society
Quarterly, 13 (1958), 13-19.  See work by Perry
Miller (1958).

1784 _____.  "Approaching Thoreau Through Modern

Scholarship. "  Emerson Society Quarterly, 18
(1960), 23-26.

1785          , ed.  A Week on the Concord and Merrimack
Rivers.  New York:  Scribner, 1921.

1786          , ed.  The Heart of Thoreau's Journals.  Boston:  Houghton Mifflin, 1927.  Reprinted New York:
Dover, 1961.

1787  SHERMAN, Stuart Pratt.  "Emotional Discovery of
America, " in American Academy of Arts and Let-
ters:  Four Addresses in Commemoration of Its
Twentieth Anniversary.  New York:  Scribner, 1924,
pp. 144-188.  Reprinted in Sherman, The Emotional
Discovery of America and Other Essays, ed.  Jacob
Zeitlin.  New York:  Farrar and Straus, 1932, pp.
3-34.  Published posthumously; Sherman died in
1926.  Also reprinted in Loomis, R. S. , and D. L.
Clark, eds. , Modern English Readings.  New York:
Farrar and Straus, 1934, pp. 131-143.

1788          .  "Thoreau Returns from Abroad, " in Main
Stream.  New York:  Scribner, 1927, pp. 37-47.

1789  SHERWIN, J. Stephen, and Richard C. Reynolds.  A
Word Index to Walden, with Textual Notes.  Char-
lottesville:  University Press of Virginia, 1960.  Re-
printed in a corrected edition, Emerson Society
Quarterly, 57 Supplement (1969); also in book form,
Hartford, Conn. :  Transcendental, 1969.

1790  SHERWOOD, Mary P.  "Thoreau's Lecture on Sir
Walter Raleigh. "  Thoreau Society Bulletin, 75
(Spring, 1961), 4.

1791          .  "Fanny Eckstorm's Bias. "  Massachusetts
Review 4 (1962), 139-147.  Reprinted in Hicks, John
H. , ed. , Thoreau in Our Season (1966), pp. 58-66.

1792          .  "Thoreau's Penobscot Indians. "  Thoreau
Journal Quarterly, 1 (1969), 1-13.

1793          .  "Did Thoreau Foreshadow a Third Culture
Synthesis?"  Thoreau Journal Quarterly, 1 (1969),
22-29.

1794          . "The Fowlers of Thoreau's Maine Woods. "
Thoreau Journal Quarterly, 4 (1972), 23-30.

1795          . "Thoreau's Minnesota Trail in 1978, " Part
I. Thoreau Journal Quarterly, 10 (1978), 25-34.

1796   SHUKLA, Kamal Kant. "Emerson and Hindu Thought. "
Ph. D. diss. , Wayne State, 1973. DA, 34 (1974),
7246A. Thoreau, passim.

1797   SHUMAN, R. Baird. "Thoreau's 'Of Books and Their
Titles': A New Edition. " Emerson Society Quarterly, 18 (1960), 26-34. Includes reproduction of
manuscript.

1798          . "Thoreau's Passage on the 'Frozen-Thawed'
Apple. " Emerson Society Quarterly, 18 (1960), 34-
39.

1798a  SILBER, Mark, ed. Thoreau Country. Photographs
and Texts selected from the Works of Henry David
Thoreau by Herbert Wendell Gleason. Introduction
by Paul Brooks. San Francisco: Sierra Club,
1975.

1799   SILLEN, Samuel. "Thoreau in Today's America. "
Masses and Mainstream, 7 (December, 1954), 1-9.

1800          . "Thoreau in Our Time, " in Looking For-
ward. New York: International, 1955, pp. 153-163.
Marxist approach.

1801   SILVERMAN, Kenneth. "The Sluggard Knight in Thoreau's Poetry. " Thoreau Journal Quarterly, 5
(1973), 6-9.

1802   SIMON, Gary. "What Henry David Didn't Know About
Lao Tzu: Taoist Parallels in Thoreau. " Literature East and West, 17 (1973), 253-274.

1803          . "1845 and Walden: Triumph and Despair. "
Thoreau Journal Quarterly, 9 (1977), 2-10.

1804   SIMON, Myron, and Thornton H. Parsons, eds. Transcendentalism and Its Legacy. Ann Arbor: University of Michigan Press, 1966. "Personality and
Style in Concord, " by Gilman and Brown, pp. 87-122;

and "American Transcendentalism...", by Herbert
Schneider, pp. 215-228.

1805    SIMPSON, Lewis P.   "The Short Desperate Life of
        Henry Thoreau." Emerson Society Quarterly, 42
        (1966),   46-56.

1806    _____ .   The Man of Letters in New England and the
        South. Baton Rouge:   Louisiana State University
        Press, 1973.   Thoreau, passim.

1807    SINGH, Brij Mohan.   "Walden:   A Study in the Creation
        of Selfhood." Punjab University Research Bulletin
        of the Arts, 3 (1972),  121-132.

1808    SKINNER, B. F. Walden Two.   New York:   Macmillan,
        1948.   Condensed version in Orrick, ed., Designs
        (1959),  pp. 55-62.

1809    _____ .   "Walden (One) and Walden Two." Thoreau
        Society Bulletin, 122 (Winter, 1973),  1-3.

1810    SKWIRE, David.   "A Check-List of Word-plays in
        Walden." American Literature, 31 (November,
        1959),  282-289.

1811    SLATER, Joseph.   "Caroline Dall in Concord." Tho-
        reau Society Bulletin, 62 (Winter, 1958),  1-2.

1812    SLATER, Philip. The Pursuit of Loneliness.   Boston:
        Beacon, 1970.   Thoreau, passim.

1813    SLETHAUG, Gordon Emmett.   "Thoreau's Use of the
        Pastoral and Fable Tradition." Ph. D. diss. Ne-
        braska, 1968.   DA, 29 (1969),  4504A-4505A.

1814    SLOTKIN, Richard. Regeneration Through Violence:
        The Mythology of the American Frontier, 1600-
        1860.   Middletown:   Wesleyan University Press,
        1973.   Thoreau, pp. 518-538.

1815    SMITH, Bradford.   "Thoreau:   Civil Disobedience,"
        in Smith, Men of Peace.   Philadelphia:   Lippincott,
        1964,  pp. 144-156.

1816    SMITH, Edwin S.   "A Thoreau for Today." Main-
        stream, 13 (April, May, 1960),  1-24, 42-55.

1817   SMITH, F. M. "Thoreau." Critic, 37 (July, 1900),
       60-67.

1818   SMITH, George W., Jr. "Thoreau and Bacon: The
       Idols of the Theatre." American Transcendental
       Quarterly, 11 (1971), 6-12.

1819   SMITH, Herbert F. "Thoreau Among the Classical
       Economists." Emerson Society Quarterly, 23
       (1977), 114-122.

1820   SMITH, John S. "The Philosophic Naturalism of Henry
       David Thoreau with Special Reference to Its Epi-
       stemological Presuppositions and Theological Impli-
       cations." Ph. D. diss., Drew (Religion), 1948.

1821   SNOW, Edward Rowe. A Pilgrim Returns to Cape
       Cod. Boston: Yankee, 1946.

1822   SNYDER, Helena Adele. "Henry David Thoreau's
       Philosophy of Life with Special Considerations of
       the Influence of Hindoo Philosophy." Ph. D. diss.,
       Heidelberg, 1902.

1823   SOUTHWORTH, James G. "Thoreau, Moralist of the
       Picturesque." PMLA, 49 (September, 1934), 971-
       974. Reply to William D. Templeman.

1824   SOWD, David Howard. "Emerson's Correspondence with
       Peter Kaufman." Ph. D. diss., Bowling Green,
       1973. DA, 34 (1974), 7204A. Thoreau, passim.

1825   SPENCER, Clare Bennett. "Orestes Brownson on Civil
       Religion: Conflicts in the Evolution of a Concept of
       a National Faith." Ph. D. diss., Case Western Re-
       serve, 1973. DA, 34 (1974), 5047A.

1826   SPERBER, Murray, ed. Literature and Politics.
       Rochelle Park, N. J.: Hayden, 1978. Thoreau
       passim.

1827   SPILLER, Robert E. The Cycle of American Litera-
       ture. New York: Macmillan, 1955. Reprinted
       New York: New American Library, 1957. "The
       Affirmation: Emerson and Thoreau," pp. 47-66.

1828   _____. The Third Dimension. New York: Mac-
       millan, 1965. Thoreau, passim.

1829 _____. The Oblique Light. New York: Macmillan, 1968. Thoreau, passim.

1830 _____. Milestones in American Literary History. Foreword by Robert H. Walker. Westport, Conn.: Greenwood, 1977. Consists of 32 reviews by Spiller, 1923-1960. Thoreau, passim.

1831 _____, et al., eds. Literary History of the United States, 3 vols. New York: Macmillan, 1948. Volumes I and II issued in a one-volume edition, 1957. "Thoreau," Vol. I, pp. 388-415, by Townsend Scudder; Thoreau Bibliography, Vol. III, pp. 742-746, by Thomas Johnson.

1832 SRINATH, C. N. "Notes from 'Chrysalis': Some Glimpses of Thoreau's Poetry," in Chander and Pradhan, eds., Studies (1976), pp. 183-193.

1833 SRIVASTAVA, Ramesh. "Thoreau's Wit and Humour," in Chander and Pradhan, eds., Studies (1976), pp. 169-182.

1834 STANLEY, Hiram M. "Thoreau as Prose Writer." The Dial, 21 (October, 1896), 179-182. Reprinted in Glick, ed., Recognition (1969), pp. 130-138.

1835 STANSBERRY, Gloria J. "Let Wild Birds Sing: A Study of the Bird Imagery in the Writings of Henry David Thoreau." Ph.D. diss., Kent State, 1973. DA, 35 (1974), 417A-418A.

1836 STAPLETON, Laurence. The Elected Circle: Studies in the Art of Prose. Princeton, N.J.: Princeton University Press, 1973. "Thoreau: The Concrete Vision," pp. 195-232.

1837 _____, ed. with Introduction. Henry David Thoreau: A Writer's Journal. New York: Dover, 1960; London: Heinemann, 1961.

1838 STAUFFER, Donald B. A Short History of American Poetry. New York: Dutton, 1974. "Transcendental Poets," pp. 93-113. Includes Thoreau.

1839 STEEL, Kurt. "Prophet of the Independent Man." Progressive, 9 (September 24, 2945), 9.

1840   STEIN, William Bysshe. "Walden: The Wisdom of
       the Centaur." English Literary History, 25 (Sep-
       tember, 1958), 194-215. Reprinted in Vickery,
       John B., ed., Myth and Literature. Lincoln: Uni-
       versity of Nebraska Press, 1966, pp. 335-347.

1841   _____. "Melville Roasts Thoreau's Cock." Modern
       Language Notes, 74 (March, 1959), 218-219.

1842   _____. "Thoreau's Hound, Bay Horse, and Turtle-
       dove." Thoreau Society Bulletin, 67 (Spring, 1959),
       1.

1843   _____. "The Motif of the Wise Old Man in Wal-
       den." Modern Language Notes, 75 (March, 1960),
       201-204.

1844   _____. "Thoreau's Walden and the Bhagavad-Gita."
       Topic, 6 (1963), 38-55.

1845   _____. "Thoreau's First Book, a Spoor of Yoga:
       The Orient in A Week on the Concord and Merri-
       mack Rivers." Emerson Society Quarterly, 41
       (1965), 4-25.

1846   _____. "Walden and the Sambita of the Sama-Veda."
       Thoreau Society Bulletin, 96 (Summer, 1966), 6.

1847   _____. "A Bibliography of Hindu and Buddhist
       Literature Available to Thoreau Through 1854."
       Emerson Society Quarterly, 47 (1967), 52-56.
       Lists some 75 Oriental texts, English and French
       translations of Veda, Epic, Purana, Kanya, etc.

1848   _____. "An Approach to Thoreau." Emerson So-
       ciety Quarterly, 56 (1969), 4-6. Introduction to
       "New Approaches: Symposium," listed below.

1849   _____. "The Yoga of Walden: Chapter I, 'Econo-
       my.'" Literature East and West, 13 (1969), 1-26.

1850   _____. "The Hindu Matrix of Walden: The King's
       Son." Comparative Literature, 22 (1970), 303-318.
       Refers to Chapter II, "Where I Lived, and What I
       Lived For."

1851   _____. "The Yoga of 'Reading' in Walden." Texas

Studies in Literature and Language, 13 (1971), 481-495.

1852 _____. "Thoreau's A Week and Om Cosmography."
American Transcendental Quarterly, 11 (1971), 15-37.

1853 _____. "The Yoga of 'Sounds' in Walden." Literature East and West, 16 (1972), 111-135.

1854 _____, ed. with Introduction. Two Brahman Sources
of Emerson and Thoreau. Gainesville, Fla.:
Scholars' Facsimiles and Reprints, 1967. Contains
Rajah R. Roy, trans., Texts of the Veds (London,
1832); and William Ward, A View of the History,
Literature, and Mythology of the Hindoos, Vol. II
(London, 1822).

1855 _____, ed. with Introduction. "New Approaches to
Thoreau: A Symposium." Emerson Society Quar-
terly, 56 (1969), 1-60. Also published as book,
Hartford, Conn.: Transcendental, 1969.

1856 STEINBRINK, Jeffrey. "The Organization of Perception in A Week." Thoreau Journal Quarterly, 5
(1973), 14-17.

1857 STEPHENSON, Edward. "Longfellow Revised." Thoreau Society Bulletin, 118 (Winter, 1972), 4-5.
Thoreau changed a line of Longfellow's poem.

1858 STERN, Madeleine B. "Approaches to Biography."
South Atlantic Quarterly, 45 (July, 1946), 362-371.

1859 STERN, Philip Van Doren, ed. The Annotated Walden.
New York: Potter, 1970.

1860 STEVENS, Bertha, ed. Thoreau, Reporter of the Uni-
verse: A Selection of His Writings. New York:
Day, 1939.

1861 STEVENSON, Lionel. "A Forgotten English Poem on
Thoreau." Thoreau Society Bulletin, 66 (Winter,
1959), 2.

1862 STEVENSON, Robert Louis. "Henry David Thoreau:
His Character and Opinions." Cornhill Magazine, 41

(June, 1880), 665-682. Reprinted in Stevenson, Familiar Studies of Men and Books. London: Chatto and Windus, 1882; New York: Scribner 1895, pp. 129-171. Excerpt reprinted in Elwin, Malcolm, ed., Essays by Robert Louis Stevenson. New York: Coward-McCann, 1950, pp. 196-222. Also reprinted in Harding, ed., A Century (1954), pp. 59-83; and in Glick, ed., Recognition (1969), pp. 65-88.

1863      . "A Recantation," in Familiar Studies of Men and Books, revised edition. New York: Scribner, 1911, pp. 9-12. Reprinted in Harding, ed., A Century (1954), pp. 84-86; and in Glick, ed., Recognition (1969), pp. 88-90.

1864 STEWART, Charles D. "A Word for Thoreau." Atlantic, 156 (July, 1935), 110-116.

1865 STEWART, Randall. "The Concord Group." Sewanee Review, 44 (October-December, 1936), 434-446.

1866      . "The Growth of Thoreau's Reputation." College English, 7 (January, 1946), 208-214.

1867 STIBITZ, E. Earle. "Thoreau's Humanism and Ideas on Literature." Emerson Society Quarterly, 55 (1969), 110-116.

1868 STILWELL, R. L. "Literature and Utopia: B. F. Skinner's Walden II." Western Humanities Review, 18 (1964), 331-341.

1869 STOCKTON, Edwin Jr. "Henry David Thoreau, Terrener or Mariner?" Radford Review, 20 (1966), 143-154.

1870 STOEHR, Taylor. "Transcendentalist Attitudes Toward Communism and Individualism." Emerson Society Quarterly, 20 (1974), 65-90.

1871      . "'Eloquence Needs No Constable'--Alcott, Emerson, and Thoreau on the State." Canadian Review of American Studies, 5 (1974), 81-100.

1872      . Nay-Saying in Concord: Emerson, Alcott, and Thoreau. Hamden, Conn.: Shoe String, 1979.

1873 STOLLER, Leo. "Thoreau and the Economic Order:
The Later Years. " Ph. D. diss. , Columbia, 1955.
DA, 16 (1956), 1456-1457.

1874 _____. "A Note on Thoreau's Place in the History
of Phrenology. " Isis, 47 (June, 1956), 172-181.

1875 _____. "Thoreau's Doctrine of Simplicity. " New
England Quarterly, 29 (December, 1956), 443-461.

1876 _____. After Walden: Thoreau's Changing Views
on Economic Man. Stanford, Calif. : Stanford University Press, 1957.

1877 _____. "Civil Disobedience: Principle and Poli-
tics. " Massachusetts Review, 4 (1962), 85-88.
Reprinted in Hicks, John H. , ed. , Thoreau in Our
Season (1966), pp. 40-43.

1878 _____. "Christopher A. Greene: Rhode Island
Transcendentalist. " Rhode Island History, 22
(1963), 97-116. Little-known follower of Emerson
and Thoreau.

1879 _____. "American Radicals and Literary Works of
the Mid-Nineteenth Century: An Analogy, " in
Browne, Ray B. , Donald M. Winkleman, and Allen
Hayman, eds. , New Voices in American Studies.
West Lafayette, Ind. : Purdue University Press,
1966, pp. 13-20. Papers given at the Mid-America
Conference on Literature, History, Popular Culture,
and Folklore, Purdue University, 1965.

1880 _____, ed. "Henry David Thoreau, 1817-1862:
Books, Manuscripts, and Association Items in De-
troit and Ann Arbor. " Thoreau Society Booklet,
No. 18 (1963), 13pp. See also under Sweetland,
Harriet.

1881 _____, ed. with Introduction. Preface by Alexander C. Kern. Huckleberries. Iowa City and New
York: Windhover Press and New York Public Library private printing, 1970. Based on Thoreau's
"Notes on Fruits. "

1882 STOVALL, Floyd. American Idealism. Norman University of Oklahoma Press, 1943. "Contemporaries
of Emerson, " pp. 55-78.

1883       , ed. Eight American Authors. New York: Modern Language Association, 1956. Reprinted New York: Norton, 1963. "Thoreau," by Lewis Leary, pp. 153-206. Revised edition, edited by James Woodress, New York: Norton, 1971. "Thoreau," by Lewis Leary, pp. 129-171.

1884 STOWELL, Robert F. A Thoreau Gazetteer. Calais: Poor Farm, 1948. Edited by William L. Howarth, and reprinted Princeton, N. J.: Princeton University Press, 1970.

1885       . "Thoreau's Influence on an English Socialist, Robert Blatchford." Thoreau Society Bulletin, 98 (Winter, 1967), 1-3.

1886       . "Poetry About Thoreau: 19th Century." Thoreau Society Bulletin, 112 (Summer, 1970), 1-3.

1887       . "Twentieth Century Poetry About Thoreau." Thoreau Society Bulletin, 116 (Summer, 1971), 1-2.

1888       . "A Note on Two Additional Maps Copied by Thoreau." Thoreau Society Bulletin, 125 (Fall, 1973), 1-2.

1889       . "Thoreau and a Map of Nantucket." Thoreau Society Bulletin, 126 (Winter, 1974), 6-7.

1890 STRAENER, Stephen D. "Walden: Thoreau's Vānaprasthya." Thoreau Journal Quarterly, 5 (1973), 8-12.

1891 STRAKER, Robert L. "Thoreau's Journey to Minnesota." New England Quarterly, 14 (September, 1941), 549-555.

1892 STRAUCH, Carl F. "The Essential Romanticism of Thoreau's Walden," in Strauch, ed., "Symposium" (1960), pp. 21-23.

1893       . "Emerson Rejects Reed and Hails Thoreau." Harvard Library Bulletin, 16 (July, 1968), 257-273. Analysis of an unpublished Emerson poem, "S. R." (Sampson Reed).

1894       , ed. "A Symposium on Teaching Thoreau." Emerson Society Quarterly, 18 (1960), 2-23.

1895    STRIVINGS, Suzanne Marie. "Thoreau and His Sources:
        A Reading of Cape Cod." Ph. D. diss., Texas
        (Austin), 1974. DA, 35 (1975), 5366A.

1896    STROMBERG, R. N. "Thoreau and Marx: A Century
        After." Social Studies, 40 (February, 1949), 53-
        56.

1897    STRONKS, James B. "The Rivals as a Possible Source
        for Walden." Thoreau Society Bulletin, 96 (Spring,
        1966), 5.

1898    STRUTZ, William. "Ellery Channing's Copy of A
        Week." Thoreau Society Bulletin, 94 (Winter, 1966),
        2.

1899    SULLIVAN, John O. "The Rise of Man and the Fall
        of the Wilderness." Thoreau Journal Quarterly, 8
        (1976), 9-15.

1900    SUMMERLIN, Charles T. "The Possible Oracle:
        Three Transcendental Poets." Ph. D. diss., Yale,
        1971. DA, 34 (1973), 3435A-3436A. Studies Emer-
        son, Thoreau, and Jones Very.

1901    SUNDQUIST, Eric John. "Home as Found: Authority
        and Genealogy in Cooper, Thoreau, Hawthorne, and
        Melville." Ph. D. diss., Johns Hopkins, 1978. DA,
        39 (1978), 2279A-2280A.

1902    SUTCLIFFE, Denham, ed. with Foreword. A Week
        on the Concord and Merrimack Rivers. New York:
        New American Library, 1961.

1903    SWAN, Michael. "Living in Concord," in Swan, A
        Small Part of Time. London: Jonathan Cape,
        1957. Reprinted Chester Springs, PA.: Dufour,
        1961, pp. 95-108.

1904    SWANSON, Donald R. "Far and Fair Within: 'A Walk
        to Wachusett.'" Emerson Society Quarterly, 56
        (1969), 52-53.

1905    SWANSON, Evadene B. "The Manuscript Journal of
        Thoreau's Last Journey." Minnesota History, 20
        (June, 1939), 169-173.

1906    SWEENEY, James Ross.  "The Cosmic Drama in Tho-
        reau's 'Spring.'"  Emerson Society Quarterly, 24
        (1961), 3-6.

1907    SWEETLAND, Harriet M.  "The Significance of Tho-
        reau's Trip to the Upper Mississippi in 1861."
        Transactions of the Wisconsin Academy of Sciences,
        Arts, and Letters, 51 (1962), 267-286.

1908    _____, ed. with Annotations.  Henry David Thoreau,
        1817-1862:  Books, Manuscripts, and Association
        Items in Detroit and Ann Arbor.  Detroit.  Wayne
        State University Library, 1962.  Annotated catalog
        for the centennial exhibition.  Also published as
        Thoreau Society Booklet, No. 18 (1963), 13pp.  See
        Leo Stoller.

1909    SWIFT, Lindsay.  Brook Farm:  Its Members, Schol-
        ars, and Visitors.  New York:  Macmillan, 1900.
        Reprinted New York:  Corinth, 1961.

1910    TANNER, Stephen L.  "Current Motions in Thoreau's
        A Week."  Studies in Romanticism, 12 (1973), 763-
        776.

1911    _____.  "Nature as Spiritual Frontier:  Melville,
        Thoreau, Whitman."  Iowa English Yearbook, 26
        (1977), 14-17.

1912    TANNER, Tony.  The Reign of Wonder:  Naivete and
        Reality in American Literature.  Cambridge, Eng-
        land:  Cambridge University Press, 1965.  Reissued,
        1977.  "Thoreau and the Sauntering Eye," pp. 46-63.
        Also contains "Saints Behold:  The Transcendental
        Point of View," pp. 19-25.  Reprinted in Barbour,
        ed., American Transcendentalism (1973), pp. 53-58.

1913    TATALOVICH, Raymond.  "Thoreau on Civil Disobedi-
        ence:  In Defense of Morality or Anarchy?"  South-
        ern Quarterly (Mississippi), 11 (1973), 107-113.

1914    TAYLOR, Horace.  "Thoreau's Scientific Interests as
        Seen in His Journal."  McNeese Review, 14 (1963),
        45-59.

1915    TAYLOR, J. Golden.  Neighbor Thoreau's Critical Hu-

mor.  Logan:  Utah State University Press, 1958.
Monograph Series, No. VI.

1916 _____ .  "Thoreau and the Integrity of the Individual," in Thoreau Society Booklet, No. 19 (1963),
pp. 16-28.

1917 _____ .  "Thoreau's Sour Grapes."  Proceedings of
the Utah Academy of Science, Arts, and Letters,
42 (1965), 38-49.

1918 _____ , ed.  The Western Thoreau Centenary.  Logan:  Utah State University Press, 1963.  Monograph Series, No. X.  Also published as Thoreau
Society Booklet, 19 (1963), 67pp.

1919 TAYLOR, John Fulton.  "A Search for Eden:  Thoreau's Heroic Quest."  Ph. D. diss., Maryland,
1970.  DA, 32 (1971), 3334A.

1920 TAYLOR, Walter Fuller.  A History of American Let-
ters.  New York:  American Book Co., 1936.
Thoreau, pp. 159-167.  Revised and reprinted as
The Story of American Letters.  Chicago:  Regnery,
1956.  Thoreau, pp. 145-152.  Bibliographies by
Harry Hartwick.

1921 TEALE, Edwin Way.  The Lost Woods:  Adventures of
a Naturalist.  New York:  Dodd, Mead, 1945.  "On
the Trail of Thoreau," pp. 81-91.  Also relates to
John Thoreau.

1922 _____ .  "Wild Life at Walden," in The Lost Woods
(1945), pp. 273-283.

1923 _____ .  "Thoreau's Walden."  Life, 23 (September
22, 1947), 70-71, 73.  Illustrated.

1924 _____ .  North with the Spring.  New York:  Dodd,
Mead, 1951.

1925 _____ .  Circle of the Seasons.  New York:  Dodd,
Mead, 1953.

1926 _____ .  "Henry Thoreau and the Realms of Time."
Thoreau Society Bulletin, 64 (Summer, 1958), 1-2.

1927    _____. Wandering Through Winter. New York:
        Dodd, Mead, 1965.

1928    _____, ed. with Introduction. Walden. Illustrated
        with 142 photographs. New York: Dodd, Mead,
        1946. Reprinted, 1955.

1929    _____, ed. with Introduction. The Thoughts of Tho-
        reau. New York: Dodd, Mead, 1962. Arranged
        topically.

1930    TEMPLE, F. J. "Thoreau, poète et philosophe." In-
        formations et Documents, 33 (December 15, 1963),
        21-29. In French.

1931    TEMPLEMAN, William D. "Thoreau, Moralist of the
        Picturesque." PMLA, 47 (September, 1932), 864-
        889. See reply by James G. Southworth, PMLA,
        49 (1934), 971-974.

1932    THOMAS, Owen, ed. Walden and Civil Disobedience.
        New York: Norton, 1966. Norton Critical edition.

1933    THOMAS, Robert Kedzie. "The Tree and the Stone:
        Time and Space in the Works of Henry David Tho-
        reau." Ph. D. diss., Columbia, 1969. DA, 31
        (1970), 1776A.

1934    THOMAS, William Stephen. "Thoreau as His Own
        Editor." New England Quarterly, 15 (March, 1942),
        101-103.

1935    _____. "José Martí and Thoreau: Pioneers of
        Personal Freedom." Dos Pueblos (Havana), August,
        1949, pp. 1-3.

1936    _____. "Thoughts of Martin Buber on Henry Tho-
        reau." Thoreau Society Bulletin, 85 (Fall, 1963),
        1. Based on conversation with Buber.

1937    THOMPSON, Wade Clayton. "The Impractical Thoreau:
        A Rebuttal." College English, 19 (November, 1957),
        67-70.

1938    _____. "The Aesthetic Theory of Henry David Tho-
        reau." Ph. D. diss., Columbia, 1959. DA, 20
        (1960), 3756.

1939 _____. "The 'Uniqueness' of Henry David Thoreau. "
Paunch, 24 (1965), 18-25.   Thoreau's a-sociality.

1940 THOREAU JOURNAL QUARTERLY.   Established 1969.
Published at Old Town, Maine.

1941 THOREAU JOURNAL QUARTERLY, Special Issue,
1971. Vol. 3, 4 quarters.   Articles as follows:

I.   Richard B. Fleck, "Concord Rebel, " a play,
1-6; Daniel Smythe, "Memorandum to Thoreau, " a
poem, 6; Douglas Noverr, "An Essay-Review of
Hildenbrand's Bibliography of Thoreau Scholarship, "
7-11; Wendell Glick, "An Early Encounter with Joe
Polis?" 12-15; Alan Seaburg, "Thoreau as Hope, "
16-19; Paul O. Williams, "Thoreau, the .03 Horse-
power Poet, " 20-21; Daniel Smythe, "Thoreau Again, "
a poem, 21; Anton Kovar, "Sophia Foord, " 22;
Robert DeMott, "Song for Thoreau, " a poem, 24;
"Report on the Thoreau Center, " 25; "Future Ap-
pearances of The Night Thoreau Spent in Jail, " 33;
Kenneth Hendren, "Welcome Speech, Thoreau Bridge
Ceremony, Abol Stream, " 32-33.

II.   Charles W. Bassett, "Katahdin, Wachusett, and
Kilimanjaro:  The Symbolic Mountains of Thoreau
and Hemingway, " 1-10; Edmund Schofield, "To Thoreau, " a poem, 10; Anton Kamp, "Samoset's Long
Walk, " 11-16; Henry Minott, "The Minott Family
and Thoreau's Birthplace, " 17-18; Peter Hooper,
"Homage to Thoreau, " a poem, 19-20; "The Poten-
tial of Our Thoreau Center, " 21-26; Mary P. Sherwood, "The Valley of the Penobscot, " 27-31.

III.   A. J. Anderson, "Thoreau:  A Provisional
Interpretation, " 1-10; Mario L. D'Avanzo, "Walden,
'The Bean Field, '" 11-13; Mary P. Sherwood, "The
Wellfleet Oysterman's House, " 17-19; "The Gleason
Photographs, " 20; Daniel Smythe, "Robert Frost's
Indebtedness to Henry Thoreau, " 21; Martin Beard-
sley, "A Catalog of Errors, " 22; Florence B. Len-
non, "Report to the Fore-Runner, " a Poem, 23;
Daniel Smythe, "Thoreau at Walden, " a poem, 23.

IV.   Harold F. Mosher, Jr. , "The Absured in Thoreau's Walden, " 1-9; Kenneth G. Johnston, "Thoreau's Star-Spangled Losses:  The Hound, Bay Horse,

and Turtle Dove, " 10-20; Daniel Smythe, "Friend
Henry, " a poem, 21; Austin H. Wilkins, "Dedica-
tion Ceremony at Abol Campsite, Near Mt. Katahdin, " 26-28; "Thoreau's 'Ktaadn' Guides, Family
Records, " 29; "The Old Fisk House at Medway, "
30.

1942 THOREAU SOCIETY BOOKLET.   Published at irregular
intervals since 1942.   Each issue contains one subject.  No. 29 published in 1978.

1943 THOREAU SOCIETY BULLETIN.   Established 1941.
Published quarterly at State University College,
Geneseo, New York.

1944 THOREAU, Henry David.   Complete Writings, 20 vols.
Boston:   Houghton Mifflin, 1906, 1916.   Reprinted
New York:  AMS, 1968.   Walden edition.

1945 THOREAU, Sophia, ed.   The Maine Woods.   Boston:
Houghton Mifflin, 1892.   Reissued, 1906.

1946 THORP, Willard.   "Thoreau's Huckleberry Party. "
Thoreau Society Bulletin, 40 (Summer, 1952), 1-2.

1947 _____, ed. with Introduction.   Walden.   Columbus
Ohio:   Merrill, 1969.   Merrill edition.

1948 THORPE, James.   "English and American Literature
in the McCormick Collection:   Some Bibliographical
Notes. "   Princeton University Library Chronicle,
10 (November, 1948), 16-41.

1949 _____.  Thoreau's Walden.   San Marino, Calif. :
Huntington Library, 1977.   24-page pamphlet.  Illustrated with emphasis on materials at Huntington.

1950 TILLINGHAST, C. A.   "The West of Thoreau's Imagination:   The Development of a Symbol. "   Thoth, 6
(1965), 42-50.

1951 TILLMAN, James S.   "The Transcendental Georgic in
Walden. "   Emerson Society Quarterly, 21 (1975),
137-141.

1952 TIMPE, Eugene F.   "Thoreau in Germany. "   Thoreau
Society Bulletin, 93 (Fall, 1965), 1-3.

1953 _____. "The Macrocosm of Walden," in Jost, François, ed., Proceedings of the IVth Congress of the International Comparative Literature Association, 4 (1966), 73-79. Meeting at Fribourg, 1964; published The Hague: Mouton, 1966.

1954 _____. "Thoreau's Developing Style." Emerson Society Quarterly, 58 (1970), 120-123.

1955 _____, ed. Thoreau Abroad: Twelve Bibliographical Essays. Hamden, Conn.: Shoe String, 1971.

1956 TODD, Mabel Loomis. The Thoreau Family Two Generations Ago. Geneseo, N.Y.: Thoreau Society Publisher, 1958. Also published as Thoreau Society Booklet, No. 13 (1958), 23pp.

1957 TOMLINSON, Henry Major. "Travel Books," in Tomlinson, Waiting for Daylight. New York: Knopf, 1922, pp. 28-30. Refers to A Week on the Concord and Merrimack Rivers.

1958 _____. "Two Americans and a Whale." Harper's, 152 (April, 1926), 618-621.

1959 _____. "Thoreau," excerpt from "Two Americans ..." (1926), in Harding, ed., A Century (1954), pp. 136-139.

1960 TOPEROFF, Sam. "Dollars and Sense in Walden." Emerson Society Quarterly, 43 (1966), 87-88.

1961 TORREY, Bradford. "Thoreau." Atlantic, 78 (December, 1896), 822-833.

1962 _____. "Thoreau as Diarist," Atlantic, 95 (January, 1905), 5-18.

1963 _____. "Thoreau," in Torrey, Friends on the Shelf. Boston: Houghton Mifflin, 1906, pp. 89-129. Reprinted in Glick, ed., Recognition (1969), pp. 138-149.

1964 _____, "Thoreau's Demand upon Nature," in Torrey, Friends on the Shelf (1906), pp. 131-150.

1965 _____, and Francis H. Allen, eds. The Journal of

Henry David Thoreau, Vols. VII-XX of the Walden
Edition. Boston: Houghton Mifflin, 1906. Published separately in 14 vols in 1916. New edition
with Foreword by Henry Seidel Canby in 1949. Reprinted in two large volumes (four pages per sheet),
with new Foreword by Walter Harding, New York:
Dover, 1962. Reprint carries same pagination as
1906 edition.

1966   TOWNSEND, Harriet A., ed. In Touch with Thoreau.
Buffalo: Privately printed by the editor, 1907.
Quotations from writings of Thoreau.

1967   TRACY, Bruce H. "Walden as a Novel: A Psychological Reading." Ph.D. diss., New Mexico, 1971.
DA, 33 (1972), 2346A.

1968   TRACY, Henry Chester. "Henry David Thoreau,"
in Tracy, American Naturists. New York: Dutton,
1930, pp. 67-85. Refers to nature-worshippers, as
distinguished from naturalists, who study nature.

1969   TRANQUILLA, Ronald E. "Henry David Thoreau and
the New England Transcendentalists." Ph.D. diss.,
Pittsburgh, 1973. DA, 35 (1974), 1065A.

1970   TREAT, Robert and Betty. "Thoreau and Institutional
Christianity." American Transcendental Quarterly,
1 (1969), 44-47.

1971   TRENT, William P. A History of American Literature: 1607-1865. New York: Appleton-Century,
1923. Thoreau, pp. 337-346.

1972   _____, and John Erskine. Great American Writers.
New York: Holt, 1912. "The Transcendentalists,"
pp. 108-134.

1973   _____, et al., eds. Cambridge History of American
Literature. New York: Macmillan, 1917-1921.
Reprinted in one-volume edition, 1944. Thoreau,
Vol. II, pp. 1-15, by Archibald MacMechan.

1974   TRIPP, Raymond P., Jr. "Thoreau and Marcus Au-
relius: A Possible Borrowing." Thoreau Society
Bulletin, 107 (Spring, 1969), 7.

1975            . "Three-Stage Argument in Walden. " Tho-
          reau Society Bulletin, 118 (Winter, 1972), 5-6.

1976    TRYON, Warren S. , and William Charvat, eds.    The
          Cost Books of Ticknor and Fields and Their Pre-
          decessors, 1832-1858.  New York:  Bibliographical
          Society of America, 1949.

1977    TUERK, Richard Carl.  "Circle Imagery in the Prose
          of Emerson and Thoreau from Nature (1836) to Wal-
          den (1854). "  Ph. D. diss. , Johns Hopkins, 1967.
          DA, 28 (1967), 1798A.

1978            . "Thoreau and Chaucer's Dream. "  Thoreau
          Society Bulletin, 103 (Spring, 1968), 1.

1979            . "An Echo of Virgil in Walden. "  Thoreau
          Society Bulletin, 117 (Fall, 1971), 4-5.

1980            . "Thoreau's Early Versions of a Myth. "
          American Transcendental Quarterly, 10 (1971), 32-
          38.

1981            . "The One World of Thoreau's Verse. "
          Thoreau Journal Quarterly, 6 (1974), 3-14.

1982            . Central Still:  Circle and Sphere in Tho-
          reau's Prose.  The Hague:  Mouton, 1975.

1983    TURNER, Lorenzo Dow.  Anti-Slavery Sentiment in
          American Literature Prior to 1865.  Washington,
          D. C. :  U. S. Government Printing Office, 1929.
          Reprinted Port Washington, N. Y. :  Kennikat, 1966.
          Thoreau, p. 98 and passim.

1984    UHLIG, Herbert.  "Improved Means to an Unimproved
          End. "  Thoreau Society Bulletin, 128 (Summer,
          1974), 1-3.  Thoreau on Darwinian philosophy.

1985    ULLYAT, A. G.  " 'Wait Not Till Slaves Pronounce the
          Word':  Thoreau's Only Anti-Slavery Poem in the
          Context of Civil War Poetry. "  Thoreau Society
          Bulletin, 132 (Summer, 1975), 1-2.

1986    UNRUE, Darlene.  "John Smith and Thoreau:  A-Fish-
          ing in the Same Stream. "  Thoreau Journal Quar-
          terly, 8 (1976), 3-9.

1987   UPHAUS, Willard E. "Conscience and Disobedience."
       Massachusetts Review, 4 (1962), 104-108. Re-
       printed in Hicks, John H., ed., Thoreau in Our
       Season (1966), pp. 22-26.

1988   URBANSKI, Marie. "Henry David Thoreau and Mar-
       garet Fuller." Thoreau Journal Quarterly, 8
       (1976), 24-29.

1989   UTLEY, Francis L. "Thoreau and Columella: A Study
       in Reading Habits." New England Quarterly, 11
       (March, 1938), 171-180. Refers to Lucius Columel-
       la, a Roman writer on agriculture around A. D. 45.
       Thoreau read Of Husbandry in 1830.

1990   VAN DORE, Wade. " ' Only That Day Dawns...' "
       Thoreau Journal Quarterly, 5 (1973), 6-9.

1991   _____. "Thoreau Haiku." Thoreau Journal Quar-
       terly, 5 (1973), 11-13.

1992   VAN DOREN, Mark. Henry David Thoreau: A Critical
       Study. Boston: Houghton Mifflin, 1916. Reprinted
       New York: Russell and Russell, 1961.

1993   _____. "Position," excerpt from Henry David Tho-
       reau (1916), reprinted in Glick, ed., Recognition
       (1969), pp. 187-198.

1994   VAN NOSTRAND, A. D. "Thoreau Beside Himself,"
       in Van Nostrand, Everyman His Own Poet. New
       York: McGraw-Hill, 1968, pp. 92-112.

1995   VINCENT, Leon Henry. American Literary Masters.
       Boston: Houghton Mifflin, 1906. Thoreau, pp. 321-
       333.

1996   VIVAS, Elizeo. "Thoreau: The Paradox of Youth."
       New Student, 7 (1928), 5-8, 15.

1997   VOLKMAN, Arthur G. "The Hound, Bay-Horse, and
       Turtle Dove." Thoreau Society Bulletin, 103 (Spring,
       1968), 6-7.

1998   _____. "Thoreau as a Seer." Thoreau Society Bul-
       letin, 111 (Spring, 1970), 2-3.

1999 _____. "Thoreau and N. C. Wyeth--a Vignette."
     Thoreau Society Bulletin, 125 (Fall, 1973), 5-6.

2000 _____. "A Mythological Rainbow." Thoreau Society
     Bulletin, 129 (Fall, 1974), 7.

2001 _____. "Henry David Thoreau:  Obscurity or Im-
     mortality?" Thoreau Journal Quarterly, 8 (1976),
     19-20.

2002 WADE, J. S. "Friendship of Two Old-Time Natural-
     ists." Science Monthly, 23 (August, 1926), 152-
     160. Refers to Thoreau and Thaddeus William Har-
     ris.

2003 _____. "Henry Thoreau and His Journals." Nature
     Magazine, 16 (July, 1927), 153-154.

2004 _____. "A Contribution to a Bibliography from 1909
     to 1936 of Henry David Thoreau." Journal of the
     New York Entomological Society, 47 (June, 1939),
     163-203.

2005 WAGGONER, Hyatt H. American Poets from the
     Puritans to the Present. Boston:  Houghton Miff-
     lin, 1968. Thoreau, pp. 115-122.

2006 _____. "'Grace' in the Thought of Emerson, Tho-
     reau, and Hawthorne." Emerson Society Quarterly,
     54 (1969), 68-72. Reprinted in Cook, Reginald L.,
     ed., Themes, Tones, and Motifs (1969), pp. 68-72.

2007 WAGNER, C. Roland. "Lucky Fox at Walden," in
     Hicks, John H., ed., Thoreau in Our Season (1966),
     pp. 117-133.

2008 WAITE, Robert George. "'Linked Analogies':  The
     Symbolic Mode of Perception and Expression in
     Emerson and Melville." Ph. D. diss., Kentucky,
     1973. DA, 34 (1974), 6668A.

2009 WALCUTT, Charles Child. "Thoreau in the Twentieth
     Century." South Atlantic Quarterly, 39 (April,
     1940), 168-184.

2010 _____. "Walden as a Response to 'The American
     Scholar.'" Arizona Quarterly, 34 (1978), 5-30.

2011   WALKER, Edyth. "Walden--A Calming Influence."
       Thoreau Society Bulletin, 42 (Winter, 1953), 1-2.

2012   WALKER, Eugene A. "Touchstones." Thoreau Society
       Bulletin, 136 (Summer, 1976), 1-2. Evaluating Tho-
       reau.

2013   WALKER, Linda Kay. "A Fruitful Profusion: The
       Wild Berry Motif in Thoreau's Journal." Ph. D.
       diss., Oklahoma, 1976. DA, 37 (1977), 5131A-
       5132A.

2014   WALKER, Roy. "The Natural Life: An Essay on
       Thoreau." Vegetarian News (London), 26 (Spring,
       1948), 3-8.

2015   WALLIS, Charles L. "Gandhi's Source Book." Chris-
       tian Registrar, 128 (September 23, 1949), 31-32.

2016   WALTER, Nicholas. "Disobedience and the New
       Pacifism." Anarchy, 14 (April, 1962), 112-115.

2017   WALTERS, J. C. "Henry David Thoreau." Manches-
       ter Quarterly, 145 (January, 1918), 25-43.

2018   WARDERS, Donald F. "Excursion in Understanding."
       CEA Critic, 37 (1975), 20-24.

2019   WARNCKE, Wayne. "Walden Re-envisioned." Southern
       Humanities Review, 11 (1977), 331-336.

2020   WARREN, Austin. "Lowell on Thoreau." Studies in
       Philology, 27 (July, 1930), 442-462.

2021   _____. "Thoreau," in Warren, The New England
       Conscience. Ann Arbor: University of Michigan
       Press, 1966. Thoreau, passim.

2022   WASSERSTROM, William. "Howells' Mansion and Tho-
       reau's Cabin." College English, 26 (February,
       1965), 366-372.

2023   WATANABE, Toshio. "The Murderous Innocence:
       Henry David Thoreau and the American Wilderness."
       Studies in English Literature, 50, Japanese number
       (1973), 79-100. Abstract of article in English in
       Studies in English Literature, 51, English number
       (1974), 230-232.

2024  WATKINS, Thomas Coke, ed.  Henry David Thoreau:
       A Little Book of Nature Themes.  Portland, Me.:
       Mosher, 1906.

2025  WATSON, Ella.  "Thoreau Visits Plymouth."  Thoreau
       Society Bulletin, 21 (Fall, 1947), 1.

2026  WEAVER, Richard M.  "Two Types of American In-
       dividualism."  Modern Age, 7 (1963), 119-134.
       Compares Thoreau with John Randolph of Roanoke
       (1773-1833).

2027  WEIDMAN, Bette S.  "Thoreau and Indians."  Thoreau
       Journal Quarterly, 5 (1973), 4-10.

2028  WEISS, John.  "Weiss on Thoreau."  Christian Ex-
       aminer, 79 (1865), 98-101.  Reprinted in Thoreau
       Society Bulletin, 21 (Fall, 1947), 3.

2029  WELCH, Donovan Le Roy.  "A Chronological Study of
       the Poetry of Henry David Thoreau."  Ph. D. diss. ,
       Nebraska, 1966.  DA, 27 (1967), 3435A-3436A.

2030  WELLS, Henry W.  The Modern American Way of
       Poetry.  New York:  Columbia University Press,
       1943.  Reprinted New York:  Russell and Russell,
       1964.  Thoreau, pp. 67-77.

2031  _____ .  "An Evaluation of Thoreau's Poetry."
       American Literature, 16 (May, 1944), 99-109.  Re-
       printed in Harding, ed. , A Century (1954), pp. 150-
       161.

2032  WENDELL, Barrett.  A Literary History of America.
       New York:  Scribner, 1900.  Thoreau, pp. 332-337.
       Reprinted in Glick, ed. , Recognition (1969), pp. 150-
       154.

2033  WERGE, Thomas.  "The Idea and the Significance of
       'Economy' Before Walden."  Emerson Society Quar-
       terly, 20 (1974), 270-274.

2034  WESOLOWSKI, Daniel.  "Thoreau's Nutrition."  Tho-
       reau Society Bulletin, 141 (Fall, 1977), 7.

2035  WEST, Herbert Faulkner.  "Values in Thoreau."  Tho-
       reau Society Bulletin, 20 (Summer, 1947), 1.

2036 _____. "Strange Interlude--Thoreau as the Voice
of America," in West, Rebel Thought. Boston:
Beacon, 1953, pp. 196-210.

2037 _____. "Thoreau and the Younger Generation."
Thoreau Society Bulletin, 56 (Summer, 1956), 1.

2038 WEST, Michael. "John Evelyn, Sir Kenelm Digby,
and Thoreau's Vital Spirits." Thoreau Society Bulletin, 117 (Fall, 1971), 8.

2039 _____. "Charles Kraitsir's Influence upon Thoreau's
Theory of Language." Emerson Society Quarterly,
19 (1973), 262-274. Refers to Dr. Charles Kraitsir, a Hungarian, who championed a theory of language that would unlock and make all language study
easy.

2040 _____. "Scatology and Eschatology: The Heroic
Dimensions of Thoreau's Word Play." PMLA, 89
(1974), 1043-1064.

2041 _____. "Walden's Dirty Language: Thoreau and
Walter Whiter's Geocentric Etymological Theories."
Harvard Library Bulletin, 22 (1974), 117-128.

2042 _____. "Versifying Thoreau: Frost's 'The Quest
of the Purple Fringed' and 'Fire and Ice.'" English Language Notes, 16 (1978), 40-47.

2043 WESTBROOK, Perry D. Acres of Flint: Writers of
Rural New England, 1870-1900. New York: Scare-
crow, 1951. Revised edition, Metuchen, N.J.:
Scarecrow, 1980. Thoreau, passim.

2044 _____. "The Theme of the Quest: Thoreau."
English Record, 8 (Winter, 1957), 13-18.

2045 _____. "John Burroughs and the Transcendentalists."
Emerson Society Quarterly, 55 (1969), 47-55. In-
cludes Emerson, Thoreau, and Whitman, on whom
Burroughs wrote a total of some 50 essays.

2046 _____. John Burroughs: A Biography. New York:
Twayne, 1974. "Emerson and Thoreau," pp. 50-63.

2047 WHALING, Anne. "Studies in Henry David Thoreau's

Reading of English Poetry and Prose, 1340-1660."
Ph. D. diss., Yale, 1946.  DA, 29 (1968), 1238A.

2048    WHEELER, Jo Ann.  "Duty of Civil Disobedience."
        Money, 14 (June, 1949), 4.

2049    WHEELER, Ruth Robinson.  "The Thoreau Houses."
        Thoreau Society Bulletin, 31 (April, 1950), 2-3.

2050    _____.  "Thoreau's Farm."  Thoreau Society Bul-
        letin, 42 (Winter, 1953), 2-3.  Thoreau's birthplace.

2051    _____.  "Thoreau and Capital Punishment."  Tho-
        reau Society Bulletin, 86 (Winter, 1964), 1.  Re-
        cent discovery of 1849 petition signed by Thoreau
        to protest the hanging of a murderer.

2052    _____.  "Thoreau's Village Background."  Thoreau
        Society Bulletin, 100 (Summer, 1967), 1-6.

2053    _____.  Concord:  Climate for Freedom.  Concord,
        Mass.  Concord Antiquarian Society, 1967.  Tho-
        reau, pp. 156-157 and passim.

2054    _____.  "Thoreau's Concord," in Harding et al.,
        eds., Henry David Thoreau:  Studies (1972), pp. 25-
        33.

2055    WHEELER, Wilfred.  "Thoreau in Concord."  Thoreau
        Society Bulletin, 45 (Fall, 1953), 2.  Reminiscence
        of Thoreau by a Concordian.

2056    WHICHER, George Frisbie.  Walden Revisited:  A
        Centennial Tribute to Henry David Thoreau.  Chi-
        cago:  Packard, 1945.

2057    WHIPPLE, Edwin P.  Recollections of Eminent Men.
        Boston:  Ticknor and Fields, 1887.  Thoreau, p.
        134, and passim.

2058    WHISHNANT, David E.  "The Sacred and the Profane
        in Walden."  Centennial Review, 14 (1970), 267-
        283.

2059    WHITAKER, Rosemary.  "A Week on the Concord and
        Merrimack Rivers:  An Experiment in the Communi-
        cation of the Transcendental Experience."  Ph. D.
        diss., Oklahoma, 1969.  DA, 31 (1970), 737A.

2060 _____ . "A Week and Walden:  The River vs the
        Pond." American Transcendental Quarterly, 17
        (1973), 9-13.

2061 WHITCOMB, Robert. "The Thoreau 'Country.'" Book-
        man, 73 (July, 1931), 458-461.

2062 WHITE, E. B.  "One Man's Meat." Harper's, 179
        (August, 1939), 329-332.  Also printed as "Walden,"
        in White, One Man's Meat. New York:  Harper,
        1939.

2063 _____ . "Transcendental Retort," in White, Second
        Tree from the Corner.  New York:  Harper, 1953,
        pp. 94-96.

2064 _____ . "Walden--1954." Yale Review, 44 (August,
        1954), 13-22.

2065 _____ . "A Slight Sound at Evening," in The Points
        of My Compass.  New York:  Harper, 1954.  Re-
        printed in White, Essays of E. B. White.  New
        York:  Harper and Row, 1977, pp. 234-242.

2066 _____ . An E. B. White Reader, ed. William W.
        Watt and Robert W. Bradford.  New York:  Harper
        and Row, 1966.  Reprints "Walden" (1939), pp. 226-
        233; and "A Slight Sound at Evening" (1954), pp.
        234-243.

2067 WHITE, F.  "Thoreau's Observations on Fogs, Clouds,
        and Rain." Nature Study, 17 (October, 1921), 296-
        298.

2068 WHITE, Viola C.  "Thoreau's Opinion of Whitman."
        New England Quarterly, 8 (June, 1935), 262-264.
        Thoreau's letter to Harrison Blake about Whitman.

2069 _____ , ed.  The Concord Saunterer:  Including a
        Discussion of the Nature Mysticism of Thoreau and
        a Checklist of Thoreau Items in the Abernethy Li-
        brary of Middlebury College.  Middlebury, Vt.:
        Middlebury College Press, 1940.

2070 WHITE, William.  "A Henry David Thoreau Bibliogra-
        phy, 1908-1937." Bulletin of Bibliography and Dra-
        matic Index, 16 (1938-1939), 90-92, 111-113, 131-

132, 163, 181-182, 199-202. Collected and published as a book, Boston: Faxon (publisher of Bulletin of Bibliography), 1939.

2071 _____ . "Three Unpublished Thoreau Letters."
New England Quarterly, 33 (September, 1960), 372-
374.

2072 _____ . "An Unpublished Thoreau Poem." American Literature, 34 (March, 1962), 119-121.

2073 _____ . "An Unpublished Thoreau Poem: A Correction." Thoreau Society Bulletin, 82 (Winter,
1963), 2.

2074 _____ . "A Week in the Feinberg Collection." Thoreau Society Bulletin, 85 (Fall, 1963), 2.

2075 _____ . "A Thoreau Letter." Serif, 1 (December,
1964), 28-29.

2076 WHITFORD, Kathryn. "Thoreau and the Woodlots of
Concord." New England Quarterly, 23 (September,
1950), 291-306.

2077 WHITFORD, Philip and Kathryn. "Thoreau: Pioneer
Ecologist and Conservationist." Scientific Monthly,
73 (November, 1951), 291-296. Reprinted in Harding, ed., A Century (1954), pp. 192-205.

2078 WHITTEMORE, Robert Clifton. "Henry David Thoreau," in Whittemore, Makers of the American
Mind. New York: Morrow, 1964, pp. 185-196.

2079 WIDMER, Kingsley. "The Prophets' Passional Ethos:
Henry David Thoreau." Paunch, 24 (1965), 40-50.

2080 WIENER, Hervey S. "'To a Fairer World': Thoreau's
Last Hours." Journal of Historical Studies, 1
(1968), 361-365.

2081 WILDER, Thornton. "The American Loneliness."
Atlantic, 190 (August, 1952), 65-69. Reprinted
in Weeks, Edward, and Emily Flint, eds., Atlantic
Monthly Jubilee. Boston: Little, Brown, 1957,
pp. 165-174.

2082  WILLAUER, G. J. , Jr.  "Ambiguity and the Land-
      scape of Thoreau, " in Deguise, Pierre, and Rita
      Terras, eds. , Symposium on Romanticism:  An In-
      terdisciplinary Meeting.  New London:  Connecticut
      College, 1975.  Given at Connecticut Conference,
      April 21-26, 1975, pp. 58-62.

2083  WILLIAMS, Donald H.  "Thomas Wentworth Higginson
      on Thoreau and Maine. "  Colby Library Quarterly,
      7 (1965), 29-32.

2084  _____.  "Whose Woods These Are ... "  Thoreau
      Journal Quarterly, 4 (1972), 27-28.

2085  WILLIAMS, Paul Osborne.  "The Transcendental Move-
      ment in American Poetry. "  Ph. D. diss. , Pennsyl-
      vania, 1962.  DA, 23 (1962), 1372-1373.  Studies
      Emerson, Thoreau, Jones Very, Christopher Cranch,
      and Ellery Channing.

2086  _____.  "The Borrowed Axe:  A Biblical Echo in
      Walden?"  Thoreau Society Bulletin, 83 (Spring,
      1963), 2.

2087  _____.  "Thoreau's 'It is no dream of mine';  A
      New Proposal. "  Thoreau Society Bulletin, 86 (Win-
      ter, 1964), 3-4.

2088  _____.  "The Concept of Inspiration in Thoreau's
      Poetry. "  PMLA, 79 (September, 1964), 466-472.

2089  _____.  "Emerson Guided:  Walks with Thoreau and
      Channing. "  Emerson Society Quarterly, 35 (1964),
      66-68.

2090  _____.  "Thoreau and Purslane. "  Thoreau Society
      Bulletin, 91 (Spring, 1965), 3.

2091  _____.  "Thoreau in the 'Boatswain's Whistle. ' "
      Emerson Society Quarterly, 38 (1965), 133.  Refers
      to Cape Cod; first published posthumously as a prose
      piece in 1864.

2092  _____.  "Thoreau's Growth as a Transcendental
      Poet. "  Emerson Society Quarterly, 19 (1973), 189-
      198.

2093    _____. "The Influence of Thoreau on the American
        Nature Essay. " Thoreau Society Bulletin, 145 (Fall,
        1978), 1-5.

2094    WILLIS, Lonnie Leon. "Folklore in the Published
        Writings of Henry David Thoreau: A Study and a
        Compendium-Index. " Ph. D. diss. , Colorado, 1966.
        DA, 28 (1967), 1412A-1413A.

2095    WILLSON, Lawrence S. "The Influence of Early North
        American History and Legend on the Writings of
        Henry David Thoreau. " Ph. D. diss. , Yale, 1944.

2096    _____. "Thoreau and Roman Catholicism. " Catho-
        lic History Review, 42 (July, 1956), 157-172.

2097    _____. "Thoreau and the Natural Diet. " South
        Atlantic Quarterly, 57 (Winter, 1958), 86-103.

2098    _____. "From Thoreau's Indian Manuscripts. "
        Emerson Society Quarterly, 11 (1958), 52-55.

2099    _____. "Thoreau's Canadian Notebook. " Hunting-
        ton Library Quarterly, 22 (May, 1959), 179-200.

2100    _____. "Thoreau--Citizen of Concord. " Emerson
        Society Quarterly, 14 (1959), 7-12.

2101    _____. "The Great Reversal. " Dalhousie Review,
        39 (Spring, 1959), 5-18.

2102    _____. "Thoreau and the French in Canada. " Re-
        vue de l' Universite d'Ottawa, 29 (July-September,
        1959), 281-297.

2103    _____. "Thoreau's Medical Vagaries. " Journal of
        the History of Medicine and Allied Sciences, 15
        (January, 1960), 64-74.

2104    _____. "The Transcendental View of the West. "
        Western Humanities Review, 14 (1960), 183-191.

2105    _____. "Another View of the Pilgrims. " New Eng-
        land Quarterly, 34 (June, 1961), 160-177.

2106    _____. "Thoreau: Defender of the Savage. " Em-
        erson Society Quarterly, 26 (1962), 1-8.

2107 WILSON, Edmund, ed. The Shock of Recognition.
Garden City, N.Y.: Doubleday, Doran, 1943. "Thoreau," by James Russell Lowell, pp. 229-243.

2108 WILSON, John B. "The Aesthetics of Transcendentalism." Emerson Society Quarterly, 57 (1969), 27-
34.

2109 WINN, Ralph Bubrich. "Henry David Thoreau," in
Winn, ed., American Philosophy. New York: Philosophical Library, 1955, pp. 259-261.

2110 WINTER, Julie. "Thoreau: An Astrological Birth
Chart." Thoreau Society Bulletin, 126 (Winter,
1974), 3-4.

2111 WINTERICH, J. T. "Romantic Stories ... Walden."
Publishers Weekly, 116 (September 21, 1929), 1363-
1368. Reprinted in Twenty-Three Books and the
Stories Behind Them. Philadelphia: Lippincott,
1938, pp. 165-174.

2112 WITHERELL, Elizabeth. "An Editor's Nightmare:
'It is No Dream of Mine' in the Princeton Edition
of Thoreau's Poetry." Concord Saunterer, 12
(1977), 5-9.

2113 WITHERINGTON, Paul. "Thoreau's Almost Unpassable
Test." Research Studies, 41 (1973), 279-281.

2114 WOLF, William J. Thoreau: Mystic, Prophet, Ecologist. Philadelphia: Pilgrim, 1974.

2115 WOOD, James Playsted. "English and American Criticism of Thoreau." New England Quarterly, 6 (December, 1933), 733-746.

2116 _____. "Henry David Thoreau: Biographical
Sketch," in Wood, ed., One Hundred Years Ago
(1848). New York: Funk and Wagnalls, 1947, pp.
1-4.

2117 _____. "Mr. Thoreau Writes a Book." New Colophon, 1 (October, 1948), 367-376. Refers to A
Week.

2118 _____. A Hound, A Bay Horse, and a Turtledove.
New York: Pantheon, 1963. For young readers.

2119 WOODBURY, Charles J. Talks with Ralph Waldo Emerson. New York: Baker and Taylor, 1890. Thoreau, pp. 76-91 and passim.

2120 WOODLIEF, Annette Matthews. "Style and Rhetoric in the Sentences of Walden." Ph. D. diss., North Carolina (Chapel Hill), 1972. DA, 33 (1973), 4372A-4373A.

2121 _____. "Walden: A Checklist of Literary Criticism Through 1973." Resources for American Literary Study, 5 (1975), 15-58.

2122 _____. "The Influence of Theories of Rhetoric on Thoreau." Thoreau Journal Quarterly, 7 (1975), 13-22.

2123 WOODRESS, James, ed. American Literary Scholarship: An Annual Survey. Durham, N. C.: Duke University Press, 1963--to date. See "Emerson, Thoreau, and Transcendentalism" by different authors.

2124 _____, ed. Ph. D. Dissertations in American Literature, 1891-1966. Durham, N. C.: Duke University Press, 1968.

2125 _____, ed. Eight American Authors. New edition, New York: Norton, 1971. See also Stovall, Floyd (1956).

2126 WOODRUFF, Stuart. "Thoreau as Water-Gazer: 'The Ponds.'" Emerson Society Quarterly, 47 (1967), 16-17.

2127 WOODS, Frederick. "Henry David Thoreau: The Artist as Individualist." Stand (London), 10 (Summer, 1955), 10-12.

2128 WOODSON, Thomas M. "Thoreau's Prose Style." Ph. D. diss., Yale, 1963. DA, 32 (1972), 4639A.

2129 _____. "The Two Beginnings of Walden: A Distinction of Styles." English Literary History, 35 (1968), 440-473.

2130 _____. "Thoreau on Poverty and Magnanimity." PMLA, 85 (1970), 21-34.

2131 _____. "Thoreau's Excursion to the Berkshires and
Catskills." Emerson Society Quarterly, 21 (1975),
82-92.

2132 _____. "Thoreau's Walden, Chapter I, Paragraph
63." Explicator, 33 (1975), Item 56. Reply to
article by F. DeWolfe Miller.

2133 _____. "Notes for the Annotation of Walden."
American Literature, 46 (1975), 550-555.

2134 _____. "Thoreau's Attitudes Toward His Prospec-
tive Readers During the Evolution of Walden." Annual Report for 1975. American Literature Sec-
tion, MLA. Abstract, p. 16.

2135 _____. "The Title and Text of Thoreau's 'Civil
Disobedience.'" Bulletin of Research in the Hu-
manities (formerly Bulletin of the New York Public
Library), 81 (1978), 103-112.

2136 WOODWARD, Robert H. "Thoreau's 'Ferule': A
Textual Note on Walden." Thoreau Society Bulletin,
123 (Spring, 1973), 1-2.

2137 WORTHINGTON, John W. "Thoreau's Route to Katahdin." Appalachia, 26 (1946), 3-14.

2138 WRIGHT, Nathalia. "Emily Dickinson's Boanerges and
Thoreau's Atropos: Locomotives on the Same Line?"
Modern Language Notes, 72 (February, 1957), 101-
103.

2139 WU, Ta-Cheng. "T'ao Ch'ien and Thoreau: A Note
on Two Different Attitudes Toward Nature," in Yen,
Yuan-Shu, ed., Proceedings from the International
Comparative Literature Conference. July 18-24,
1971, at Tamkang College of Arts and Sciences,
Taipei, Taiwan, Republic of China, 1972, pp. 387-
393.

2140 WYATT, Edith Franklin. "Two Woodsmen--Thoreau
and Muir," in Great Companions. New York: Ap-
pleton, 1917, pp. 341-365.

2141 WYETH, N. C. "Thoreau, His Critics, and the Public." Thoreau Society Bulletin, 37 (Fall, 1951),

1-2.  Written in 1919, remained unpublished until
this date.  Reprinted in Glick, ed. , Recognition
(1969), pp. 227-232.

2142   WYLLIE, E. M. "Thoreau Trails." Holiday, 4,
(September, 1948), 105-114.

2143   WYLLIE, John Cook.  "Delugeous or Detergeous or?"
Center for Editions of American Authors Newsletter,
2 (1969), 3.  See article by Harding (1968).

2144   YAHAGI, Kodo.  "On the Position of Henry David
Thoreau in Relation to the Formation of American-
ism." Taisho Daigaku Kenkyukiyo, 44 (March,
1959), 1-40.  Japanese publication; article in English.

2145   ZAHNISER, Howard.  "Thoreau and the Preservation
of Wildness." Concord Journal, July 18, 1957.
Reprinted in Thoreau Society Bulletin, 60 (Summer,
1957), 1-2.

2146          . "Thoreau and the Wilderness." Thoreau
Society Bulletin, 80 (Summer, 1962), 3-4.

2147   ZALAMEA, Luis.  "Thoreau Today." Américas, 14
(March, 1962), 27-32.

2148   ZEITLIN, Eugenia.  "Henry in the Desert." Thoreau
Society Bulletin, 126 (Winter, 1974), 1-2.

2149   ZIFF, Lazar, ed. with Commentary and Notes.  Walden:  A Writer's Edition.  New York:  Holt, Rinehart, and Winston, 1961.

2150   ZIMMER, Jeanne M.  "A History of Thoreau's Hut and
Hut Site." Emerson Society Quarterly, 18 (1972),
134-140.  Reprinted in The Concord Saunterer, December, 1973.

## INDEX OF COAUTHORS,
## EDITORS, TRANSLATORS

# SUBJECT INDEX

Bellew, Frank  391
Bergson, Henri  188
Bible  291, 611, 664, 1275, 1276, 2086
Bibliography (Primary and secondary)  43, 44, 59, 77, 85,
    114, 138, 285, 290, 414, 497, 507, 766, 855, 875, 878,
    884, 919, 946, 947, 956, 968, 1011, 1016, 1026, 1123,
    1208, 1244, 1247, 1292, 1449, 1516, 1540, 1693, 1831,
    1883, 1955, 2004, 2070, 2121, 2123, 2124, 2125
Biographical Studies of Thoreau
    Short articles, character sketches, appreciations,
        memories, etc.  5, 36, 37, 46, 47, 50, 56, 61, 63,
        66, 70, 71, 90, 106, 108, 109, 129, 131, 133, 160,
        197, 205, 210, 211, 217, 235, 251, 260, 262, 266,
        269, 270, 286, 295, 297, 298, 342, 430, 431, 432,
        435, 436, 437, 442, 445, 446, 447, 462, 467, 473,
        481, 491, 509, 511, 527, 567, 568, 575, 576, 577,
        583, 585, 626, 627, 628, 629, 647, 656, 659, 663,
        669, 685, 687, 688, 697, 698, 701, 702, 703, 716,
        717, 718, 721, 739, 740, 747, 753, 755, 756, 757,
        760, 762, 799, 812, 860, 862, 876, 901, 918, 960,
        1004, 1007, 1008, 1013, 1019, 1064, 1069, 1070,
        1091, 1115, 1122, 1125, 1133, 1135, 1148, 1150,
        1161, 1225, 1231, 1241, 1245, 1252, 1253, 1254,
        1264, 1287, 1314, 1339, 1399, 1402, 1415, 1443,
        1469, 1470, 1471, 1478, 1512, 1515, 1535, 1584,
        1612, 1632, 1644, 1660, 1688, 1763, 1764, 1779,
        1781, 1805, 1858, 1862, 1863, 1864, 1915, 1917,
        1939, 1993, 1996, 1998, 2017, 2028, 2078, 2079,
        2080, 2110, 2116, 2148
    Book-length biographical studies  107, 125, 153, 168,
        415, 440, 517, 610, 619, 650, 661, 750, 768, 924,
        970, 1035, 1051, 1059, 1098, 1099, 1121, 1186,
        1199, 1248, 1249, 1281, 1306, 1353, 1476, 1510,
        1547, 1559, 1563, 1652, 1697, 1706, 1709, 1718,
        1992, 2118
Birds  86, 93, 560, 824, 1835
Blake, H. G. O.  27
Botany (see also Columella)  655, 1545, 1546, 1782, 1989
Brady, Kate  916
Bremer, Fredrika  887
Brook Farm  566, 1704, 1909
Brown, John  78, 79, 402, 463, 599, 803, 888, 1459, 1495,
    1541
Brown, Theodore  928
Brownson, Orestes  389, 1261, 1825
"Brute Neighbors"  252
Buber, Martin  1936

Excursions 1368
Journals 111, 183, 184, 185, 186, 218, 1296, 1413,
    1721, 1786, 1837, 1924, 1925, 1926, 1927, 1965
Letters 219
Maine Woods 1293, 1430, 1431, 1945
Poems (Collections of) 200, 215, 1702
Walden (includes "Civil Disobedience," usually reprinted
    in the same volume) 110, 126, 127, 448, 840, 875,
    878, 884, 950, 991, 1181, 1318, 1414, 1561, 1569,
    1630, 1657, 1722, 1774, 1775, 1859, 1928, 1932,
    1947, 2133, 2149
A Week on the Concord and Merrimack Rivers 951,
    1295, 1785, 1902
Education (see also Teacher, Thoreau as a) 198
Emerson, Edward 6, 661
Emerson, Ralph Waldo 58, 95, 152, 179, 230, 266, 278,
    285, 314, 316, 324, 325, 331, 336, 343, 359, 364,
    366, 369, 370, 375, 400, 409, 410, 414, 415, 416,
    451, 460, 470, 496, 497, 499, 508, 519, 555, 557,
    640, 653, 654, 663, 717, 748, 769, 773, 790, 793,
    816, 818, 852, 919, 971, 976, 982, 1038, 1052, 1073,
    1089, 1132, 1140, 1146, 1157, 1162, 1180, 1196, 1224,
    1246, 1371, 1441, 1458, 1462, 1485, 1500, 1540, 1541,
    1542, 1548, 1598, 1600, 1601, 1618, 1633, 1668, 1675,
    1679, 1707, 1710, 1723, 1725, 1796, 1824, 1854, 1871,
    1872, 1893, 1900, 1977, 2006, 2008, 2010, 2089, 2119
England (includes English) 584, 589, 1526, 1627, 1708, 1885,
    2047, 2115
Epicurus 999
Ether see Drugs
Excursions 1365, 1368, 1752


Finland 1462
First Editions (includes Rare Editions; see also Manuscripts)
    43, 412, 565, 692, 937, 938, 939
Flagg, James Montgomery 144
Flowers, B. O. (includes the magazine Arena) 1638
Flynn, Errol 267
Folklore (see also Mythology) 320, 1283, 1813, 2094, 2095
Francis, Robert 156
Franklin, Benjamin 174, 247, 305
Franklin, Nora C. 1317
French Critics, translations, articles in French, etc. 92,
    153, 341, 466, 470, 471, 673, 701, 702, 743, 1255,
    1256, 1398, 1473, 1511, 1610, 1626, 1930
French, Richard C. 239

1329, 1439, 1599, 1601, 1609, 1610, 1646, 1666, 1741,
1745, 1773, 1820, 1822, 1823, 1867, 1875, 1882, 1930,
1931, 1984, 1998, 2109
Photographers and Thoreau  45
Phrenology  1874
Pindar  89, 380
Plato  1416
Poe, Edgar Allan  561, 744, 1157
Poems (written to Thoreau)  292, 609, 741, 1173, 1228, 1312,
1728, 1861, 1886, 1887
Poetry, Thoreau's  88, 200, 209, 215, 242, 254, 322, 327,
351, 356, 362, 404, 478, 512, 532, 536, 558, 563, 570,
608, 675, 705, 719, 731, 732, 733, 782, 792, 809, 849,
914, 973, 1131, 1193, 1194, 1220, 1263, 1284, 1285,
1375, 1380, 1381, 1473, 1646, 1656, 1667, 1681, 1702,
1703, 1801, 1832, 1838, 1930, 1981, 1985, 1990, 1991,
1994, 2005, 2029, 2030, 2031, 2072, 2073, 2085, 2087,
2088, 2092, 2112
Politics  see  Social Criticism
"Pond in Winter, The" (includes Ponds, etc.)  231, 256, 320,
352, 558, 559, 684, 1127, 1301, 1744, 2011, 2060,
2126
Psychological Studies  509, 807, 808, 1092, 1248, 1249, 1307,
1967
Publishers, Thoreau's (includes Editors)  204, 233, 234, 694,
937, 938, 1976


Quarles, Francis  1259
Quebec, Thoreau's Journey to  338


"Raleigh, Sir Walter" (see also Lectures)  1166, 1390, 1790
Reading, Thoreau's (includes Thoreau's Books)  355, 367,
371, 377, 380, 381, 406, 485, 486, 490, 895, 1347,
1353, 1369, 1539, 1641, 2047
Recordings  1116, 1338
Reform (includes Rebel, Freedom, Radical, etc.)  123, 243,
821, 1267, 1281, 1297, 1298, 1496, 1497, 1502, 1543,
1655, 1724, 1750, 1765, 1839, 1879, 2036
Reform Papers  796, 952, 1762
Religion (includes Puritanism)  31, 248, 869, 1060, 1167,
1261, 1435, 1458, 1534, 1605, 1820, 1970, 2096
Renaissance, American  74, 287, 416, 417, 531, 850, 988,
1377, 1486, 1642
Reputation (includes Contemporary Recognition of Thoreau)
2, 39, 817, 838, 900, 911, 1866